Realist Nights
and
Heritage Mornings

(Representations of British National Identity 1955-1965 and 1980-1990)

by

Dr Justin Christopher Hindmarsh

Grosvenor House
Publishing Limited

All rights reserved
Copyright © Dr Justin Hindmarsh, 2018

The right of Dr Justin Hindmarsh to be identified as the author of this
work has been asserted in accordance with Section 78
of the Copyright, Designs and Patents Act 1988

The book cover picture is copyright to Inmagine Corp LLC

This book is published by
Grosvenor House Publishing Ltd
Link House
140 The Broadway, Tolworth, Surrey, KT6 7HT.
www.grosvenorhousepublishing.co.uk

This book is sold subject to the conditions that it shall not, by way of
trade or otherwise, be lent, resold, hired out or otherwise circulated
without the author's or publisher's prior consent in any form of binding or
cover other than that in which it is published and
without a similar condition including this condition being imposed
on the subsequent purchaser.

A CIP record for this book
is available from the British Library

ISBN 978-1-78623-279-3

For My Dad Always

Abstract

Over the course of this book I shall endeavour to identify the significant social and cultural aspects which together help to articulate and illustrate changing perceptions of British national identity with specific reference to two periods: 1995-65 and 1980-1990. In doing so I shall be revisiting the themes and debates first articulated in my Theses "Realist Nights and Heritage Mornings: Comparing Representations of British National Identity 1955-1965 and 1980-1990." (2001). These aspects will detail the areas of affluence and consumerism, social mobility, imperial decline- and national restoration, moral change, immigration and ethnic difference. I shall then utilise a qualitative thematic analysis involving specific cultural artefacts from these periods in the form of judiciously selected British cinema and television texts. Particular attention will be given to examples from the British Social Realist productions of the early 1960s and the Heritage period dramas two decades later. I will analyse the aforementioned aspects with regard to the ways they have been represented through the characteristics of the selected British media texts in terms of their social, moral and political commitment toward broader social and cultural changes within Britain and their similar and different consequences for firstly the questioning, and then the reclaiming of national identity during these two periods.

It is this focus which links the historical and cultural analysis of the book together.

Table of Contents

ACKNOWLEDGEMENTS   xi

PREFACE   xiii

CHAPTER I. INTRODUCTION

    UNDERSTANDING NATIONAL IDENTITY   1

1.1 PERSPECTIVES ON NATIONAL IDENTITY   2

1.2 THE ROOTS OF BRITISH NATIONAL IDENTITY   8

    THE EMERGENCE OF BRITISH NATIONAL IDENTITY   8

        (A) Emergence (1362-1750)   8
        (B) Consolidation (1750-1950)   11
        (C) Decline (1950 - present)   15

1.3 QUESTIONING NATIONAL IDENTITY 1955-65   15

1.4 RECLAIMING NATIONAL IDENTITY 1980-1990   31

CHAPTER II.

    GREAT BRITAIN: A SOCIAL, POLITICAL AND CULTURAL PERSPECTIVE 1955 – 1965   49

2.1 INTRODUCTION   50

2.2 GREAT BRITAIN: THE INTERNATIONAL CONTEXT   51

    THE SUEZ CRISIS   51
    THE COMMONWEALTH   56
    EUROPE   57

2.3	CONVERGENT AND CONFLICTING IDENTITIES	58
	Economic Change and Political Crises	58
	Cultural Change and Social Division	67

CHAPTER III.

	Questioning National Identity - Great Britain in 1955 - 1965	87
3.1	INTRODUCTION	88
3.2	AFFLUENCE, CONSUMERISM AND SOCIAL MOBILITY	92
3.3	MORALITY IN QUESTION	113
3.4	POST-WAR IMPERIAL DECLINE	137
3.5	CONTRIBUTING TO THE CULTURE OF CHANGE	148

CHAPTER IV.

	Great Britain: A Social, Political and Cultural Perspective 1980 – 1990	167
4.1	INTRODUCTION	168
4.2	THE POLITICS OF CHANGE: CONSENSUS TO CONVICTION	169
4.3	THATCHERISM: IDENTITY CONSTRUCTION IN THE 1980S	172
	Economics and Enterprise Culture	172
	The Politics of Confrontation	180
	Heritage and Nostalgia	187
4.4	THATCHERISM: THE INTERNATIONAL CONTEXT	197

THE FALKLANDS AND THE NATIONAL PAST	197
CONTRASTING RELATIONS: EUROPE, USA AND IMMIGRATION	205

CHAPTER V.

RECLAIMING NATIONAL IDENTITY - GREAT BRITAIN IN 1980 - 1990	213
5.1 INTRODUCTION	214
5.2 CLASS, AFFLUENCE AND SOCIAL MOBILITY	218
5.3 MORALITY	239
5.4 ENGLISHNESS, NATIONALISM AND THE IMPERIAL HERITAGE	254
5.5 CONTRIBUTING TO THE CULTURE OF CHANGE	271
CONCLUSION	276
APPENDIX – SELECTED FILMOGRAPHY	294
BIBLIOGRAPHY	301
ABOUT THE AUTHOR	322

Acknowledgement

My sincere thanks to my brother Simon for his strong moral support throughout the writing of this book which has proved invaluable to me. John Hill's seminal thesis has always provided inspiration and motivation for which I am most grateful.

I am deeply indebted to my late father John Cowens Hindmarsh who inspired me at all times and gave me the confidence and encouragement to embark on a career in Academia and I should also like to thank my Mum, Noreen, probably the most remarkable woman I shall ever know and brother Adrian for their love and patience.

Preface - Objective

What I will endeavour to illustrate here is the significant role which national identity plays in shaping, forming and influencing both individual and community consciousness within the social, political, cultural and moral spheres of British life. My comparison is formed by the analysis of the historical and social processes which lay behind the questioning of traditionally accepted perceptions of national identity during 1955-65 and the forceful reclaiming of versions of these images from 1980-90, whilst highlighting the ways the specific cultural artefacts of both periods represent these changing notions of identity.

The pre-war British conception of an historic imagined community was increasingly being undermined as rises in affluence and consumerism gave post-war society a new found confidence to question the social, political and cultural institutions and symbols of a crumbling imperial superstructure. A range of fundamental social, cultural and economic changes allowed a nation, structured and related by the ties of language, inherited ideas and beliefs, and the common experiences of a national community, to unravel. As the ramparts of establishment rule were scaled, weakened by a declining empire and an outdated class structure, the rigorous social and moral controls, which had been in place since the beginning of the century, were abandoned. This social restlessness communicated itself through a diverse range of conflicting cultural constructions: commercial television, popular culture, and sectional identities such as those associated with sexuality, class, race, youth, gender, which competed within this national vacuum vacated by the imperialist establishment. 1960s Social Realism foregrounds the new diversity in social and cultural identities of post-war Britain, whilst re-evaluating questions of morality and Englishness in the light of these post-war societal changes.

As Britain's economic and political status continued its gradual decline the socio-cultural diversity and sectional interests which had developed through the 1960s/70s severely compromised those whose sentiments lay in the sphere of traditional notions of national identity. Hence a rejection of the consensus politics of committee and negotiation led to demands from the right for a dynamic renewal in the 1980s of a national mood of "optimism", "confidence" and "self-respect".

Through the Thatcherite ethos of the Enterprise and Heritage culture a nostalgic, imperialist version of the national past was fondly reconstructed and aggressively marketed in order to reclaim the national "territory" which had been "lost" in the intervening years to the disparate, sectional interests of class, local community, trade unionists, bureaucrats and ethnic groupings. Such minority identities, and the socio-cultural and ideological beliefs by which they were defined, were absorbed into or alienated from a reclaimed nationhood under the unitary Thatcherite banner of the "British people". This new sense of "Britishness", according to Thatcher, revolved around the "rediscovered values" of strict morality, individual responsibility and national allegiance, as if they were characteristic collective British attributes.

The 1980s Heritage media products were concerned, much like the Thatcherite Heritage culture in general, with a nostalgic representation of British, or, rather, bourgeois English history - an image culture - to be packaged and sold as a commodity to an international market. Again, like Heritage culture, these media artefacts ignored the insecurities and uncertainties of a confused chaotic present and reconstructed a nostalgic period of imperialist dominance with apparently more settled and aesthetically pleasing images of national identity - projecting notions of an authentic inheritance of Englishness anchored in an idyllic and nostalgic pastoral culture.

Chapter I.
Introduction
Understanding National Identity

1.1 Perspectives on National Identity

In this chapter, I intend to focus on issues of national identity looking at the leading sociological and historical theories and the varying extent to which they are workable tools of analysis. I shall consider the extent to which they can be applied in later contextual chapters as a framework for comparing and contrasting the cultural, political and economic manifestations of national identity in Britain. I will make specific reference to two periods: 1955-65 and 1980-90. Fundamentally, I will contend that imperialism lies at the heart of British national identity. It is my belief that perceptions of British national identity inherently and inextricably incorporate notions of imperialism. These imperialist references permit the creation of an imagined national identity by depicting the perceived unity and commonality of values that are essential for and integral to any construction of national identity.

I do not claim that this relationship is inherently symbiotic or that it must inevitably endure indefinitely. It may well be that a century hence other arguments will emerge proposing an entirely different base for a construction of national identity, one perhaps rooted in plurality. However, it is my assertion that during the two periods studied the relationship is central. This is perhaps not surprising given the history of Empire. From its earliest stirrings during the reign of the first Elizabeth to its decline under the reign of the present Elizabeth, the Empire has subsisted in some recognisable form for approximately 400 years. There are Britons alive today who remember the Empire at its height. Adults who were children in the 1960s may recall their schoolteachers pointing to parts of the globe and advising them that another obscure portion of Africa was about to gain its independence. When measured in terms of territorial acquisition the Empire continued to expand until the 1930s. Its demise is extremely recent and it is therefore perhaps not surprising that its influences are still present and that imperialist references provide the key to an understanding of British national identity.

I shall now review the relevant socio-historical literature in relation to national identity. This is not a comprehensive survey and it focuses on those sources most germane to the task in hand.

CHAPTER I - UNDERSTANDING NATIONAL IDENTITY

One of the most prominent and most quoted theorists of national identity Benedict Anderson (1985: 12-13) claims: "Nation, Nationality, Nationalism - all have proved notoriously difficult to define, let alone to analyse. In contrast to the immense influence that nationalism has exerted on the modern world, plausible theory about it is conspicuously meagre". Hugh Seton-Watson (1977), who writes on Nationalism, from a social science and liberal historiography perspective, acknowledged the existence of the nationalist phenomenon and yet concluded that no "scientific definition" could be constructed. Tom Nairn (1977, 1997) who cites a Marxist historiography and social science background claims that the theory of nationalism represents Marxism's great historical failure, both from a theoretical and a political perspective.

However, despite such apparent pessimism in formulating a definition of nationalism, Anderson goes on to stress the idea of nation as an imagined political community. He says "the members of even the smallest nation will never know most of their fellow-members, meet them, or even hear of them, yet in the minds of each lives the image of their communion" (Anderson 1985:15). Anderson argues that the nation is imagined as limited because of the finite if elastic boundaries beyond which lie other nations. It is also sovereign and the emblem of a free nation is the sovereign state. Lastly a nation is imagined as a community, because, regardless of the social inequalities and exploitation that may occur in each, it is always perceived as a "deep, horizontal comradeship" (Ibid. 1985: 15-16). According to Anderson, such imaginings have engendered an allegiance in people, making it possible for them to be willing to die for such notions as the nation.

Anderson expands further on his theory. He asserts the base for making communities imaginable and the cultural roots of nationalism. He finds a relationship between the system of production and productive relations (capitalism); a technology of communications (print); and the "fatality of human linguistic diversity". One feels socially and culturally closer to those who speak one's own language than to those who do not (Ibid. 1985: 16-17). Anderson identifies the role played by the development of print as an important feature in the growth of nationalism. This makes it possible for rapidly growing numbers of individuals to think about themselves, and to relate themselves to others, in distinctively new ways by identifying themselves in terms of national identity. In this Ross Poole (1999) concurs with Anderson, but also stresses that, if the nation is an imagined community, then it also serves as a form of "self-consciousness" as it is the public composition of the nation's notion of itself (Ibid. 12-13). As a mode of identity, it exists as a form of individual and other-awareness which can be understood more appreciably at a cultural level.

The nation is culturally specific and exists through a common language spoken by the populace, the shared public symbols they acknowledge, the history and literature they learn, the currency they spend, and the common news, television, film and music they share. According to Poole the nation also exists through the process of one's "self-formation" whereby an individual feels more at home in one social environment as opposed to another (Ibid.: 14-15).

Ernest Gellner (1983, 1997) retains a concern with culture and delineates national identity as the consequence of an educated, culturally homogenous, industrialised, modern, society. However, Smith (1991) categorises Gellner's approach as a language based theory of nationalism in which language is the key aspect of any culture, articulating most distinctively the collective personality of the society. Nationalism is essentially a linguistic movement and differences in language will under certain social criteria, result in dissension and lead to national secession. Schlesinger (1991) on the other hand defines Gellner's theory more as a cultural understanding of national identity in which the essence of the culture has definite preconditions in industrial progression. Indeed it is what might be called the "culturalist" elements contained within these various approaches to national identity which are of particular significance within this book.

Smith (1984) defines a nation (and therefore the features of national identity) as a population, which shares an historic terrain, common myths and historical memories, a widespread, public culture, a common economy and common legal rights. Moreover, Smith emphasises the complex process involved in defining national identity. He includes other kinds of collective identities such as class, religious or ethnic identity. He highlights the shifting changes of nationalism and its ideology, with other ideologies like liberalism, fascism and communism, depending on whichever political system prevails. British imperialism tended to incorporate aspects of many of these divergent ideologies and operated as an apparently unifying force. Regional, religious or class divisions could be overridden whilst pursuing national objectives.

This tended to obscure the multidimensional facets of a construction of national identity. Apart from political, economic and legal elements, other processes are assigned to individuals by way of national identity such as the socialisation of individuals as "nationals" and "citizens". This is perhaps most frequently attained in modern society with national curricula, education systems through which a degree of loyalty and a distinctive, uniform culture are developed. Notions of common values, symbols and traditions are also developed; by the use of symbols - flags, coinage, artefacts, anthems, uniforms, monuments and ceremonies. Citizens are reminded of their shared heritage and cultural domain, strengthening and enhancing the nobility of his or her notion of a common identity and sense of belonging (Smith 1984, 1991). The apparatus of Empire allowed for a profusion of totemic symbols of Britain as a united dominant international force. Indeed as Smith goes on to warn, national identity can also

> "... offer a narrow, conflict-laden legitimisation for political community, which inevitably pits culture-communities against each other... people have allegedly been willing to surrender their own liberties and curtail those of others. They have been prepared to trample on the civil and religious rights of ethnic, racial and religious minorities whom the nation could not absorb. International, or more accurately inter-state, relations have similarly suffered, the ideal of the nation, transplanted across the globe from its western heartland, has brought with it confusion, irritability, strife and terror, particularly in areas of mixed ethnic and religious character" (Smith 1984: 17-18).

Homi Bhabha (1990) claims that in order to identify the construction of what he calls the Janus-faced discourse of the nation one has to first explore the Janus-faced ambivalence of the language itself involved within this process (Ibid. 1990: 4-7). Bhabha further cites the nation as a means of ambivalent narration that locates culture as a tool for marginalising, discontinuity, dispersing and reproducing, as much as producing, constructing, forcing and guiding within society, and warns against a danger amongst theorists of confusing race with nation, associating a sovereignty appropriate to the identities of indigenous peoples to ethnographic or linguistic groups (Ibid.: 7-8).

Breuilly (1985) identifies nationalism as a force utilised by political movements in search of or exercising state power and qualifying such actions with nationalist arguments. A nationalist polemic can, in this context, be seen as a political doctrine constructed upon what Breuilly identifies as three basic declarations:

a) That there exists a nation with a clear and particular character.
b) The interests and values of this nation take precedence over all other interests and values.
c) The nation must be as independent as possible, meaning it must have political sovereignty.

Breuilly concurs with Smith (1984) in highlighting the danger of confusing nationalism with ethnocentrism. However, he also stresses that this can be avoided by emphasising that the idea of a nation belonging exclusively to a particular race of people be established as the foundation of political claims. This can be the main argument adopted by a political movement (Ibid.). Nazi Germany took this argument to a horrific conclusion.

Giddens (1981) characterises the nation-state as an administrative structure the power of, which covers clear territorial boundaries, whereas the nation is the unification of this apparatus. Nationalism can therefore be a set of symbols or beliefs representing a community of experience to those belonging to a particular regional, ethnic or linguistic grouping. They may or may not come together within the boundaries of the aforementioned nation-state.

CHAPTER I - UNDERSTANDING NATIONAL IDENTITY

However, according to Hobsbawm (1990, 1993) some of these theoretical models, such as Gellner's fail to highlight or sufficiently gauge the views of the nation as understood by the ordinary people who are the matter of the official national ideologies of states and movements. Consequently, these cannot be indications of mindset of even the most committed members. In addition, one cannot assume that for most people national identification excludes or subordinates, the remaining group of identifications, which comprise the social make-up. Indeed, national identity is always taken together with other types of identities (cf Smith 1984, 1991). Furthermore, national identification can change and shift in time, even over short periods. Hobsbawm believed that nations would gradually be subordinated to a new global reordering along supranational boundaries (Ibid. 1990).

Leaving aside issues of explicitly constructed nationalism, and the various excursions in the literature into specific histories and political events, the culturalist thread of analysis appears to have four main aspects of relevance here:

a) The concept of an imagined community (Anderson 1985).
b) The multidimensionality of the contributory elements of national identity (Smith 1984, 1991).
c) National identity's potential for cultural division as well as unification (Smith 1984, 1991).
d) The diversity of different levels of identity construction. (Bhabha 1990; Hobsbawm 1990).

All these elements are significant in the construction of British national identity. Imperialism required the presentation to the world of a shared belief system and of a nation with a singularity of purpose. This provides a vital focus and totemic core for the imagined community discussed by Anderson above. I will demonstrate below how this acquisition of Empire began at broadly the same time as the United Kingdom came into being as a recognisable territorial political and economic entity.

Significantly, the construction of Empire accelerated after the Act of Union joined England and Scotland. The Scots would come to play a major role in Empire building and to some extent, this suppressed any latent nationalist tendencies toward Scottish independence. The build up of Empire served, then, to broadly obscure the plurality and multiplicity of identities that existed in terms of class and region. With an Empire to run and a 'Great Britain' to defend differences that might have been expected to emerge from class conflict could be suborned and overridden in order to achieve the common purpose of serving the Empire. Hence the centrality of imperialism to the constitution of British National Identity.

1.2 The Roots of British National Identity

The Emergence of British National Identity

British national identity can usefully be conceptualised in terms of three historical phases:

a) emergence; the early development of British / English national identity up until the mid eighteenth century (1362 – 1750).
b) consolidation; the establishment of Empire and the influence of evangelical Protestantism and monarchy in cementing a more defined national identity in nineteenth century Britain (1750 – 1950).
c) decline; the lessening influence and increasing uncertainty experienced in late twentieth century Britain in relation to both the nation's sense of identity and position in the world manifested by the rise in Celtic nationalism and the question of European integration and the disintegration of Empire (1950 -).

I shall consider the first two phases and then move on to look at the two key periods of the third phase in more detail since they constitute the central focus of my argument.

(A) Emergence (1362-1750)

According to Seton-Watson (1977) in the fourteenth and fifteenth centuries the gradual flowering of the English language was to be a

CHAPTER I - UNDERSTANDING NATIONAL IDENTITY

significant development for English national consciousness. The year 1362 was a date of symbolic national importance. In this year English replaced Norman French in the law courts, and the opening of Parliament proceeded in English for the first time (Seton-Watson 1977, Wood 2000). Indeed by this time Parliament had a clear political role. In Edward II's reign, a calendar was compiled on what Parliament did, the **Modus Tenendi Parliamentum**, which dealt with issues of foreign policy, war, matters concerning the Royal family and the laws of the kingdom (Wood 2000). Anderson (1985) concurs, highlighting the arrival of Wycliffe's vernacular manuscript bible which followed in 1382.

Seton-Watson claims that though England had been a land of civilisation from before the time of Julius Caesar an English nation complete with its own distinctive language only came to fruition in the fourteenth century. However, it is only the history of England rather than the history of the British people which can be traced back to this period.

An English national consciousness, and the educated Englishman's pride in his own language, were given greater clarity through the Anglo-French wars and by discontented churchmen, increasingly disillusioned with the foreign establishment (The Vatican) of a church divided against itself (Jones 1998: 12-13). In the sixteenth century different influences converged to create a potent sense of national identity. The Reformation served as a platform for national change as well as a rejection of strong overseas influences[i] (Jones 1998, Wood 2000). The English translations of the Bible enhanced the language, whilst a significant flourishing of poetry was also taking place. The severe practices of the Tudor reign between 1485-1603 found favour with avaricious landowners and merchants.

---

[i] "Christianity, before the Reformation, meant primarily the body or Community of Christ's people, whereas afterwards it often came to mean a body of different nationalisms. This was a key insight into pre-Reformation assumption of thought. It was the Church which had been the main force in creating community at every level of life, from local parish to the whole of Europe. To attack the Church was to attack society. After the Reformation, the open division in Christianity, there was no centrifugal force strong enough to create community at an international level, and there was no international law yet to replace the Canon Law" (Jones 1998: 239-240).

They were envious of the wealth possessed by the monasteries and indignant towards foreigners such as the French, England's long-standing foe, and the Spanish whose shipping, weigh-laden with riches provided valuable cargo for English ships (Richards 1997, Storry and Childs 1997, Greenfield 1992). During the reign of Elizabeth I there was an increase in the popularity of literature with its emphasis on land, history, language and institutions. The enthusiasm surrounding religious and political ideas and the threat to England's shores posed by the Spanish Armada, all helped to enhance the emergence of an English nation (Helgerson 1992, Storry and Childs 1997). By this stage in English history much of the population, even hundreds of thousands, gave allegiance to the nation as well as to the established authorities represented by a feudalistic or religious or sovereign leader (Helgerson 1992, Richards 1997).

Linda Colley (1992) provides an interesting and insightful account of the emergence of the notion of a British nationality which, she argues, emerged in the eighteenth century following a convergence of historical elements. The notion of Great Britain as a single entity was made easier to imagine by the Protestant religion (Colley 1992: 54). According to David Vincent (1989), the common culture characteristic of Britain from the eighteenth century onwards could be located within the seminal works of popular Protestantism such as the Bible, Milton, Bunyan and Foxe. This Protestantism was glorified in a series of mysticised triumphs over the increasingly alien culture of Catholicism which was vicariously manifested in the Spanish Armada, the Glorious Revolution and the Jacobean Rebellion. This resulted in some members of the establishment elite seeing themselves as a chosen few, equating themselves and contemporary Britain with the Israelis of the Bible (Richards 1997: 6). The most popular 'British' composer during this era was the German George Frederick Handel whose work *The Messiah*, could be interpreted as a glorification of Protestant Christianity (Ibid.). Linda Colley claimed:

> "Protestantism, broadly understood, provided the majority of Britons with a framework for their lives. It shaped their interpretation of the past and enabled them to make sense of the present. It helped them to identify and confront their

enemies. It gave them confidence and even hope" (Colley 1992: 54).

(B) Consolidation (1750-1950)

The series of triumphant wars against the French helped forge a British nationality and delineated a marked contrast between a "Protestant, democratic, parliamentary, commercial and progressive" Britain and a "Catholic, aristocratic, agrarian, backward and poor" France (Richards 1997: 6). The outcome for Britain of such an aggressive and belligerent international policy was the appropriation and acquisition of an enormous global empire. The Welsh and the Scots played an integral and proactive role as imperial governors, military leaders, commercial traders and religious missionaries. Glasgow and Cardiff were increasingly seen, like London, as imperial cities (Ibid.: 6).

According to Richards (1997: 7) a distinctively British identity was emerging, which also and simultaneously complemented the cultural diversity of the four ingredient British "nations". Regional and local cultures remained important to regional and provincial identity, and did not compromise national and imperial pride. For example both the political apparatus itself was national and the principal political parties (Liberal and Conservatives) were specifically constructed and articulated as national. As Richards noted:

> "Parliament was the embodiment of the Whig theory of history, of the gradual and inexorable evolution of democracy, the recognition and incorporation of Catholics, Jews, the working classes and women into the body politic and the operation of political parties that were cross-class and transnational" (Richards 1997: 7).

The rapidly expanding Empire proved a greater force than any national divisions and, significantly, was looked upon as "supranational", with the English, Irish, Scots, and Welsh fighting shoulder to shoulder in the British Imperial Army (Ibid.: 7). The existence and growing significance of Empire led to an increasing tendency for national identity to become predicated upon the national role in the world at large. A British culture started to take root. Influential Victorians numbered several Scots amongst their ranks such as John Ruskin, Samuel Smiles and Edward Irving. However, the central power base of the Empire remained England. The intrinsic identity of Britain was English and there could be no potent Celtic/Gaelic challenge to this identity. Unlike England these other areas of the British Isles were culturally bisected according to Highlands and Lowlands (Scotland), north and south (Wales), and Welsh and non-Welsh speakers, and between Catholics and Protestants (Ireland) (Richards 1997: 8).

However the most significant development of the past two centuries according to Richards, is that "both Anglo-Saxon and Celt... were accommodated within the British Empire, making Britishness compatible with Englishness, Welshness and Scottishness" (Richards 1997: 9).

Gerald Newman (1987) has explored how British national identity came to be constructed by England. He argues that notions of British identity became problematised during the latter part of the eighteenth century. This was the background for the expansion of an explicit national identity, caused primarily by a virulent response to the international but largely French-inspired Enlightenment. The national rejection of the Gallicised influence within English aristocratic society was principally initiated by the bourgeois English intelligentsia (Newman 1987, Richards 1997).

In response to such foreign cultural influence there emerged growing cultural and intellectual movements. There was a marked increase in academic work incorporating virulently nationalistic anthologies. In 1755 Dr. Johnson's Dictionary raised concerns regarding risks to the English language from "Gallicisation" (Richards 1997: 9). Similar anthologies in English painting, music and poetry were all produced in the second half of the eighteenth century. Indeed these were all overtly national projects which aimed to celebrate English culture whilst at the same time downgrading any French achievements. However, the British Museum, the Royal Academy, the Encyclopaedia Britannica which had all

CHAPTER I - UNDERSTANDING NATIONAL IDENTITY

started were clearly more British than English in terms of their cultural aspirations (Ibid.: 9). Great English writers from former times were re-acclaimed, and represented as exponents of the language in an attempt to identify national literary heroes. Geoffrey Chaucer, Edmund Spencer, John Milton, Dr. Johnson and especially William Shakespeare were all lauded with regard to notions of the "national genius" (Richards 1997: 10).

Also during this period there was an interest amongst English writers in rediscovering an ancient and primordial past, a pre-1066 Anglo-Saxon culture which was free of Norman domination. This was also seen as a thinly veiled reference to contemporary concerns regarding French social influences through the Enlightenment (Richards 1997: 10-11). In addition iconographical representations pertaining to a "national personality" were created during this period, especially those of John Bull and Britannia. "Originally invented in 1712, John Bull was eventually to be identified with, and hold the appearance of, a sturdy and robust early-nineteenth-century country squire in swallow-tail coat, waistcoat and boots, and carrying a riding crop". He became the epitome of bluff, decent, commonsensical Englishness, as opposed to Britishness" (Richards 1997: 10).

Britannia, developed in the mid eighteenth century occupied a more general function as the "iconographic personification of the nation, a symbol of the virtues relevant to national life - patriotism, dedication, honesty, selflessness, discipline and simplicity" (Richards 1997: 10, Taylor 1992). The makeup of the national ethos was supplemented, during this period, by the combination of two significant and influential beliefs. One was Evangelical Protestantism:

> "The Evangelicals, characterised by an intense seriousness of purpose, immense industry and enthusiastic missionary spirit, censorious highmindedness and a puritanical abstention from worldly pleasures, mounted a full-scale and successful assault on every level and aspect of society, promoting philanthropy, religion, education, duty and hard work, and attacking cruelty, frivolity and vice" (Richards 1997: 11).

The Evangelicals helped to abolish slavery, put an end to public executions, and banned bull baiting and prize fighting, sports now considered to be barbaric. This movement also curtailed gambling and the consumption of alcohol and introduced ascetic guidelines in relation to sexual behaviour instilling moral sense and an obligation to duty and service. These beliefs were taught in schools and privileged in literature and at law. They became "British national values" across the United Kingdom (Richards 1997: 11).

At the same there was a renewed interest in chivalry predicated upon the values of the English gentlemen, that is: "courtesy, bravery, modesty, purity, compassion and a sense of responsibility towards women, children, the weak and the helpless. This permeated the literature of the period and was adopted by youth organisations like the Boy Scouts and Boys Brigade. It became enshrined in the codes and regulations of sports like football and cricket and embodied in the public school ethos (fair play, team spirit, modesty, loyalty) absorbed... by schoolboys everywhere through popular fictions from <u>Tom Brown's Schooldays</u> to the Greyfriars stories in <u>The Magnet</u>" (Richards 1997: 12).

Sir Ernest Barker claimed in 1947 that these values had become an intrinsic aspect of British national character. "The idea of the gentleman is not a class idea, it is the idea of a type of character... a mixture of stoicism with medieval lay chivalry, and of both with unconscious national ideals, half Puritan and half secular" (Barker cited in Richards 1997: 12). The notion of the gentleman was a significant form of representation for the ruling establishment of the whole nation. Evangelicalism and chivalry combined to produce a form of legitimacy for an Empire appropriated in order to enhance Britain's political, economic and military standing:

> "The Evangelical missionary impulse, the desire to bring the heathen to the light of God, and the Calvinist idea of the elect, the British as the greatest nation in the world obliged to provide justice and good government for inferior races, intertwined with a chivalric vision of empire as a vehicle for young

Englishmen to demonstrate the virtues that made them gentlemen". This confluence inspired a continued theme in imperial writing and nurtured the improbable notion that the British ran their Empire primarily for the benefit of its subjects. Lord Curzon, the Viceroy of India, summed up this largely imaginary belief. He wrote that in Empire "we had found not merely the key to glory and wealth but the call to duty and the means of service to mankind" (Richards 1997: 12).

(C) Decline (1950 - present)

The sub-sections Emergence and Consolidation have provided a necessary background for the main substance of my detailed concerns which relate to two phases (1955-65; 1980-90) from the period of Decline.

1.3 Questioning National Identity 1955-65

The Suez crisis of 1956 was a critical moment in modern British history. This humbling if not humiliating event marked clearly for the attention of the world the end of Britain as a first rate independent imperial power. This coincided with a break up of Empire that began to accelerate and acquire a degree of inevitability that had not been apparent during the move towards the independence of India in 1947. This significance was reflected culturally in the fact that 1956 was also the year which saw the Royal Court Theatre stage the premiere of "Look Back In Anger" and the "angry young" authors emerge from an industrialised provincial working class England.

Issues surrounding British identity have occupied the centre-ground of domestic political, social and cultural life since then. This has been especially so in relation to post-war Commonwealth immigration, British membership of the European Economic Community, and today, the beginnings of "the break-up of Britain" through Devolution programmes in Scotland, Wales and Northern Ireland. Political and economic divisions have surfaced between regions, entwined with ideological and class concerns. According to Laing a multitude of social and political allegiances have put at risk the possibility of national unity by undermining the components which helped to solidify pre-war perceptions of national belonging. He included cultural and racial uniformity, class and religious loyalties and the notion of public duty (Laing 1986). This traditional imagery of nationhood was famously evoked in Orwell's English romanticism in 1940. To him a British citizen returning to England from a foreign land had "the immediate sensation of breathing different air". This was furthered by the characteristic signs of English stability including "gloomy Sundays... red pillar boxes, policemen in blue uniforms" and not to mention... "solid English breakfasts... and the curious passion for herrings" (G. Orwell cited in S. Orwell and I. Angus 1970: 97).

Without the cohesive bonds of Empire holding together the disparate strands, socio-cultural differences have emerged which collectively stretch any notion of a uniform national identity. Imperialism functioned in such a way as to require the nation to define itself and its identity for presentation globally and this overriding need became privileged at the expense of more locally rooted senses of identity. Class and regional differences were submerged. Imperial Britain looked outward and whilst the Empire flourished with the tacit or overt approval of the nation it operated to project internationally a single sense of identity and a set of peculiarly 'British values' such as integrity, honesty and endeavour.

This section will examine the ways in which these 'British values' and previously accepted notions of national identity, characteristic of a pre-war class-based imperial establishment, were questioned by post-war British society. Changing attitudes in the political, social, cultural, racial and moral spheres became apparent in the light of increasing affluence and consumerism. At the same time re-assessment of Britain's role as an influential global force took place against a backdrop of vanishing empire and Cold War. I will examine these social and cultural issues and argue that a British national cinema, predicated upon the sectional class-based interests of a specific form of nationalism, emerged and found representation in the so called 'Social Realist' discourse of 1959-63.

CHAPTER I - UNDERSTANDING NATIONAL IDENTITY

At the height of Empire cinematic portrayal of the working class tended to be comic as in George Formby or the class and containment films of Gracie Fields. Other than these examples representation of the working class tended towards the fulfilling of a role in the furtherance of Empire and national defence. With the dismantling of Empire in the 1950s came a shift in the cinematic depiction of the masses. The Social Realist films arrived at a time when the working class had been empowered by the Education Act of 1944, the rise of welfare capitalism, full employment and the Butskellist policies of the post war years. Now something of an economic and political force for the first time it became clear from the Social Realist films that working class interest in Empire was of somewhat less than paramount importance.

The Social Realist film and some of the contemporary television productions, notably <u>Coronation Street,</u> adopted a highly localised perspective. This assumed that working class interests were essentially governed by the more immediate parameters of the pub, corner shop and factory. Hence this working class environment was portrayed in very specific regional and usually industrial terms and bore little resemblance to any traditional pastoral notions of England, as expressed by Blake, as a "green and pleasant land". By contrast middle class or mercantile terms of reference reject localised modes of speech, dress and demeanour and are inclined towards the supranational or imperialist. The relationship between Empire and the mercantile classes is historic and almost symbiotic. India was for example largely colonised by the East India Company, Canada by the Hudson Bay Company and Rhodesia by the diamond prospector Cecil Rhodes. All three, especially India, came to be essential elements of Empire but originated as business prospects for an ambitious, aspirant mercantile class.

The desire to construct business organisations overseas and to colonise the territory is not prominently associated with the aristocracy. Having already invested in extensive areas of Britain and thus establishing a form of domestic Empire they seemed to feel no urge to venture abroad. This is the paradox of Empire. The middle or mercantile class were drawn to the colonies as a means of escaping the stifling class restrictions of Britain only to set up their own version of a class based society overseas. In the carefully constructed society of Empire however they occupied the positions of power.

It will be my contention that the fall of Empire contributed towards an undermining of the mercantile middle class and weakened its position in the national class hegemony, which in turn privileged the portrayal of the newly nascent working class. This collision between the classes marked a period of tension and great social change and the cinematic artefacts studied depict a marked shift in emphasis. National identity moves from a supranational or imperialist foundation to a more fragmented, pluralist basis. This is reflected to some extent by the first cinematic portrayals of issues of race, gender and sexuality. Without the template of Empire, and its adherence to a strictly defined social order, opportunities for social fluidity emerged. I will argue that Joe Lampton (in Room at the Top) was very much a creature of and for his time finding and forcing open doors of opportunity that would probably have been closed to him a decade earlier.

As British power diminished American influence increased. The post-war emergence of the giant Soviet nuclear superpower increased British dependence on the military protection of its relatively recent ally. World War II collaboration, culminating in the Anglo-American Alliance and the "Special Relationship", was aligning Britain ever more closely to American foreign policy. A nascent NATO coupled with the nation's declining world influence followed the Suez fiasco and coincided with the country's rapidly shrinking empire.

Wartime consumption of national wealth compounded by the growing global influence of the Soviet Union made Britain less likely to contemplate future conflict predicated upon imperial self-interest. Furthermore, opinion polls towards the end of the 1950s demonstrated general public resistance to conscription and defence spending (Sinfield 1989: 74). Britain, previously used to being a leading player within the diplomatic sphere, was uncomfortable with the multilateral negotiations characteristic of the United Nations whilst also being excluded from the EEC. The government's desire for Britain to remain a sole power within Churchill's "Three Circles" of global influence (Commonwealth and Empire, the English-speaking world and a United Europe) became an aspiration rather than an achievement.

Uncertain of the nation's role on the world's stage, there was scant political consolation to be found at home. The British were still struggling with the constraints of wartime austerity. As greater affluence helped enhance public confidence the British people started to contemplate an alternative form of political governance to an exhausted, antiquated, and paternalistic class ordered imperialism. The presentation of national unity necessitated by war and encouraged by Empire was fragmenting and pluralist cracks in the fabric were appearing. A stench of moral and institutional decay had undermined the perceived integrity of the British conservative establishment during the early 1960s. This reached its apotheosis with the potent blend of sexual scandal and state security revealed by the highly public cases of Soviet spy William Vassall and War Minister John Profumo.

The Tories' post-Suez Prime Ministers had personified the anachronistic image of Britain's establishment leadership. Harold Macmillan, an admirer of Edwardian patrician culture, and the grouse-shooting aristocrat Sir Alec Douglas Home, who once admitted to counting with matchsticks, and their imperial imagery were no longer typical of a post-war world. The new affluence drove social and cultural changes and encouraged a greater sense of freedom and an increasing rejection of Empire. Harold Wilson was Labour's relatively young and articulate leader. He sought to define his party and his leadership (largely through utilising the modern medium of television) through a new, vibrant British identity based on the dual aspirations of a modern meritocracy and the "white heat of technological revolution". Significantly Wilson appeared to adopt the trappings of the newly classless, conspicuously smoking a pipe and wearing a raincoat instead of an overcoat. He gave every impression of consciously discarding the iconography of Empire.

Technological advances helped drive domestic consumption, materially and culturally. Cars, washing machines, refrigerators and other domestic appliances became more freely available in newly affluent post war Britain. The significance of this affluence lies not in its relation to gross national wealth but in its increasing availability to sections of society formerly largely excluded from personal prosperity. Consumerism would begin to act as a focus for a society now looking away from external considerations of Empire and global standing but towards individual advancement. A commitment to Empire required a willing and steady supply of soldiers, administrators and colonisers. The individuals needed were now seduced elsewhere by consumerist aspirations.

Commercial television and radio, the Sunday tabloid newspapers such as *The News of the World*, youth culture, the Teddy Boy phenomenon and Rock'n'Roll connected a dramatic growth in consumerism with a "new culture of representation" (Hebdige 1988, Sinfield 1989). This commercialisation of British social and cultural life drew resentment across the spectrum of society. Together with the New Left of the late 1950s and early 1960s and CND, there emerged a group of novelists and poets. John Wain, Philip Larkin, Thom Gunn, John Osborne, Stan Barstow, Alan Sillitoe, Shelagh Delaney, David Storey and John Braine eventually became the "angry authors".

However they were not consciously part of any movement and their political beliefs did not always coalesce. John Braine was notably right wing and there were aspects of misogyny in John Osborne's Look Back In Anger (1959). Their emergence acted as evidence of the increasing visibility of pluralist groupings and the collisions resulting from a clash with the existing social and class hegemony. Collectively this group warned of the "moral" dangers imperilling a way of life which, they felt, was threatened by the material blandishments of the new consumerist culture. Amid the Butskellist driven prosperity of the 1950s fears emerged of a bourgeois corruption of the traditional British working-class principles of community and kinship, substituting for them class condescension, consumerism, and a new consensus predicated upon supposed middle-class values.

Real incomes amongst British workers rose by 50% over the course of the decade and 1958-59 witnessed a radical reduction in

CHAPTER I - UNDERSTANDING NATIONAL IDENTITY

purchase tax. This enabled cars and hitherto unaffordable electrical products including washing machines, refrigerators and especially televisions to become achievable symbols of an affluent and socially fluid working class. Whilst acknowledging the material improvements brought about by a rise in prosperity the new mass culture was condemned by respected left-wing writers such as E. P. Thompson and John Saville, of the *New Left Review,* for its cultural depravity and spiritual isolation. Richard Hoggart (1958) in *The Uses of Literacy* delineated the social customs, domestic relations and cultural characteristics of the working-classes in the harsh industrial environment in which he grew up in the north of England. Whilst placing great emphasis on the influence of popular culture, Hoggart criticised the erosion of the traditional pre-war lower-class culture in favour of the "generalised emotional responses" and the "mass opinion, mass recreational" American model prevalent in 1950s English society (Sinfield 1989).

Clearly, Hoggart perceived a nobility of culture in the pre-war working class, which was now under threat. The decline of Empire allowed for such a debate to achieve social significance and earnest cinematic attention. Similarly Raymond Williams (1962), another influential writer on British cultural life, stressed the importance of culture to those discontented individuals and groups on the left who believed domestic culture could be used as a medium for social change. This disparate group of historical revisionists believed in the foregrounding of "history from below". Here alternative folk myths and radical achievements by workers were recounted and celebrated. This acted as a counter point and response to a perceived sense of alienation springing from the new culture of popular music, television, social and political apathy and a lack of self-questioning of contemporary society.

In short, a cultural process was at work which, freed from the constraints of Empire, could imagine and re-create a 'lost' working class culture of vitality and moral purity under attack from insidious consumerism and the corruption of indifference. This alternative British cultural history was mediated through a combination of emerging repertory theatres, Arts Council sponsorship for young new playwrights, The English Stage Company at the Royal Court Theatre and a new "vital theatre" (Laing 1986).

The young contemporary dramatists were "angry" and anxious to tackle the concerns of modern society. Arnold Wesker's Roots was a criticism of the cultural condition of the contemporary working-classes. In 1960 Wesker's Centre 42, utilised visual exhibitions, theatrical events and folk and jazz music, in attempting to foreground cultural modes of protest which were aligned with the beliefs and values of the Trade Union movement. Joan Littlewood created the Theatre Workshop which communicated radical political messages in a popular form, employing improvisation techniques, as opposed to conventional scripts, and topical material. Littlewood produced Brendan Behan's The Hostage concerning the IRA and Shelagh Delaney's A Taste of Honey, set in the squalid back streets of working class Salford. Both plays transferred successfully to the West End whilst Oh, What a Lovely War criticised the imperial establishment and the futility of war.

The structure of British social and cultural life was changing and this was influencing the West End theatre. The Royal Court, with the assistance of The English Stage Company, was producing theatre more radical than the immediate post-war bourgeois diet of Noel Coward, Terence Rattigan and The Mouse-Trap. Arnold Wesker's Roots and Chips with Everything, John Arden's Sergeant Musgrave's Dance and John Osborne's Look Back in Anger, all endeavoured to promote wider social and cultural horizons for the likes of miners, peasants, foot-soldiers and working-class graduates. Jimmy Porter, the new English anti-hero of John Osborne's Look Back in Anger, attracted much publicity and critical acclaim, allowing the Royal Court to prosper commercially. The Royal Court gained a reputation, which distinguished it from conventional West End theatre. They nurtured the writers Osborne, Wesker, Arden and Joe Orton whose interest in the changing character of Britain's social and cultural identity appealed to audiences seeking a more thought-provoking form of theatre.

The new drama of the 1950s/60s articulated the anger and frustrations of a generation increasingly disillusioned with the imperial establishment but seemingly divorced from the pre-war culture of the working class cherished by Hoggart and Williams. Directors Tony Richardson, Karel Reisz and Lindsay Anderson having been schooled in the Free Cinema documentaries of the 1950s and influenced by French New Wave pioneers such as Truffaut and Godard developed a "new cinema whose commitment was to "realism" a determination to tackle "real" social issues and experiences in a manner which matched and a style that was honest and "realistic" as well" (Hill 1986: 127).

Social Realism endeavoured to inculcate a similar social impulse and invigorating sense of life that the "angry young man" cycle had addressed in contemporary theatre and literature. With location shooting, working class protagonists and contemporary social issues, films such as Room at the Top (1959) and the influential Saturday Night and Sunday Morning (1960) conveyed "a raw brand of Englishness". This was set in opposition to both the artificial conventions of studio-based cinema and the insular "metropolitan southern English middle class culture" (Anderson cited in Laing 1986: 116). This new domestic social and cultural diversity was not merely limited to the sectional interests of class but also extended beyond the boundaries of an imagined indigenous white community.

The British Nationality Act of 1948 coupled with the continuing post-war policy of de-colonisation resulted in increased immigration. Racial tensions became a cause for increasing social concern particularly following inner city disturbances in Nottingham and Notting Hill. The establishment's response was to insist upon employment as a pre-condition for entry into the country, therefore making coloured migration more problematic than white. This reinforced the belief that racial enmity was seen as an institutional as well as an individual characteristic amongst those who had only recently entered Britain (Hill 1986, Marwick 1998). However it can also be seen as further evidence of a national turn away from Empire. The decision to grant all former subjects of the Empire admission to the United Kingdom sprang from that rather odd but traditional aristocratic patrician blend of guilt, compassion and responsibility. It did not survive the Empire and its effective removal from governmental thinking by the Act is an indicator of the beginning of a national identity rooted in introspection.

The authorities were therefore attempting to constrain the movements of their former imperial subjects but simultaneously the strict moral and social controls employed by the conservative establishment were loosening. Capital punishment was abolished in 1964, abortion and homosexuality became legal, censorship of the arts was eased greatly, sexual habits altered as contraceptives became more readily attainable and divorce was made easier. The high profile Wolfenden Report, which was published in 1957 had recommended a more tolerant social attitude toward sexual matters (Hill 1986, Aldgate 1995).

Affluence and consumerism took root in post-war Britain and social and cultural identities became less homogenised and more distinctive. This visible emergence of pluralism coincided with the decline of Empire and the fading from power of the traditional imperial class ordered establishment. Actions and beliefs changed in the spheres of domestic and international politics, culture, race and morality. Debates about the meaning of being working class and its culture began to find expression in the media. The loss of Empire and the removal of imperialism as a focus for national unity allowed these disparate strands to emerge. As the archetypal "angry young man" Jimmy Porter raged against the lack of "good brave causes" whilst the patrician, Edwardian, Colonel Redfern mourned the fact that he "knew in his heart it was all over". This period of intense social change incorporated a lament for Empire from a sympathetic but nonetheless overtly establishment figure and a cry of anger from a young working class man. Common to their distress is the loss of Empire and the focal point it provided for all sides in the class divide.

In this next section I am concerned with the issues surrounding the idea of a British national cinema during the period 1955-65 as first articulated in my 2001 Theses "Realist Nights and Heritage Mornings." Specifically I shall be focussing upon the arguments advanced by John Hill and Andrew Higson as typical of the arguments prevalent within debates concerning British cinema.

CHAPTER I - UNDERSTANDING NATIONAL IDENTITY

Historical and Conceptual Framework (1955-1965)

I wish to argue that there was a British national cinema predicated upon the fore-grounding of community and class-based interests within a framework of national identity which was manifested in the work of the British Social Realist cinema between 1959-63. Here I am employing the term "Social Realist Cinema" as used by John Hill in his seminal work from 1986, <u>Sex, Class and Realism</u>. In this book Hill defines Social Realism as a new cinema which had a "commitment to realism, a determination to tackle real social issues and experiences in a manner which matched, a style which was honest and realistic as well." (Hill 1986: 127). Hill goes on to contrast the "realism" of this British "new wave" cinema, through its use of location shooting and the deployment of little known northern actors with the "phoney conventions of character and place characteristic of British studio procedure." (Ibid: 127). Indeed Social Realism's focus upon issues of class, sexuality and the regions had a refreshing effect upon the previously staid and rigid environment of British cinema. (Hill 1986). This new drama emerged from the social and cultural changes of the late 1950s which had encompassed the decline of the empire, an increase in the affluence of the working-class, the birth of a discernible youth culture and the emergence of the New Left. Social Realist cinema was based on the contemporary novels of writers like Alan Sillitoe, Shelagh Delaney, John Braine, Stan Barstow and the theatre productions of the "Angry Young Men" like John Osborne. In social terms, as with the novels and in the theatre, the essential concern of this film movement was to challenge a particular, and until then, deep-rooted version of Englishness.

This cinema articulated the anger and frustrations of a generation growing increasingly disillusioned with the outmoded beliefs, social mores and moral restraints of Britain's imperial establishment. Social Realism attacked the alien influence of the new American-style consumerism, materialism and popular culture upon the "Englishness" of society, especially television, advertising and Rock 'n' Roll which had all been condemned by the New Left. Untypical of commercial British cinema until then, the films explored northern working-class protagonists' desires and aspirations for "something better" as well as their ambivalent feelings concerning their own community. These films were made amidst a period in post-war Britain of relative economic growth and prosperity. However both income and class inequalities continued to persist whilst the foreign and domestic policies of both the Conservative government and Labour opposition were remarkably similar. (Bogdanor and Skidelsky 1970; Marwick 1998). Consequently the Social Realist films conveyed more of a moral and cultural polemic than a political one. Indeed the films' principal characters such as Arthur Seaton in Saturday Night and Sunday Morning (1960) and Vic Brown in A Kind of Loving (1962) rebel against the mind numbing boredom and constraints of domestic life and work as they are trapped in both their social background and their urban environment. Moreover they find themselves isolated both from the greater political and social system, which they are unable to penetrate, and their own downtrodden and increasingly consumerist-orientated working class community.

The year 1956 had been significant for social and cultural change in Britain. It was the year of the Suez Crisis, it was the year the first "angry" play, Osborne's "Look Back in Anger" made its debut at the Royal Court theatre, and it was the year when a group of young film-makers with left wing sympathies – Tony Richardson, who had directed "Look Back in Anger" at the Royal Court, Karel Reisz and Lindsay Anderson – had formed the Free Cinema documentary movement. This movement was a reaction against what Lindsay Anderson described as: "…a British cinema still obstinately class-bound; still rejecting the stimulus of contemporary life, as well as the responsibility to criticise; still reflecting a metropolitan Southern English culture which excludes the rich diversity of tradition and personality which is the whole of Britain." (Anderson cited in Laing 1986:114).

The Free Cinema belief in location shooting together with the French New Wave preference for natural lighting were to influence Anderson, Reisz and Richardson and impact upon the formal strategies of the Social Realist films they were later to direct. The

CHAPTER I - UNDERSTANDING NATIONAL IDENTITY

use of grainy black and white film, unknown regional working class actors such as Albert Finney, Rita Tushingham and Tom Courtney and location shooting in the north of England located contemporary audiences within a cinematic terrain different from that of the "metropolitan, Southern English middle-class culture" represented by British cinema until then. My argument will be, then, in chapter 3 that we must try to understand the particular version of the national past, as it is mediated through these cultural artefacts, and therefore the socio-historical function they may be performing.

Although Social Realism can be seen as part of the legacy of the British realist aesthetic tradition which dates back before Free Cinema to the documentary movement of John Grierson and Humphrey Jennings in the 1930s, films such as <u>Room at the Top</u> (1959) and <u>Saturday Night and Sunday Morning</u> (1960) can still be seen as products which achieve the verisimilitude of conventional classical Hollywood narrative. Higson (1996: 136). Although the films can be described as "realist", the text's principle objective is still to convey a linear story comprising of a beginning, middle and end. According to Higson (1996) in the Social Realist film, like the classical Hollywood product, "representation" is mediated as "presentation", in other words, the story is conveyed to the spectator as "the real world" and in turn the spectator is expected to follow the events surrounding the story rather than attend to cinematic style. Indeed the critics of the early 1960s rarely commented on the narrative forms of the British Social Realist films. (Higson 1996: 136). However according to John Hill the conventional narrative's tendency for a "problem solving" resolution can effect the way Social Realism tackles its subject-matter. (Hill 1985: 74-6). A definition of narrative is outlined by Tzvetan Todorov: "Every narrative is a movement between two states of equilibrium, which are similar but not identical. At the beginning there is always a balanced situation...then something comes along to break the calm and creates an imbalance...the equilibrium is then restored, but it is not the same as at the beginning." (Todorov cited in Andrew, 1984: 84). Both the Social Realist films, and Heritage which I shall turn to later, loosely conform to the Todorov principle. In the case of Social Realism the disequilibrium is caused by a social or sexual violation; for example Brenda's unexpected pregnancy in <u>Saturday Night and Sunday Morning</u> (1960).

According to the conventions of this narrative however there is a presumption on the part of the spectator that any such disequilibrium will be corrected. (Hill 1985:74). Similarly these narrative conventions tell us that it is the motivations of a principal character that initiates story development – Arthur's affair with Brenda – and the corrective methods of others which establish a new equilibrium – Arthur is beaten up by Jack's brother after which he stops seeing Brenda. However in this way Social Realism's attempt to represent the working class as a group is problematised by what John Hill describes as "the individualising conventions of classical narrative"... for in this instance.... "Class... is an individual as opposed to a collective experience, a moral rather than a socially and economically structured condition." (Hill 1985: 75-6). In his chapter "Working Class Realism and Sexual Reaction: Some Theses on the British "New Wave"" (1983) John Hill suggested that Social Realist cinema was by no means entirely progressive and from the point of view of sexuality and domesticity these films "end by reproducing an ideology of marital and procreative sexuality"...whilst they also reaffirm "the need for male regulation of female sexuality within the marriage institution." (Hill 1983: 310). Andrew Higson (1983: 87) on the other hand disagrees with Hill's perspective. Writing in the pages of <u>Screen</u> he accuses Hill of a "sociological desire for neatness and continuity" through a slavish devotion to the inevitable closure and resolution of the narrative. With specific reference to <u>Saturday Night and Sunday Morning</u> (1960) Higson stresses that what is surely significant in this film is not that Arthur Seaton is dragged back into the family unit with Doreen, but his general resistance and rebellion toward social constraints and domestic repression throughout the film as evidenced by both his stone throwing aggression targeted at the new housing estate, a symbol of the increasing embourgeoisement of the working class in British society at this time, and his sexual miscreance with Brenda.

(Higson 1983: 88). Indeed according to Higson what Hill is overlooking in his conclusion that the Social Realist films are "reactionary" is this very interplay between the contained and excessive behaviours in the film's narrative which helps produce an "unresolved tension in the film-viewing experience for the spectator, a tension which works over the ideological stresses of the period described by Hill." (Higson 1983: 88).

However with regard to the visual aspects of the narrative Higson (1996) argues that Social Realism's "authentic iconography... reproduces the visual and aural surfaces of a distinctively British way of life" through what is known as "surface realism". (Higson 1996: 136). The use of the authentic place (northern English locations) and character (urban/industrial/working class/unknown regional actors) breaks the conventions of studio-based classical Hollywood melodrama. Furthermore Higson stresses that surface realism involves an intense spectator interest in these iconographic details which unlike Hollywood iconography, does not dissolve into the mise-en-scene as narrative background (whereby the actors can play out the story) but also plays a "part" - through "the visual spectacle of the real" – in narrating and indeed "authenticating the fiction". (Higson 1996: 134-6). This is particularly prevalent in the landscape and townscape shots where place becomes "a signifier of character, a metaphor for the character's mood". (Higson, 1996: 134). Andrew Higson's earlier study of Social Realism's use of "place" in Screen in 1984 gave particular focus to A Taste of Honey (1961). The film's director of photography Walter Lassally expertly frames Jo in long and then medium-shot in one sequence which lasts fifty seconds without dialogue or any apparent narrative motivation as the camera tracks her meandering, amidst the mist and the fog along the canals of Salford.

In another sequence lasting twenty-seven seconds a noisy Manchester street parade is inter-cut by numerous shots of the watching crowds before we return to the narrative as the camera finally cuts to Jo. John Hill (1986) claims that these sequences help the cinematography of A Taste of Honey to aestheticise the northern industrial townscape, forcing audiences to gaze at the visual spectacle whilst narrative motivation takes a back seat. (Hill 1986: 132-4). This emphasis on place and spectacle in this film also ensures that these location sequences and others similar to them in the rest of the New Wave productions are frequently the most analysed scenes in the films. (Higson 1984, 1996, Hill 1986, Lovell 1990). As Higson states when summarising the significance of Social Realism's locations: "It is place, rather than action, which assumes importance." (Higson 1983: 84). However the need in Social Realism to foreground "both narration and description" at the same time, as outlined above, causes a "textual tension" between these two processes; involving "social problem and pleasurable spectacle". (Higson 1996: 134). In addition, Higson identifies a "moral thrust to the iconographic commitment to the representation of "ordinary people."" (Higson 1996: 137). However he claims that this "moral realism... also involves a particular construction of the social in terms of "universal human values." It is that same demand voiced by the documentarists of the 1930s that films should show the dignity of the working class man...A concern for personal relations and human values invests the landscape with a greater sense of moral urgency and a more compelling sense of human sympathy, while the real historical landscape, local and concrete, legitimates and authenticates this moral universe." (Higson Ibid: 137).

Amongst the most striking location scenes in the Social Realist films are those identified by Higson as "That Long Shot of Our Town From That Hill" (Ibid 1996: 134). The shot, such as the one featuring Vic on a hilltop high up overlooking the working-class horizon in <u>A Kind of Loving</u> or a similar point-of-view of Frank Machin in <u>This Sporting Life</u>, serves to create a space between the camera's eye and the working-class protagonist who can be seen as "an observer within the landscape" (Lovell 1990: 369). Higson claims that shots such as these act to locate the lower class male in his environment, "inscribing a middle-class observer/outsider as viewer, and as the source of the film's enunciation." (Higson in Lovell: 370). Hill agrees, however he stresses further that this point-of-view of the "outsider" ascribes to Social Realism's comparatively liberal social portrayal of sexuality a distasteful voyeuristic leaning which he attaches to "a bourgeois obsession with cleanliness, fascination with working-class squalor and sexuality." (Hill 1986: 136). Moreover Lovell acknowledges this distance between the viewer and the viewed and takes the argument a step further by suggesting this "space" which is opened up could be best enjoyed by "Hoggart's scholarship boy: the adult working-class male looking back with nostalgia at a remembered childhood landscape." Lovell believes that such an individual can empathise with and feel involved in what is being observed by bringing to the scene:

"The knowledge of the insider combined with the distance achieved by the move outside and beyond... it is...this position which can align itself most readily and personally with the point of enunciation of many of the 'New Wave' films." (Lovell, 1990: 370). Consequently Richard Hoggart's "scholarship boy" may recognise the young, restless, sexually virile worker, as the man he may have become had he remained in that environment.

1.4 Reclaiming National Identity 1980-1990.

The second part of this book begins at the end of the 1970s when the Empire had vanished save for Hong Kong and a disparate collection of economically undeveloped islands. In tandem with the loss of Empire the middle class had lost ground economically, socially and politically. Again revisiting the debates I detailed in my 2001 Theses "Realist Nights and Heritage Mornings" I will demonstrate how a pseudo class system attempted to re-assert itself and how it sought to impose essentially bourgeois, imperialist influences upon a construction of national identity. However, notions of duty and public service no longer bound this new aspirant class. I will seek to establish that it had been commandeered and undermined or, from a Thatcherite perspective, inspired and empowered by the rise of a new meritocracy.

Following this period, the policies of Thatcher's governments were frequently concerned with identifying enemies "within and without" the nation and named among others unions, miners, socialists, Europe, Argentineans and single mothers (Samuel

1989). In Thatcherite terms these were the new threat to national security and sovereignty. According to Thatcher, post-war national economic decline was the responsibility of the special interests of producers, trade unions and the bureaucratic nationalised industries in preventing change and trailing international competitors in the fight for economic efficiency and greater productivity. Thatcher saw political and economic issues in terms of Britain's potential greatness. She spoke of "inspiring a new national mood..." calling for the "...renewal of our traditional craftsmanship and civic spirit" on every plane of society, following years of the "long dismal drawling tides of drift and surrender".

At the centre of this new mood must be "... a recovery of our self-confidence and our self-respect. Nothing is beyond us!" (cited in Riddell 1989: 7-8). The distinctive Britishness of Thatcher's discourse centred on a set of "values" she claimed were in danger of being lost. She spoke of the rule of law, the family - as the font of moral discipline - thrift, ambition, hard work, individual responsibility and national pride. However, despite preaching a doctrine of individualism Thatcher defended these "British values" against any perceived alien threat such as strikes and racial unrest by employing the repressive elements of the state system. The government drew the police and the legal system into the struggle with the striking miners in 1984-85 with harsh results. A ban was imposed on secondary picketing and the police closely monitored the strikers. In addition aggressive, high-level policing was a feature of the notoriously bloody "Operation Swamp" in Brixton in 1981, and the tragic nation-wide inner city riots in the same year and in Tottenham in 1985.

The style of Thatcher's leadership amounted to authoritarian populism. It centred around a vision of popular national identity drawing upon a reconstruction of the British character which included John Bull, Churchill, the Dunkirk Spirit, and was expressed in a nationalist language, which featured the constant themes of nation and people. Thatcherism attempted to assert unity at the level of "the nation", an imagined community of shared values and beliefs. As an arch revisionist and self styled meritocrat she sought to reconstruct a middle class definition of

CHAPTER I - UNDERSTANDING NATIONAL IDENTITY

national identity by reviving imperialist references. Despite the absence of an Empire in reality, this incorporation of imperialism took the form of re-constructed notions of Empire which could be inserted effortlessly into the emergent 'heritage' industry.

Thus when assessing what role the trade unions might have in this new Britain she asked the question... "How have they affected the lives of the nation at large?..." This, according to Thatcher, was the "... natural question for trade unionists to ask themselves" (Margaret Thatcher, Conservative Trade Unionists' Annual Conference, November 1979, cited in O'Shea 1984: 23). Here Thatcher was criticising the specifically factional concerns of trade unionists, whom she referred to as the "enemy within," and who were demonised in the Tory press as a violent mob of "Marxist bully boy leftists" (O'Shea 1984: 28). She talked of "the nation" through the workers' sense of "Britishness". In so doing she was using the "isolation effect" (Poulantzas 1973) whereby social categories (classes, races, gender groups, old, young, rich, poor, socialist) are transmuted into a-political groups such as individuals, families and ultimately consumers. As Thatcher stressed when addressing the trade unionists: "...we are all consumers and as consumers we want a choice" (Ibid.: 23).

The images typically associated with Tory notions of Britishness in the 1980s were markedly different to those proffered by the Labour Party which was swinging further toward the left. It was suffering from the popular image of its ageing leader, Michael Foot, who was ridiculed by the political right as a withered and decrepit figure. It was considered to be obsessed with an increasingly antiquated discourse of hegemonic class struggle, re-nationalisation, unilateral nuclear disarmament and Jarrow-style "marches for jobs". This imagery was compounded by the Government propaganda machine and its constant references associating Labour with the repressive left-wing regimes of Eastern Europe. Meanwhile the Conservatives were promoting a populist nationalism which attempted to recreate a "Dunkirk Spirit" for the 1980s. This received a largely unexpected boost by the Falklands conflict. I will discuss this war and try to explain why an essentially anachronistic colonial skirmish, lasting for only a few weeks and incurring British casualties in the low hundreds, seemed to evoke contemporary comparison with the Second World War, a six year struggle for national survival. I will examine how the "Falklands Factor" galvanised huge public support for the sort of expedition last mounted in the XIX century. I will suggest that this conflict focused the latent middle class need for imperialist references and was an essential factor in the reconstruction of a national identity in the 1980s, another period of great social change.

The language of Thatcherism urged the people to "rejoice" at every budget rebate and veto Britain was able to extract from the growing Euro bureaucracy which threatened to "swallow up" British sovereignty inside a federal super-state. Projecting herself as a latter day Boadicia, Thatcher claimed she was protecting the nation's "self-respect... our heritage and our great past" (Thatcher cited in O'Shea 1984: 25). The loss of Empire in the physical territorial sense prevented a straightforward imperial centred construction of national identity, but there was a clear demand shown by the newly re-ascending middle or meritocratic mercantile class for such imperial fantasies.

Through an examination of the 'Heritage Films' and their commercial and critical success I will seek to establish that this form of cinema in particular was meeting this desire for themes of national nostalgia. By adopting a veneer of liberalism and humanitarian principles for contemporary consumption such films represented a reconstructed fantasy of Empire.

The Falklands war, a quintessentially imperial conflict, enabled Mrs Thatcher to energise the idea of the nation against both domestic foes as well as foreign. She seized the moment as an opportunity to use the rhetoric of nationalism as a mode of nationalistic recompense. This was intended to address the feelings of despair, inferiority and demoralisation some of the socially alienated and economically disenfranchised were beginning to endure during the painful monetarist "economic solution" of free market enterprise. This overseas military engagement operated to draw attention away from bitter domestic, economic, social and political differences that had already emerged under her term of office, at this stage still less than three years old. This imperial dispute acted as a masking agent serving to obscure the plurality of political opinion and the many socio-cultural identities which comprised 1980s national identity.

The main political and ideological thrust of Thatcherism remained individualism with its aim to free a nation of entrepreneurs, princes of industry and self-starters from the fetters of the state, to release the "energy" of enterprise and initiative. Through her Chief Policy Adviser, Sir Keith Joseph, she drew upon XIX century entrepreneur Samuel Smiles' study of the "self-made men" of the industrial revolution who attempted to counter the cultural and social snobbery which they met in Victorian society. In this, she was indirectly challenging the "caring", paternalistic establishment values of the Tory "Grandees," the privileged old Tories. This rejection of the values of *noblesse oblige*, combined with the promotion of a meritocratic, self-serving acquisitiveness, only served to clash with the traditional principles of honour and sense of public duty characteristic of the old aristocratic conservatism. Two early victims of Thatcher's first cabinet reshuffles were Frances Pym and Ian Gilmore, Tories of the "old school", who had served in Edward Heath's cabinet and had disagreed with the new Prime Minister over policy issues.

The Thatcherite emphasis on the individual pursuit of wealth and personal success generated selfishness, an uncaring attitude to those less fortunate, personal greed, and eventually, to corporate greed. For example, the recently privatised nationalised industries reduced employee numbers in order to enhance profits for the benefit of directors and shareholders. Thatcher's advocacy of the enterprise culture of risk and reward, and the Victorian values of thrift, moral virtue and public duty, had given way to acquisitive individualism, aggressive self-interest and belief in unlimited economic growth. Nationally Thatcher's monetarist economic policies placed strict control on the money supply, leading to a failure to subsidise struggling industries. The manufacturing base, which was mainly located in the North and Midlands, shrank. There was a simultaneous expansion in the service sector, and especially in financial services for London and the South. This followed Mrs

Thatcher's policies of deregulation and substantial tax reductions following a squeeze on public money and proved especially beneficial to the wealthy and high earners. Such policy decisions seemed to concentrate the majority of the nation's wealth in the bourgeois south-east at the expense of the traditional working-class north, fuelling regional frictions and enhancing a North/South economic divide.

This erosion of social cohesion presented Thatcherism with ideological as well as social problems. If the New Right employed the slogan of community in attempting to assuage social divisions it might be uncomfortably reminiscent of the tainted and rhetorical ideology of Socialism. Hence the strategy of constructing a potentially unifying cultural theme around notions of Englishness and the associated issues of family, civic respectability and nation (Hall 1988).

Events such as the Falklands crisis and much-vaunted claims of a "special relationship" with the USA allowed Britain some illusory aspirations to global status, influence and power in a post-imperial age. In this context representations of national Heritage were to play a central role in re-evaluating growing uncertainty surrounding British cultural identity during the 1980s and in encouraging the fantasy of Empire that underpinned 1980s constructions of national identity.

The Conservatives combined a nostalgic bourgeois interpretation of history with the physical manifestations of "National Heritage". These policies created a pastiche in which the social frictions and class inequalities of history were substituted by the values and achievements of the ruling classes. Working-class experience was absorbed into a picturesque, idyllic image of the past (Horne 1984). During the course of the 1980s Heritage became identifiable in a diverse range of cultural artefacts such as museums, historic buildings, country houses, reconstructed "communities", quaint industrial museums and National Trust membership.

It found cinematic representation in Heritage products such as Chariots of Fire (1981), A Passage to India (1984), Brideshead Revisited (1981) and The Jewel in the Crown (1983) - which I shall analyse in detail in later chapters. Commercial leisure also

CHAPTER I - UNDERSTANDING NATIONAL IDENTITY

helped make Heritage more widely available through television costume drama and theme parks. Against the decline of the manufacturing sector tourism had emerged in the 1980s as a principle source of foreign income, behind North Sea oil and the growing Financial Sector. "Images of friendly London "bobbies", traditional craftsmen at work and Lords and Ladies in their historic houses" abounded in the tourist guides of the time (In *Britain*, July 1988, cited in Samuel 1989: 54). Similarly according to Samuel "a localised sense of place and historical identity was also fostered" as Suffolk became "Constable Country" and Cornwall was a "smuggler's coast." Peterborough was "reinvented as 'one of the great Roman towns', York as a 'Viking Centre', whilst the Shropshire canals were promoted as the West Midlands' Lake District" (Samuel 1989: 54-55). The 1980s Heritage culture compensated symbolically for post-war social and economic decline by presenting a seductive version of British history.

Responsibility for "the Arts" fell to the Government Department of Heritage and Tourism in 1982 and government funding became more selectively targeted at high-profile "national" symbols of the performance arts such as the Royal Opera House and the Royal Shakespeare Company. The National Theatre, under increasing commercial pressure to fill all its seats began re-staging pre-war farces (Hewison 1987: 122-7). Government funding of established national arts institutions at a time when fringe theatre was in decline coupled with an emerging Heritage industry and high profile royal coverage helped to reinforce notions of an imaginary national bourgeois culture during the 1980s. Indeed Thatcher looked upon the arts as a great British success story, describing them as "... a product with which we compete on equal or superior terms with the rest of the world. The arts are both at the heart of the tourist industry, and a major diplomatic and cultural aid" (Hewison 1987: 128). In so doing Heritage culture of the 1980s conveyed a bourgeois history, where the alternative accounts of British class struggle and workers' rights were hidden behind a vision of costume drama and re-presentation.

In sum, then, with the loss of Empire and the emergence of a more conspicuously plural society, the late 1950s and the 1960s witnessed considerable social change. As the pillars of Empire weakened and fell, it is possible to see differing classes coming to the fore and new conflicts arising from the collision of those classes and the emergence of new racial and social groups. As the old, imperial social order began to disintegrate social tensions were increasingly apparent in a nation previously imagined to be untied, and it is these tensions that drive forward the characteristic cultural innovations of the period – most notably in the rise of 'Social Realist' cinema and television.

Social and cultural change then accelerates in the course of the later 1960s in ways and with consequences which are well beyond the scope of this book, although certain aspects of the culture of the period – for example the development of the key popular cinema figure of James Bond – will be given some consideration here. Sufficient to observe for present purposes, however, that after the chronic instability of the 1960s and 1970s the Thatcherite right found itself facing an acute cultural and political problem. How is a unifying national identity to be sustained in a society which has become so clearly differentiated? Their response in the 1980s was an attempt to reconstruct some of the values and attitudes once associated with Empire, thereby underpinning an effort by the mercantile meritocracy to reclaim a bourgeois version of national identity. Thus, in both the periods with which I am concerned, it is the relation to Empire, first to its loss and then to its imaginary reclamation, that is central to national identity.

In the following section I will focus upon the issues surrounding the notion of a British national cinema during the period 1980-1990. Once again as in my seminal 2001 Theses "Realist Nights and Heritage Mornings" I shall be concentrating upon the arguments articulated by Andrew Higson and John Hill as representative of the variety of arguments existing in relation to debates regarding British Cinema.

Historical and Conceptual Framework (1980-1990)

As I have articulated in "Realist Nights and Heritage Mornings" (2001) I shall again argue here that a distinctly British national cinema predicated upon the Heritage cycle of films and classic television serials emerged in the 1980s, one that employed a bourgeois view of the English national past which was then sold on a global scale, especially to the USA. Here I am using "Heritage Cinema" as Andrew Higson understands the term. (1993, 1995, 1996). Higson describes the Heritage cycle of films as one which "reinvents and reproduces, and in some cases simply invents, a national heritage for the screen." (Higson 1995: 26). Higson stresses his interest in Heritage films is in "how they represent the national past, and in how this representation works for contemporary spectators....the past is displayed as visually spectacular pastiche, inviting a nostalgic gaze that resists the ironies and social critiques so often suggested narratively by these films." (Higson 1993: 109). As Higson concludes the Heritage films "offer apparently more settled and visually splendid manifestations of an essentially pastoral national identity and authentic culture: Englishness as an ancient and natural inheritance, *Great* Britain, the *United* Kingdom." (Ibid: 110). Heritage products such as Chariots of Fire (1981), Brideshead Revisited (1981), Another Country (1984) and A Passage to India (1984) displayed a nostalgic perspective which was emblematic of changes at work in 1980s society. (Higson 1993: 109). This was a time when Britain's global status was sinking further into economic recession whilst traditional working class industries and their communities were thrown into poverty and social insecurity. Notions of identity were increasingly being questioned as the multinational European Community gained in influence and British society was increasingly being seen as ethnically diverse. Within this context the Heritage media ignored the distasteful post-imperialist economic and social uncertainty of the contemporary to reconstruct an imperialist bourgeois, picturesque national identity culture. (Higson 1993 :110-111).

These productions were, in comparison with lavish Hollywood products, low budget artefacts made by independent companies, sometimes in co-production with television, notably Channel 4. They were affiliated with the British art cinema and were mainly viewed at art-house venues or on television by a largely "middle-class audience... older than the mainstream film audience". (Ibid: 110). Heritage media operates "within a cultural mode of production, as distinct from Hollywood's industrial" (Ibid: 110), reflected in both the exhibition of the films and their grounding in culturally and historically prestigious national literature and theatre through adaptations from Edwardian writers E M Forster; *A Passage to India*, *A Room with a View* and *Maurice* or Evelyn Waugh's *Brideshead Revisited* as well as *Another Country*, adapted from Julian Mitchell's play. (Higson 1993 114-5).

The Heritage media and its particular reconstruction of the past can be seen as part of the larger tourist, recreational and heritage industry which grew out of the stark, social, economic and political changes within Thatcher's Britain. As Higson (1993: 112) states, the Thatcher government attempted to combine "tradition and modernity" through heritage - and its particular associations with "the preservation of values and traditions, and "enterprise" – with its connotations of change and innovation." Corner and Harvey develop this point further:

"What has come to be called "the heritage industry" is itself a major component of economic redevelopment, an "enterprise," both in terms of large-scale civic programmes and the proliferation of private commercial activity around "the past" in one commodified form or another." (Corner and Harvey, 1991:46).

Through the National Heritage Acts of 1980 and 1983 bourgeois values and tastes were transposed into national culture. Properties, estates and landscapes belonging to the aristocracy were re-presented as national estates and landscapes. Therefore in this context National Heritage overrides all class conflict and social opposition for the sake of national culture. (Bommes and Wright 1981: 67): "By reproducing these trappings outside of a materialist historical context, they transform the heritage of the upper classes into the national heritage."(Higson 1993: 114). Indeed properties and estates maintained by English Heritage and the National Trust such as Castle Howard and Tatton Hall, the centre of both tourist and public interest during the 1980s, feature prominently in heritage media. In tracing the origins of the contemporary heritage film

CHAPTER I - UNDERSTANDING NATIONAL IDENTITY

back to Cecil Hepworth's adaptation of the Victorian novel, Comin' Thro' the Rye (1924) Higson claims that the 1980s heritage media "invokes the idea of national heritage as part of the bid to construct a distinctive national cinema drawing on indigenous cultural traditions". (Higson 1996: 237).

The "museum aesthetic" of heritage media is consciously designed to "display" the vast country estates, beautiful landscapes, expensive furnishings, lavish costumes and the aristocratic set. Hence in the heritage media, spectator gaze is aimed as much at the mise-en-scene as with the events of the narrative. (Higson 1993: 117; 1996: 233). The characteristic narrative of these artefacts is "slow and episodic" (especially in the classic television serial adaptations) as opposed to the quick-paced "causal development of the classical film". (Higson 1996: 233). Indeed in A Room with a View there are extravagant "inter-titles" designed to reinforce this novelistic structure (Higson 1993: 117). There is a concentration on "character, place, atmosphere" as opposed to "goal-directed action". The "intertextuality" of heritage media means that the "same actors play similar ...class types" (Higson 1993: 115) in more than one production; Helena Bonham Carter (A Room With A View, Maurice), Rupert Graves (the same two films) Nigel Havers (Chariots of Fire, A Passage to India) and Peggy Ashcroft (Jewel in the Crown, A Passage to India). According to Higson the camerawork resembles an association with "art photography" and "set-piece images" through its "pictorialist" quality. (Higson 1993: 117). Furthermore "The use of long takes, deep focus and long and medium shots" enables the camera to draw the spectator's attention to the heritage setting and the properties and possessions which occupy it. (Higson 1993; 116-17, 1996: 233-34). High-angle shots, distanced from character point-of-view, enabled 1980s audiences to luxuriate in the enticing mise-en-scene. For instance in an episode of Brideshead Revisited a crane shot slowly tracks toward the staircase balcony where it pans across the "Great Hall" ostentatiously displaying the paintings, antique furniture and lavish interior designs which adorn the vast spaces, walls and high ceilings, whilst Charles and Sebastian, who are engaged in the narrative, are barely seen below on the sofa, marginalised from what Higson

(1993) describes as the "heritage space" which is reserved "for the display of heritage properties". (Ibid: 117). Moreover in <u>A Room with a View</u> there are a number of travelogue style shots of Florence framed without the "mediation" of "character point-of-view". (Higson 1993: 117). I have commented earlier that the heritage media could be seen on one level by 1980s audiences as a postimperialist denial of the socio-economic complexities of the decade, finding solace and reassurance in an imaginary, unified national identity of the past. Moreover heritage may also be looked upon as a critique of the Thatcherite present from a liberal-humanitarian perspective. (Light 1991: 63). Through the cloak of costume drama heritage can condemn the Thatcherite values of individualistic material gain by contrasting them with the Liberal-humanitarian friendships apparent in their narratives: "gay love-affairs... transclass relationships... interethnic friendships" (Higson 1993: 119). Indeed in his novels Forster stresses the need "for a Liberal-humanist refashioning of Englishness". (Ibid: 119). At a narrative level then, Higson claims that heritage "raises questions" about the "nature" and character of Englishness, about "who inherits England?" The "hybrid quality of Englishness" is suggested in the liberal humanist connections prevalent in nearly all heritage media. (Higson 1996: 239-40). The nature of inheritance stems from "the decay and decadence of aristocratic life" (Ibid: 239) as conveyed in <u>Brideshead Revisited</u> and <u>A Room with a View</u>, and a loosening of the imperial "reigns of power" (Ibid: 239) as delineated in <u>A Passage to India</u>, and <u>Jewel in the Crown</u>. However any underlying liberal narrative can be overwhelmed by the visual splendour and magnificence of the heritage iconography; country estates, sumptuous Raj banquets, idyllic Cambridge settings and white-flannelled cricketers. These scenes provide a permanent and unshakeable image of "traditional" bourgeois Englishness where "social deference" is the norm and "social transgressions forbidden". (Higson 1996: 240). Hence the visual world suggests an England of extravagant, private heritage property where cultural heterogeneity is nowhere to be seen and where England is once again imperial and strong. The visual pastoral nostalgia represented by heritage media evokes this view of the national past as unimpaired and complete.

CHAPTER I - UNDERSTANDING NATIONAL IDENTITY

In this way, the past is seen as an aesthetically appealing shelter from the harsh social, political and economic realities of the Thatcherite 1980s. In his further discussions on British cinema Andrew Higson writing initially in <u>Screen</u> in 1989 and then later in "Waving the Flag: Constructing a National Cinema in Britain" (1995) argues that any future theoretical boundaries relating to debates on national cinema should be outlined not only with regards to where the film is produced but also along the area of consumption in terms of how a nation's audience understands and makes use of the films they view, as well as to consider what Higson calls "the film culture as a whole." (Higson 1989: 36-44, 1995: 279). This then involves the wide international sphere of films, such as American, continental European and Asian which will be on view within a particular nation and the variety of exhibition outlets such as multiplexes, art-house cinemas, videos and cable television from which they are shown, as well as the location these films have "intertextually" within a nation's popular culture. (Ibid: 44-45). Higson's concern with the question of national cinema is augmented by the notion of how it can be said to be representative of a uniform national cultural identity as well as operate within a complex international cinema and television network. (Ibid 1995: 7-8). In addition Higson stresses that it is important that we attain a clearer picture of just how audiences use these variety of films, their range of gratifications and expectations, how their cinematic impressions differ according to not only class, race and gender but also the changing experiences presented by numerous modes of filmic exhibition. Higson also points out the important relationship between the various discourses surrounding film and especially what he describes as the "tension" between those intellectuals who claim a true national cinema should be one which adheres to the level of cinema as art, (and dismisses Hollywood product as culturally debased) and the alternative discourse which claims that mass-produced popular entertainment nullifies these notions of "art that is cinema" or "nationality." (Higson 1989: 45). Higson concluded at the time of writing this that Film Studies theorists needed to...

" bridge the gap between textual analysis, the analysis of critical discourses in print-form, and the vast continent of the popular audiences for film – and the question of audiences has to be crucial for the study of national cinemas. For what is a national cinema if it doesn't have a national audience?" (Higson 1989: 46).

John Hill (1992, 1997, 1999) challenges Andrew Higson's contention above that "the parameters of a national cinema should be drawn at the site of consumption as much as the site of production of films" therefore including...the activity of national audiences and the conditions under which they make sense of and use the films they watch," (Higson 1989: 36) arguing that because Hollywood films are the main cinematic diet for British audiences they actually become "part" of British national cinema. Indeed Hill stresses that confusing the difference between notions of a national cinema and a cinema in Britain, as well as to stress an accent on consumption, undermines the claims for film production to be distinctively British rather than American. Hill criticises the concept of nationalism believing that it: "seeks to impose upon the nation not only a historically frozen and hermetically sealed conception of identity but also an imaginary sense of unity which fails to take account of the variety of collective identities and forms of belonging (such as class, gender, ethnicity and region) which may exist within the national community." (Hill 1992: 15). Moreover Hill stresses that in Britain especially, due to its unique composition of distinctive national elements, this nullification of ethnic and cultural variation has been more marked especially during the nationalist reawakening of the Thatcherite 1980s which promoted an essentially English nationalism at the expense of the Celtic "nations" and other group identities within Britain. Hill's counter argument to Higson is one that involves a national cinema which can be distinctively British in terms of setting and social issues and which addresses national specificity but without being overtly nationalistic and by rejecting the homogenising assumptions associated with national identity. Through a greater definition of Britishness ethnic, gender and class groupings in films such as <u>My Beautiful Laundrette,</u> (1985) <u>Gregory's Girl</u> (1980) and <u>High Hopes</u> (1988) can become part of a hybrid British Cinema which according to Hill "does not assume the existence of a unique or unchanging "national culture," and which is quite capable of dealing with social divisions and differences," (Hill 1992: 16), adding specifically that "the "Britishness" of British cinema in the 1980s was neither unitary nor agreed but depended upon a growing sense of the multiple, national, regional, and ethnic identifications which characterised life in Britain in this period." (Hill 1999: 244). Hill warns however that such a diverse and plurastic British cinema is not usually the type which is distinctive enough to be commercially successful in the international cinematic marketplace:...'in the case of the heritage film, it is international audiences, especially American, which have become a key source of revenues as well as prestige.' (Hill 1997: 247). Indeed quoting Thomas Elsaesser (1984) Hill stresses the point that the 1980s British Heritage cinema was just the type of film cycle which a more progressive and challenging British cinema would endeavour to counter:

"British films have been rather successful in marketing and packaging the national literary heritage, the war years, the countryside, the upper classes and elite education, and, in doing so, have also succeeded in constructing and circulating quite limiting and restricted versions of "Britishness."" (Elsaesser in Hill 1992: 17).

Hill then is seeking the development of a British cinema which is driven not, like Hollywood, on economic grounds but on a social and cultural motivation to produce varied, stimulating and provocative representations of the myriad sectional concerns of modern Britain. (1992, 1997, 1999). Analysing Hill's hypothesis Philip Schlesinger suggests in "The Sociological Scope of National Cinema" that it is perhaps more prescient in a growing pan-European age to accommodate an increasingly inquisitive, restless and diverse cultural "national space" of the type outlined above within if not the parameters of a national cinema then instead those of a "state cinema:" "Hill's argument may be read as a plea for retaining the role of critical cultural discourse in thinking about cinema in the national public space." (Schlesinger 2000: 27).

In "The Limiting Imagination of National Cinema" (2000) Andrew Higson develops upon some of his concerns surrounding the issues of national cinema that he had broached in his original article outlined above in 1989. Higson (2000: 68-9), stresses that debates surrounding national cinema need to take more consideration of the variety of interpretation and signification that an audience may receive from a range of international films and the alternative aspects which these media artefacts may distil within the "home" culture: "What we call "national cinema" is always a complex of often competing local, national and international forces, not an exclusive, self-determining space." (Higson b 2000: 206). Higson rejects Hill's assertions above, (1992, 1997, 1999) that what is required is a national cinema which is regional, ethnic, diverse, independent from the power of Hollywood, and can represent the hybrid qualities of contemporary Britain, claiming instead that what Hill is actually describing is less a "national cinema" and more an inquisitive, revisionist or even "left-wing" cinema. Moreover Higson believes that Hill is really stressing the need for a particular type of film which deals with the sectional issues of a socially and culturally divergent Britain and one which presents them within a "realist" cinematic form. For example in his 1999 publication, *British Cinema in the 1980s,* Hill places greater national significance upon the films of Stephen Frears, Ken Loach and Isaac Julien than those of the Heritage cinema (Higson 2000: 70-1). Furthermore Higson identifies what he believes are two faults with Hill's hypotheses. One, is that a cinema based upon an inquisitive terrain concerning the addressing of social, gender and ethnic issues does not need to be one which is anchored within exclusively British foundations. As Higson stresses these issues can also be dealt with through a variety of international and or period films by a range of directors such as Spike Lee, Jane Campion or Emir Kusturica in ways which can still communicate powerfully with British audiences. Secondly Higson criticises Hill's selection of films from the 1980s as not being fully representative of the output of British cinema during that decade and instead only conveying a relatively narrow choice based upon Hill's own particular socio-cultural interests. Therefore Higson stresses that "The case for supporting a home-grown cinema, ...is thus weakened rather than strengthened by Hill's call for a critical cinema that promotes cultural diversity." (Higson 2000: 72).

Higson claims that the term "national" is not the only sphere or space, regardless of whether it is the correct one, in which to discuss issues of social questioning and cultural diversity:

"It (national) seems to gloss over too many other questions of community, culture, belonging and identity that are often either defiantly local or loosely transnational. Concepts like "national life" and "national culture" thus seem destined to imply a homogenising and enclosing tendency...it is inappropriate to assume that cinema and film culture are bound by the limits of the nation-state. The complexities of the international film industry and the movements of finance capital, film-makers and films should put paid to that assumption... to argue for a national cinema is not necessarily the best way to achieve either cultural diversity or cultural specificity. In any case, the contingent communities that cinema imagines are much more likely to be either local or transnational than national" (Higson 2000: 72-3).

Chapter II.

Great Britain: A Social, Political and Cultural Perspective 1955 – 1965

2.1 Introduction

In this chapter I intend to address the key issues concerning the changing social character of British national identity during the late 1950s and early 1960s. In so doing I shall again be detailing debates I first discussed in "Realist Nights and Heritage Mornings: Comparing Representations of British National Identity 1955-65 and 1980-1990." (2001). In undertaking this exercise I shall examine issues such as Suez, the Commonwealth, Diplomacy, Nuclear weapons, CND (and the role played by the New Left), as well as immigration and the impact of US imperialism on notions of British cultural identity. These areas will be analysed within the social and historical framework detailed above, as well as through two forms of identity construction. Firstly, I shall be analysing Britain's national identity as perceived on the world stage; focussing upon the nation's role in relation to "other" international cultures because these global considerations were so influential in this period while Britain was facing both a declining and changing position in the world. Secondly, British internal identity will be examined during a period when different sources of identity, both converging and conflicting, were emerging in relation to notions of the domestic cultural community.

During the late 1950s and early 1960s it became apparent that the old imperialist establishment which had been at the helm of the country's social, political and diplomatic policies during the pre-war era of <u>consolidation</u> was under threat (Sinfield 1989, Samuel 1989). This decline in the country's global capabilities was not merely smoothed over; it was anticipated that this "loss" would be greatly recompensed for by a combination of Britain's widespread international interests conveyed in the paradigm of 'the three circles', through the UK being at the head of the Commonwealth, by articulating moral leadership, through its development of nuclear weapons, through the experience and reputation of its diplomacy.[i]

---

[i] The "three circles" concept stemmed from Churchill, who expressed it as follows:

> "I feel the existence of three great circles among the free nations and democracies... The first circle for us is naturally the British Commonwealth and Empire, with all that that comprises. Then there is also the English-speaking world in which we, Canada and the other British Dominions, and

Many observers look back upon the period between the mid-fifties and early sixties as a time of great change in British society (Marwick 1990, Bogdanor and Skidelsky 1970, Sked and Cook 1984, Hill 1986). Over the course of the next few pages I intend to highlight the major political and economic transformations over this period, such as Britain's changing role in the world, the Suez crisis, and the effect of the "cold war", as well as the breakdown of the empire. The emergence of a new labour government will also be analysed as well as changes in the areas of employment, education, housing and domestic consumption.

2.2 Great Britain: The International Context

The theme of this whole section is concerned with Britain's place in the world as a significant driver of change with regard to notions of British/English identity during this period. I shall begin by analysing the Suez Crisis as a starting point in a sequence of events which symbolised Britain's changing perception toward its international status. Indeed, as we shall discover shortly, these changes were mirrored in what was happening with the Commonwealth and Europe.

The Suez Crisis

> "Few British Prime Ministers can have entered office assured of such general support as Sir Anthony Eden. Regarded more as an international statesman than a mere British politician, and possessing the charm and manners of the quintessential British gentleman (to say nothing of the looks of a cinema

---

the United States play so important a part. And finally, there is United Europe. These three majestic circles are co-existent and if they are linked together there is no force or combination which could overthrow them or even challenge them. Now if you think of the three inter-linked circles you will see that we are the only country which has a great part in every one of them. We stand in fact at the very point of junction and here is this island at the very centre of the sea-ways and perhaps of the airways also; we have the opportunity of joining them all together" (W. Churchill 1950, cited in "Europe Unite! Speeches 1947-1959": 1960: 417-418).

matinee idol), he appeared a fitting successor indeed to Winston Churchill" (Sked and Cook 1984: 125).

However, despite these and other apparent attributes such as being expert in the field of foreign affairs (Bogdanor and Skidelsky 1970), Eden appeared to meet his political nemesis during the Suez crisis of 1956.

Egyptian leader Gamal Nasser had managed to convince certain Western powers, including Britain, of the commercial benefits of building a high dam at Aswan on the Nile. However, as part of this agreement, Egypt was expected to contribute $900 million of the total $1300 million construction costs, with Britain, USA and the world Bank contributing the bulk of the remaining $400 million. However this became less likely when Nasser used Egypt's cotton crop as "security" in paying for Czechoslovak arms. This, combined with Nasser's close relationship with communist Russia, disturbed the Americans who reneged upon their initial promise of funding. This forced Britain and the World Bank to do likewise. Nasser then nationalised the Suez Canal Company, stating that its revenue would now have to finance the Dam's construction (Bogdanor and Skidelsky 1970, Sked and Cook 1984).

The British government reacted angrily to Nasser's actions comparing him with Adolf Hitler and demanding that something be done in order to stop the Egyptian leader.

Initially, Eden sought a peaceful solution to the crisis, but was quickly influenced by public and political pressure (from both Conservative and Labour), as well as frustrated by somewhat nebulous support from the Americans. He ultimately decided to gamble on military action with the help of the French, who like Britain were worried about the risks to their imperial influence (as well as trading links with the African and Asian continents), as a consequence of losing control of the canal to Egypt (Ibid. 1970, 1984).

With the help of the Israelis, whose port, Eilat was being blockaded by the Egyptians following conflict between the two countries in 1948, the British and French paratroopers attacked and captured Port Said on 5 November 1956.

However, President Eisenhower of the US was in the process of re-election. Amidst the Cold War tensions of the 1950s one of

Eisenhower's key campaign pledges was to promote international peace. This, coupled with anger at his allies' aggression compelled Eisenhower to have their actions condemned at the United Nations (UN) who consequently voted in favour of a cease-fire, stressing that a UN force should occupy the canal zone instead of the British and French. Due to pressure on the pound from the international markets, (which could only be prevented by an American backed loan from the IMF: International Monetary Fund), as well as the spectre of Soviet intervention and the personal strain on Eden, Britain agreed to a humiliating withdrawal on 6 November along with the more recalcitrant French. The last British troops left Egypt shortly before Christmas 1956.

Following the affair Eden came in for severe criticism from many quarters for this national embarrassment, with his actions being ridiculed as reckless and naive, whilst Eden himself had perhaps hoped that by overthrowing Nasser's regime in favour of an Egyptian leader who would be sympathetic to British interests, this new government would have sanctioned the international control of the canal (Ibid. 1984).

Eden faced particular enmity from the majority of the press with only "The Express" and "The Sketch" continuing to back him. The view amongst financiers in the City was one of uncertainty whilst middle-class voters had misgivings concerning Eden's leadership. The BBC retained a neutral stance over the crisis much to the government's chagrin. Moreover the air time it permitted Gaitskell following a broadcast by Eden initiated both irritation and suspicion of the BBC as an institution which was politically biased towards the Left in the eyes of the Conservative party in the years that followed (Briggs 1995). However, opinion polls suggested areas of support for Eden's hard stand - with one giving him a 12% increase in approval between 30 October and 21 November and another suggesting a rise from 40% to 53% during the first two weeks of November. Furthermore in a by-election at Chester on 15 November the Conservative vote dropped by only 5%. This would serve to suggest increasing social and political division within the United Kingdom at the time concerning the nature and objectives of Britain's post-war role. Suez had appeared therefore to be devastatingly symbolic of Britain's crumbling imperial stature during this period (Smith 1984, Sinfield 1989, Sked and Cook 1984, Samuel 1989, Marwick 1998).

Although there were differences in the Conservative Party over Suez, these were largely contained. However, Labour's policy divisions were both more vocal and virulent as evidenced by Aneurin Bevan who claimed "it isn't possible to create peace in the Middle East by jeopardising the peace of the world" (Sked and Cook 1984: 134) whilst Hugh Gaitskell's broadcast on the BBC attempted to mobilise Conservative backbenchers in an effort to remove Eden from office. Consequently there were heated and acrimonious exchanges between the two men in the commons during early November (Ibid. 1984, Briggs 1995, Marwick 1998).

The Suez affair appeared to cause serious diplomatic consequences for Britain. Firstly, the split which had occurred within the Anglo-American axis threatened to jeopardise Western solidarity at the time of the "Cold War". Secondly, world attention was directed from the events in Hungary where Soviet tanks were squashing an uprising in Budapest at the same time as the British attack on Egypt. The crisis also reaffirmed Britain's increasing reliance on the USA but above all emphasised that the former imperial giant was no longer a great global force. (Bogdanor and Skidelsky 1970, Sked and Cook 1984). As Sir Pierson Dixon, Britain's representative at the UN wrote:

> "... At the time I remember feeling very strongly that we had by our action reduced ourselves from a first-class to a third-class power. We revealed our weakness by stopping; and we threw away the moral position on which our world status largely depended. We were greater than our actual strength. So long as people knew that we went to war in defence of principle - which is what we did in 1914 and 1939..." (Sked and Cook 1984: 136).

Suez only served to accelerate the nation's international decline, questioning in the process, not only old certainties about Britain's role but contributing therefore to a sense of change, division and confrontation in British society by its undermining the traditional beliefs upon which notions of collective identity had previously been predicated. British gold reserves dropped by £100 million immediately following Suez, whilst Franco-British relations were damaged and Britain's desire for decolonisation was perhaps enhanced as a consequence of the crisis. Finally, a tired and dispirited Eden officially resigned as British premier on health grounds in January 1957. However, unofficially some have suggested that Eisenhower desired the resignation of the British Prime Minister and that Harold Macmillan, R. A. Butler and Winston Churchill helped to bring this about (Avon 1960).

Suez proved to be Britain's final imperial conflict, barring the Falklands war of 1982 and the ongoing Northern Ireland situation. It had clearly been a shock to Britain's establishment. The possibility of the nation taking any independent political and military action was now seen to be greatly reduced. Britain was now being compelled to re-evaluate its position in the world.

The man faced with this situation was Eden's replacement, Harold MacMillan - a very different individual from that of his predecessor. According to Bogdanor and Skidelsky (1970: 32): "Macmillan's Edwardianism could not have been better fashioned for the purpose. In a way it was the last authentic English style - the figure cut by patrician Englishmen when their country last unquestionably dominated the world. It was a style which carried with it the resonances of that domination. Macmillan understood this, and exploited the fact. Above all, he found it useful in his dealing with the United States."

Under Macmillan, Britain may not have retained the matter of world power but instead was attempting to utilise its long-established diplomatic traditions and connections - acting as a conduit between East and West, the USA and Europe as well as other areas of the globe.

Historically Britain's role as an international player had been enhanced further through its influence within the field of diplomacy. At first this proved to be a significant benefit. Apart from the distinctive advantage of the country's traditional abilities in negotiation, Britain also enjoyed intimate connections with the

United States and with the new Commonwealth countries, many of which continued to rely upon London for information as well as diplomatic and military aid (Bogdanor and Skidelsky 1970). However the reality was that in spite of the growing success of NATO, Anglo-American ties steadily became of less singular significance as new influential American allies emerged whilst the new Commonwealth countries emancipated themselves. Britain was unprepared for the modern multilateral mode of diplomacy which was practised in the United Nations, whilst at the same time the UK was also excluded from the new supranational EEC. Diplomacy became increasingly more difficult in a situation whereby Britain was quickly losing influence within all "the three circles" whilst maintaining the ambition to play a pivotal role in East-West relations (Bogdanor and Skidelsky 1970, Samuel 1989).

However the historical basis behind Britain's claims to be acknowledged as a global force must be stated here, particularly its role in helping to maintain international stability during the imperial era, the principal part it played during two world wars and its prominence as a major commercial player within the sphere of banking. All these aspects proved to be especially significant in the post-war period when a sense of collective national pride was fracturing as Britain's place in the world was increasingly being called into question.

The Commonwealth

> "The wind of change is blowing through this continent, and, whether we like it or not, this growth of National (African), consciousness is a political fact. We must all accept it is a fact, and our national policies must take account of it" (Macmillan, Speech in South Africa, 3 February 1960, cited in Horne 1989).

The Commonwealth was seen as a solid base of support for Britain – the heroism of its soldiers in defending British imperial interests during World War II was one example of this. The swift British withdrawal from India in 1947 culminating in India's immediate and untroubled incorporation in to the Commonwealth was another. The subsequent stabilisation of the Empire for the following decade, until the independence of Ghana and Malaya began the final stage of its abrogation, was aided considerably by this confidence in its stability. However, involvement in old style colonial wars like that which erupted in Malay, caused concern on the left wing of the Labour Party - and severe criticism from the Communist Party. The changed character of economic imperialism however manifested itself in protected markets and military bases which appeared as important symbols in flagging Britain's ailing power (Samuel 1989).

The Commonwealth could also be seen as emblematic of Britain's moral leadership. The British reputation for civilised withdrawal (Samuel 1989) contrasted with the dour and desperate struggles of other colonial powers such as the Dutch in the East Indies or the bloody French retreat in Indochina. Indeed, much of British public opinion, particularly amongst the elite, continued to retain the belief in the value of these Commonwealth ties into the 1960s. Such an attitude only began to subside at the end of that decade. Britain alone, amongst the other former imperial western European powers, could be seen to be relatively proud of its achievements in decolonising without prolonged conflict (Frankel 1975). As I shall discuss shortly the extreme leftists in the Labour Party were particularly enthusiastic for the New Commonwealth. They felt a moral duty toward the ex-colonial peoples for having ruled, alienated and exploited them within the Empire. They also agreed with Third World aspirations for national self-determination and anticipated Britain exercising the role of a leader of the new Commonwealth provided the UK undertook a policy of unambiguous neutrality and contributed generous aid (Howe in Samuel 1989).

Europe

Further doubts surrounding Britain's perception of its world role were augmented during the early 1960s when Macmillan's government initially refused to participate in a European Common Market despite both American and Continental prompting, preferring to pursue a pre-war policy in which Britain's interests were dependent upon a somewhat isolated central power balance between Europe and the USA (Bogdanor and Skidelsky 1970, Sked and Cook 1984).

However, when Macmillan finally sought entry to the European Economic Community after July 1961 concern was expressed by some of the other member states with regard to the erratic performance of Britain's welfare-capitalist economy when compared with EEC countries especially West Germany which was said to have experienced an "economic miracle" since the end of World War II. The Germans had doubled their industrial production every ten years. Britain on the other hand, having alienated itself from the modernised and competitive industrial states of Europe had merely attained incremental annual growth rates of between 2 to 3% of SDP, therefore deepening the sense of post-war decline.

Such self-imposed isolation resulted in Britain being excluded from the EEC as General de Gaulle used the French veto to keep the UK out in January 1963, fearing a domineering Anglo-American presence within European affairs (Porter in Tiratsoo 1997). Hence, post-war Britain unlike its erstwhile continental partners could not see the potential cultural diversity (Bhabha 1990, Hobsbawm 1990) inherent in the membership of a supra-national alliance of independent sovereign states such as the EEC, which illustrated the rising potential for cultural division within national identity (Smith 1984).

In this section I have attempted to articulate the significant changes regarding Britain's perceived role within the international arena, undermining old certainties about Britain's status, in relation to Suez, the collapse of Empire/Commonwealth and new moves in Europe, contributing therefore to a sense of change and uncertainty in British society through undermining traditional notions of collective identity.

2.3 Convergent and Conflicting Identities

Economic Change and Political Crises

In this section I shall analyse the different sources of identity which emerged during this period and their potential both for conflict and harmony within British society.

CHAPTER II - GREAT BRITAIN

Prime Minister Harold MacMillan had commented in 1957:

"Most of our people have never had it so good. Go round the country, go to the industrial towns and you will see a state of prosperity such as we have never had in my lifetime - nor indeed ever in the history of this country" (Hill 1986: 5).

According to Stuart Laing, this new found affluence encouraged the opinion that the class system was beginning to become outmoded and obsolete based upon the changes in the living habits of the working-class within the areas of employment, education, housing and domestic consumption. Unemployment had reached a low of 2% in June 1959 whilst white-collar workers had increased from a pre-war 23% to 36% of the work force by 1961. During the same period the number of unskilled manual workers dropped from 15% to 9% (Laing 1986: 22). Real incomes of British workers rose by 50% through the course of the 1950s. By the end of this decade education boasted an increase in expenditure, smaller classes and 20% of 15-18 year-olds still in education compared with 6% in 1931 (Ibid.: 24-5). As Laing claims:

"Such improvement was frequently cited as evidence of the general well-being, both material and spiritual, of the whole population" (Laing 1986: 25).

In terms of housing, new functional post-war suburban housing estates were being constructed throughout the country away from the traditional close-knit working class slum dwellings which were being bulldozed. These estates were frequently located in new towns with little social amenities and no community feeling like Kirby and Telford or near new industries or on the outskirts of older cities. Laing describes them as "standardised and endless, small semi-detached houses with gardens" (Ibid. 26).

Private ownership also rose from 29 per cent in 1951 to 41 per cent by 1964 whereas over the same period there was a drop in the number of council houses being built (Hall in Worswick and Ady 1962).

Large cuts in purchase tax during 1958 and 1959 allowed household electrical goods such as washing machines, vacuum cleaners, refrigerators and especially televisions to become attainable symbols of affluence to the working-classes (Ibid.).

Moreover, cars were perhaps the most potent visible signifier of affluence. Between 1948 and 1958 the number of registered cars and vans increased from 2 million to 4.5 million, and then onto 8 million by 1964 (Zweig 1961, Laing 1986: 28-9).

According to Dearlove and Saunders (1991) a number of different factors together help to explain the sustained post-war boom, of which four were particularly significant.

1. There was a substantial range of low cost imports needed by Western industries. Of these cheap Middle Eastern oil was especially useful as the world consumption of oil increased by a remarkable 7.5% per year between 1950 and 1970. In addition Third World goods and raw materials also proved cost effective for the industrialised nations, whilst the poorer countries also contributed cheap man power, either as European "guest workers" or as long-term economic migrants entering the nations of their former Imperial masters, such as the UK which actively sought immigrants from its former colonies (Dearlove and Saunders 1991).
2. The world monetary system was stabilised following the Bretton Wood conference of 1944.
3. The new inventions which had accumulated since the 1920s-30s depression because of lack of investment during a period of dipping prices and scarce profits were now commercially viable.
4. Both post-war Labour and Conservative governments employed a new interventionist or consensus policy which gave rise to the term "Butskellism" (a combination of the names of the conservative Chancellor, Butler, and the Labour leader, Gaitskell). Butskellism comprised of three fundamental beliefs. Firstly both parties supported a broad-ranging programme of welfare benefits which included free

health supervision, inclusive education, social security and the right to a house (whether private or public), amongst others (Bogdanor and Skidelsky 1970, Dearlove and Saunders 1991, Sked and Cook 1984). Secondly, Labour and Conservative believed in the so-called "mixed economy". This meant that the future employment of thousands of workers could only be guaranteed by public ownership as a number of the older more traditional industries were becoming insufficiently profitable under private ownership. Thirdly, the Keynesian economic strategy was to be used to aid economic prosperity and increased employment. Keynesian demand-management is about government attempts to sustain demand in the economy at a high enough level in order to absorb an industry producing at full capacity. This was achieved through a rise in public expenditure and an attempt to boost private spending by freeing the money supply and making credit more available.

Together these economic changes and rises in affluence gave way to an increasingly embourgoisified society, which brought with it "an accompanying conversion to consensual middle class values" (Hill 1986: 7). At the same time the British establishment's class based conception of an imagined community of post-war dominance faded. An air of moral and professional decay seemed simultaneously to pervade the Macmillan government. This was symbolised by the Vassall and Profumo sex scandals. In October 1962, a clerk at the Admiralty, William Vassall, was jailed for eighteen years for spying for the Soviet Union. Vassall was being blackmailed because he was a homosexual and the British press suspected that Vasall's activities had been kept from public knowledge, prior to his arrest, by two government ministers - Thomas Galbraith, a former civil lord of the Admiralty, and Lord Carrington, first lord of the Admiralty. In April 1963 they were exonerated by Lord Radcliffe's inquiry. By then however, Galbraith had been forced to resign and the damage not only to Macmillan's administration but also to British belief in its own national security had been done (Bogdanor and Skidelsky 1970, Sked and Cook

1984, Marwick 1998). However, worse was to follow when War minister, John Profumo's sexual relationship with high-class call girl Christine Keeler, who was simultaneously involved with Yevgeny Ivanov, Assistant Naval Attache at the Soviet Embassy, was exposed to the public. The scandal was made worse for the British establishment through Profumo's damaging and deceitful statement to the House of Commons in March of 1963 denying any "impropriety" with Keeler. This was seized upon by Labour's new young meritocratic leader Harold Wilson who was anxious to align himself and his party to a new identity construction for Britain; based on the white hot technological revolution and a classless society. In turn he articulated himself and his party against the increasingly alienated blimpish and out-dated Edwardian establishment mentality personified firstly by Macmillan, and then the aristocratic Sir Alec Douglas-Home. This notion that society was at the friction point of two divided socio-cultural identities was perhaps symbolised by evidence suggesting the public were interested rather than concerned by the sexual aspect to the Profumo affair, and that by the early 1960s British people were less moved by such behaviour than they once had been (Marwick 1998). Research undertaken amongst a sample of middle-class, earners in Cambridge and published by the *Sunday Times* "insight" team in their hastily published paperback, "Scandal 63", claimed that it was clearly the most sensual and intimate aspects of the scandal that people were most familiar with (Marwick 1991, 1998). Therefore, it seemed it was the issue of sex, as opposed to national security (an issue which had not greatly been discussed before within British public life) which was to be of greater internal significance. Britain's changing attitudes towards sexuality can also be seen in the two million copies of "Lady Chatterley's lover" sold in the year after the celebrated court case in which a Not-Guilty verdict was passed in favour of Penguin Books over the unexpurgated version of the novel. (Marwick 1991, 1998).

As the conservative establishment were being undermined by political crises the Left articulated its demand for social, political and economic change around the liberal humanitarian cause of nuclear disarmament.

"CND discovered that the cry "Ban the Bomb" implied a larger critique of British culture and society. Try as CND might to stick to "the Bomb", the culture that had produced the Bomb kept intruding upon the conversation. Many CNDers found themselves at odds with this culture. Frightened by the loss of both Britain's and the individual's capacity to control events, many middle-class men and women turned to CND as a means of realising their vision of a good society. Drawing on both the distant and the immediate past, this vision promised a world in which political and technological structures would rest on moral, rather than pragmatic, foundations. Like Tolkien's Shire and Lewis's Narnia, a Britain without the Bomb would be a world of cohesion and community" (Veldman 1994: 137).

From the late 1950s this growing movement of historical revision and socialist culture was identified as a radical left-wing form of national identity. It was originally associated with the early phases of "New Left Review" and CND, and its major intellectual motivation had arisen from the work of Edward Thompson (The Making of the English Working Class) and Raymond Williams (Culture and Society). According to Nairn (1988: 45), this seminal "movement" encouraged the idea of "history from below"; a collection of alternative folk myths, worker's proposals and radical achievement (Sinfield 1989, Ibid.) which functioned in response to the alienation felt from the dominant values of the establishment "above", which emphasised on the one hand British national identity's potential for cultural division and on the other, the growing diversity of different levels of cultural identity, fracturing and emerging within the country during this period. (Bhabha 1990, Hobsbawm 1990). Nairn describes this counter-perspective as "populist socialism" or "cultural nationalism" (Ibid.: 54). However, this is partially disputed by E. P. Thompson (1978) who regards himself a "social internationalist", belonging to a diffuse movement -part national, part international- although Thompson does acknowledge a strong national cultural commitment within his beliefs:

> "Our history and past culture presents itself to a danger-alerted mind, searching for evidences of democratic endurance and resources of cultural strength and growth. And some part of that cultural inheritance cannot but be "national" in character, with its own particular pressures, resilience and idiom; this must constitute not only some part of what we think and feel about but also some part of what we think and feel with." (Thompson 1978: 4).

Russian brutality in crushing the Hungarian uprising of 1956 had a distinctive influence upon the Left - large numbers of intellectuals and workers who were dedicated to this new diffuse movement of Left wing humanitarianism departed the Communist Party in disgust following these actions. As Thompson stressed: "what must be seen to have "failed" is the revolutionary potential - not within Russian society alone - but within any society, within man himself" (Thompson 1978: 11). This is why, as with Osborne's Jimmy Porter, "it seemed there were no good brave causes left"! (Taylor and Pritchard 1980: 3). The drama which emerged between 1955-65 articulated this feeling concisely. It was determined and progressive concerning the possibility of social change but at the same time contemptuous and depressed about the new age of affluence. CND thus became a platform for the energy and anger of this generation of protestors who believed that the principles and mores of the old imperial establishment were becoming increasingly alien and outmoded to them. This was the social and cultural void from which CND emerged, becoming symbolic and emblematic of the frustrations and aspirations of this amorphous mass of left-wing discontented; both young and old.

> "What better symbol of the insane, corrupt, crassly materialistic yet technologically sophisticated, society could there be than the H-Bomb? Here was a cause indeed, and the new generation - or a substantial proportion of it - flocked to its banners" (Taylor and Pritchard 1980: 3).

CND attracted support from a number of diverse groups such as the Pacifists, the New Left, the Communists and Anarchists, the

Quakers, the left wing of The Labour Party and others. This disparate collection were however not solely concerned with unilateral nuclear disarmament but also represented a diverse range of objectives which they felt would be enhanced through association with the campaign (Parkin 1968, Sinfield 1989). During the course of the 1950s opinion polls revealed 25% to 40% of the British people were against increasing involvement in the war in Korea, as well as to rises in defence spending and the Suez crisis. The result of this poll also showed support for unilateralism (Sinfield 1989). This last policy was predicated, quite apart from the obvious humanitarian and moral arguments, upon the notion that Britain could use its "moral leadership" as one of the three world nuclear powers, in order to unilaterally disarm and then influence the USA through the "special relationship," and then in turn the Soviets to do likewise, therefore rendering the nuclear arms race obsolete. However, the "bomb" was an emblem of Britain's post-war national identity as a leading power on the planet, even though it proved to be a crippling strain upon UK finances as Britain lavished 8% to 10% of its annual GNP, which amounted to 33% of its entire tax receipts on nuclear spending in order to retain a perception, however deluded, of world dominance. (Sinfield 1989). Consequently the disarmament policy had still to permeate the political consciousness which was fixed on the notion of global influence imagined by both Tory and Labour governments during this period. Even Aneurin Bevan, who, as the opposition spokesman for defence, stated that Britain would not be prepared to negotiate over nuclear weapons without having a substantial cache of armaments behind it to bargain with. Such opinions voiced by a leading Socialist politician only served to increase the sense of frustration and social and political alienation felt by Left - wing campaigners (Parkin 1968, Frankel 1975).

The important institutions and value systems which could be argued to have perpetuated the hegemonic values within British society during this period, from which the malcontents of the New Left were culturally divided and alienated, included Royalty, the forces of Business, Church, the military and bourgeois perceptions of Nationalism. The alternative values which the Left attempted to foreground included Republicanism, Socialism, secularism, pacifism and the notion of internationalism (Parkin 1968). CND gained its groundswell of support from the educated middle classes. The organisation's supporters were frequently aligned into "occupational groups - teachers' section, architect's and social workers'" - which closely defined their allegiance to the movement in relation to its aspirations and the "humanistic values of their respective professions" (Parkin 1968: 181).

The emergence of the post-war era had resulted in many on the left believing that the process of de colonisation – and the development of the Commonwealth - would result in a marked transformation within Britain itself (Howe 1989). The prospect was promoted by a number of socialist intellectuals, articulated by the communist party, the Bevanites, as well as the movements for colonial freedom and through certain Labour Party policy. Basil Davidson, one of the most belligerent post-war campaigners for colonial freedom felt that Britain would be able to emancipate and galvanise its own sense of collective identity and culture by unburdening itself of its strong colonial legacy (Davidson 1994). Therefore Empire could be seen, not as "another country", like the past or India, but as part of the British themselves.

The growing policy of de-colonisation, which had attracted purposeful backing from the left and was signified by the British Nationality Act of 1948, resulted in 25% of the world's populace being lawfully allowed to settle in the UK. Sadly, a rise in immigration was perceived by some of the indigenous population as a threat to both their concept of an imagined community and in turn the cultural boundaries implicit in such a community. Racial frictions began to surface in British Society, particularly during the 1958 riots in Nottingham and Notting Hill. (Sked and Cook 1984, Hill 1986, Marwick 1998).

The government had failed to anticipate or prevent such problems from occurring since the implementation of the 1948 Act. The Commonwealth Immigrants Act of 1962 was limited to permit only those who held work vouchers, those engaged in full-time study, and parents or dependant-relatives of those already present, perhaps in order to buttress these perceptibly declining imperial boundaries. However, some 60 to 70,000 white Irish immigrants, as well as white Europeans, were settling in the UK every year and numbered the most sizeable migrant group in the country. Although they were also victims of racism, the regulations of the Act did not apply to them in the way it did black immigrants. Hence this fuelled the belief amongst newly arrived migrants that it was the issue of coloured immigration as opposed to immigration in principle, which the government was blocking. In the context of national identity an absence of an institutionalised anti-racist campaign may have helped to create a feeling of scepticism toward the notion of an imagined community under threat from an "alien" culture of "otherness" (Hall 1997). Combined with such a physical "presence" came a perceived challenge to both cultural boundaries and the notion of sovereignty.

Consequently Black and Asian immigrants could not, in relation to Smith (1984), share in a historical British territory with its own particular nationalistic infrastructure of common myths and historical memories as well as symbols, flags and anthems, but instead were seen by many to represent an opposing collective identity as well as reinforcing a sense of post-war decline amongst the indigenous population concerning Britain's fracturing imperial edifice.

In this section I have articulated the widening impact affluence played in changing internal perceptions of British society through embourgoisification, as well as analysing the simultaneous questioning of traditional notions of a shared national community which were being undermined, problematised and fractured by political crises, problems consequent upon immigration and the rise of New Left politics and CND.

Cultural Change and Social Division

In this section I shall analyse the dramatic cultural changes of the period through the spheres of literature, theatre, the role of the BBC and the New Left's criticisms of Welfare Capitalism, in order to illustrate how various distinctive and antithetical shifts were under way during this period.

A central self-proclaimed tenet of British identity at this time was welfare-capitalism, the notion of Britain as emblematic of a civilised, tolerant and peaceable society, a perceived symbol of a "just" imagined community, both for capitalist countries persecuted by the demands of competition and by those ruled through the fear of communism; as well as the new Commonwealth states struggling both for economic growth and for social egalitarianism (Frankel 1975).

However, the cultural policy of the New-Left challenged this premise in demanding that the promise by the two leading political parties regarding welfare-capitalism actually be adhered to. That is, a national community must possess the social capability to widen the nets of financial security, education, health-care provision, respectable housing - and notions of "good" culture" to include all cultures and classes and not just an elite few (Sinfield 1989: 260). With regard to this last issue limited efforts had already been made, including the BBC Third Programme, The Arts Council and local authority arts funding in order to try and fulfil this aspiration.

However, the left's cultural appanage and its lasting identity during this period was symbolised within British theatre. The Royal Court and Osborne's "Look Back In Anger" articulated the New-Left's discontent both with the bourgeois establishment and the cultural erosion of working class life, as they campaigned for a new egalitarian, shared sense of British identity (Sinfield 1989). Osborne's "The Entertainer", a Royal Court production in April 1957, was set during the time of the Suez crisis, and counterpoints this with Osborne's "symbolism" of the modern Britain as a worn out "music-hall act".

Raymond Williams (1962) when defining British cultural identities within contemporary society located two divided cultural constructs in operation. The first was a working-class culture predicated upon the traditional values of communal co-operation. The second, a middle-class culture which could be seen as more competitive, individualistic and potentially isolating from the notion of a shared community. Williams' promotion of the values of co-operation over the alienating aspects of individualism expressed the desire of left-culturalists' for greater welfare and less capitalism, a policy which would help to prevent the erosion of traditional working class mores and ways of life (Sinfield 1989).

Indeed, according to the left the relative failure of the welfare-capitalist construct, were the elements which had initially rendered it useful. These were "mass production, consumerism, advertising - which seemed to be what D. H. Lawrence described as "anti-life" (Sinfield 1989: 245). These had all marginalised working people, smoothing over national cultural divisions. Increased prosperity was corrupting the pride of the working class whilst weakening their powers of resistance against a corruptive social change; "it all seemed a failure at the level of culture" (Sinfield 1989: 245).

Therefore, as the standard of living of the working-classes rose, their cultural values and social identities changed and fractured. In other words, an "embourgeoisification" of the working-class was occurring creating divisions predicated upon affluence, where little had previously existed (Hill 1986, Laing 1986). This "embourgeoisement" was also symbolic in forcing the Labour party to re-evaluate their own identity within a changing national structure, culminating in Wilson's post-imperialist meritocratic modernisers of which the New Left was suspicious. Emblematic of the fear felt by amongst others, Potter (1960), Hoggart (1957) and Frankenburg (1966) was the decomposition of the traditional working-class community, precipitated by the corrosive effects of an other invading "mass" culture. Within this national cultural struggle the New-Left subculture, comprised principally of the discontented middle-class, evaluated themselves in terms of notions of good culture and working-class culture. Therefore, if embourgeoisement was to have a destructive influence upon the traditions and culture of a class then middle class intellectuals looked upon it as a social and cultural obligation to criticise it (Sinfield 1989).

The New Left believed that culture could play a significant role toward influencing social change within Britain during this period.

The proliferation of "mass" culture which had derived from the USA was identified by the left as symbolic of US imperialism poisoning and encroaching upon an indigenous working class culture (Williams 1962). The left attacked British society's appetite for pseudo-American identities as an escape from the alienating effects of the multifarious and divisive British class and cultural system - a legacy of the era of imperial consolidation. They cited "rock music... the horror film, the Sunday strip-paper and the latest tin-pan drool" (Sinfield 1989: 241) as the cultural artefacts of this "otherness".

Bill Haley was one of the earliest teenage heroes as Rock'n'Roll mesmerised the British youth. "Teddy Boys" rioted in August 1955 during the showing of <u>Rock Around the Clock</u> in spite of the film's far from radical values (Nuttall 1962, Sinfield 1989). The general antagonism toward the growth of Rock'n'Roll by religious, legal and educational institutions only served to enhance its cultural significance within the psyche of youth. Deviance, atrophy, havoc and above all, an anti-establishment mentality were associated with Rock 'n' Roll in the minds of much of the contemporary youth, as well as sowing the seeds of a popular American cultural identity within people's consciousness (Ibid. 1962, 1989).

Perhaps the most notorious, oppositional sub-culture to force its way onto the national psyche was that of the Teddy Boy (Hebdige 1988: 70): "whose tastes were most clearly conditioned by exposure to American imports, to American popular music and American films - (the style according to Barnes (1979) was strongly influenced by Hollywood gangster and Western stereotypes), - The Teds, after all, were predominantly drawn from the alienated lower working-class youth." Hence the Teds as a distinctive emerging sub-culture only served to accentuate emerging social and cultural divisions within a Britain which was becoming increasingly uncertain as to its modern identity.

The Communists, especially, sought to defend the identity of a "British cultural heritage", which featured Shakespeare, Shaw and Shelley, Blake and Byron as well as Chaucer and Dickens. However, according to Sam Aaronovitch, who was the Communists' spokesperson on cultural issues, this clarion call did not only apply to the left but to "millions" of other British people "of the most varied political and social opinions" (Taylor 1958, Sinfield 1989: 243). This belief therefore revealed the perceived threat to the conception of an imagined British community, from the capitalist imperialist culture of the USA, creating cultural divisions within an imagined uniform British way of life.

However, one acceptable form of US culture as perceived by the left was that of Jazz (Sinfield 1989). Rebellious and oppositional, Jazz was appropriated by and became symbolic of the New Left's disparaging of the otherness of American commercialism, becoming emblematic of its struggle for a British cultural identity. Significant Jazz performers with left wing sympathies included Humphrey Lyttleton, Johnny Dankworth and George Melly. Ken Coyler's band marched with CND during protests and Jazz played an important role in Anderson's 1958 film "March to Aldermaston" (Ibid. 1989). Hence, this alternative musical form offered the ideal unification of the cultural divisions between New-Left and lower-class: it was the "good" music which the working class would have been performing and enjoying had they not been corrupted by US cultural imperialism (Ibid. 1989).

In 1956 the Russians invaded Hungary, and Britain became embroiled in one of its final imperial conflicts, which culminated in national embarrassment during the Suez invasion of Egypt. This all coincided with the appearance in Britain of distinctive new writers concerned with contemporary issues such as Allan Sillitoe and John Braine, as well as the first performance of John Osborne's "Look Back in Anger" at the Royal Court Theatre. John Hill describes these writers as being: "...far from satisfied and complacent", with this new society at that time, and claims that with the help of Suez and Hungary they were able to articulate the "disaffections and tensions" prevalent within society by: "Binding together all the key issues of the period: youth, class, affluence and the status of women" (Hill 1986: 21).

Post-war novelists such as John Wain's "Hurry on Down" (1953) and Kingsley Amis' "Lucky Jim" (1954) had focussed on the young lower-middle-class hero counter-pointed against an upper-middle-class environment of snobbery and privilege. The contemporary novelists of the mid-to-late fifties conveyed a determined realism which delineated an ambivalent critique of both the material advantages and moral erosion they argued characterised the modern affluent Britain (Hill 1986, Sinfield 1989, Marwick 1998).

The aforementioned group of writers became known as the "angry young men," and played a pivotal role in the distinctive pattern of dramatic cultural change taking place in Britain during this period (Elsom 1976, Morrison 1980, Hill 1986). John Hill (1986) goes on to identify what he describes as the "myth of the 'angry young man' " which drew together a wide and varied spectrum of novelists and poets including Philip Larkin, Wain and Amiss, John Osborne, Stan Barstow, Shelagh Delaney, David Storey, John Braine and Stuart Holroyd, who all highlighted contemporary class frictions frequently wrought by the new affluence and social injustices in their work (Ibid.: 21).

The work of writers such as Braine, Sillitoe, Storey and Delaney were set specifically in the north of England and acted as an overt and uniform criticism on the material gains and moral losses of the new affluence.

The central protagonist in these contemporary works was usually clever and well-educated but significantly always from the working class. For example, Joe Lampton in Braine's "Room at the Top" is characterised as an ambitious white-collar worker who represents a new working-class desire to attain social, cultural and economic respectability and not be condemned to the margins of society by an outdated class-conscious establishment. Lampton pursues the material attractions provided by Susan, a wealthy businessman's daughter. However with Alice, Joe has a more passionate, honest and fulfilling sexual relationship. With the upper-middle class Susan Joe utilises his sexuality in order to attain the wealth and social status he craves. Joe has difficulty articulating to his traditional working-class aunt and uncle the reasoning behind his liaison with Susan other than what she represents "her father's brass" as Joe's uncle reminds him (Braine 1957, Walker 1974, Hill 1986, Murphy 1992). Other works along a similar social and cultural theme during this period included Sillitoe's "Saturday Night and Sunday Morning" (1958), Barstow's "A Kind of Loving" (1960), and David Storey's "This Sporting Life" (1960). Most of this literature had been finished in the mid-1950's. However, publishers and editors were initially somewhat recalcitrant in expressing any substantive interest in working-class life as portrayed by these novelists. For example, it took Alan Sillitoe five visits to different publishers before his final version was accepted and likewise David Storey was frustrated eight times before encountering success (Laing 1986, Marwick 1991). Marwick (1991) argued that such rejections were particularly problematic and disheartening for the contemporary novelist who was attempting to foreground a new range of social concerns. However, Laing (1986) stresses that by the end of the 1950's the rise in affluence coupled with the increased volume of paper-back copies and cinematic adaptation presented the writings of Storey, Barstow and the others with more social exposure and broader circulation - something which was not achievable under the limited scope within hardback publication described above. As Laing elucidates:

> " 'Saturday night and Sunday Morning' appeared in Pan paperback in 1960 and was reprinted thirteen times by 1964. The first novels of Storey and Barstow were published in Penguin in 1962... This suggests not only the comparative attractiveness of the novels for a general readership... but also the critical importance of the film version in securing a wide readership" (Laing 1986: 64-65).

Critics such as Hill (1986) believe that most of the "anger" which derived from the contemporary writers of the period was not aimed at social or economic inequity but the "materialistic freedom" arising from modern consumerism, which in turn fed class snobbery and superficial morality: "an embourgeoisement process was taking place in the traditional working-class" (Hill 1986: 7). Writers such as Colin Wilson and Stuart Holroyd encouraged greater independence from this other, conflicting mass culture and stressed the need for a social understanding concerning its cultural depravation upon domestic society. Holroyd identified this cultural regression by contrasting new technology and consumerism and its accompanying sense of isolation to the writings of established English poets like Yeats and T. S. Eliot. Other critics such as D. E. Cooper emphasise the "angry writers" criticism of "effeminacy" through their condemnation of what Cooper sees as women's negative characteristics such as "snobbery, superficiality and materialism", which are especially prevalent in John Osborne's writing (Hill 1986: 24-5). However a <u>detailed</u> textual analysis of both primary, literary and audio-visual material will take place in the forthcoming chapters.

Other writers of the period apart from the "angries" also voiced tones of disenchantment. E. P. Thompson and John Saville having resigned from the communist publication "The Reasoner" after criticising the Russian invasion of Hungary initially formed another left-wing publication "The New Reasoner" before teaming up with "Universities and Left Review" in 1959 to form "New Left Review"[ii]. This new journal criticised old-style Stalinist communism as well as the new welfare-capitalist nation. Accepting a growth in "affluence" the review, criticised the cultural depravity and paucity resulting from a stifling and stultifying system, which they felt was restricting communication modes and constraining creativity (Ibid.: 26).

Other influential writers concerned with the emergent effects of popular culture and the working-class during this period were Richard Hoggart and Raymond Williams. Both were tutors in adult education. Hoggart at the University of Hull where he taught literature and Williams at Oxford University.

Hoggart's key work, "The Uses of Literacy" (1957), outlines and analyses the social practices, domestic relations and cultural characteristics of the working-classes in which the author himself grew up. Hoggart pays specific attention to the impact of popular culture, especially pop music and popular fiction upon the lives of the working-class (Ibid. 1957). His main criticism concerns an attack upon what he regards as the new superficial American mass culture which in 1950's England was displacing the traditional pre-war working-class brand which had grown out of and was at

---

[ii] The opening editorial of the newly founded Universities and Left Review (itself a manifestation of the changed intellectual atmosphere in Britain) said farewell to "that comfortable womb world in which conservatives and socialists still held hands". Its first issue contained articles by E. P. Thomson and David Marquand on Kingsley Amis's Fabian pamphlet; its second featured a symposium on "Socialism and the Intellectuals", all the contributors agreeing that it was important to move away from the negative character of Amis's politics.

the same time consumed by those people from the same social background, or as Hoggart himself stresses:

> "... No doubt many of the old barriers of class should be broken down. But at present the older, the more narrow but also more genuine class culture is being eroded in favour of the mass opinion, the mass recreational product and the generalised emotional response" (Hoggart 1959: 280).

However, perhaps the particular aspect which correlates closest between the writings of the "angry" authors and those of Hoggart is through the personification of Hoggart's "Scholarship boy", the working-class boy who goes through the process of further education by way of scholarships and then finds himself both ambivalent towards his own environment and on the cusp of two cultures (Hoggart 1959). Terry Lovell (1990) believes that the adult scholarship boy takes the role of the "middle-class observer/outsider... looking back with nostalgia at a remembered childhood landscape" (Lovell 1990: 370). Lovell argues that the "knowledge of the insider combined with the distance achieved by the move outside and beyond" may help Hoggart's scholarship boy to recognise the "young, restless, sexually virile worker", such as Arthur Seaton in Sillitoe's "Saturday Night and Sunday Morning" as the man he may have grown into had he not moved away from that environment.

In his first publication, "Culture and Society" (1958), Raymond Williams identifies four definitions of the word culture: that of being a whole way of life, material, intellectual and spiritual (Williams 1966). Therefore Williams would appear to be interested in the whole cultural interaction of literature, words and actions.

In his next book "The Long Revolution" (1961), Williams focuses more on the contemporary debates surrounding the contemporary cultural influences upon the media. In this text Williams concentrates on a holistic anthropological definition of culture as opposed to the more traditional literary and artistic approach. He clarifies his wider definition of culture thus:

"Culture is a description of a particular way of life, which expresses certain meanings and values not only in art and learning but also in institutions and ordinary behaviour. The analysis of culture, from such a definition, is the clarification of the meanings and values implicit and explicit in a particular way of life, a particular culture..." this will include "... analysis of elements in the way of life that to followers of other definitions are not "culture" at all: the organisation of production, the structure of the family, the structure of institutions which express or govern social relationships, the characteristic forms through which members of the society communicate" (Williams 1961: 57).

Hence, Williams is fore-grounding the role of both culture in politics and political influences within the sphere of culture. In "Communications" (1962), Williams believes that the cultural revolution can be achieved with the aid of modern mass communications - themselves a manifestation of cultural change. Perhaps, the most significant proposal made by Williams in terms of its long term cultural impact were the suggestions for the study and teaching of communications such as media institutions, media production and a mode of textual analysis applicable to all cultural forms- recommendations which have subsequently been implemented.

It is widely held that significant changes occurred in British theatre commencing from 1956 onwards. Taylor (1962) cites the opening of John Osborne's "Look Back in Anger" at the Royal Court Theatre in London as the dramatic cultural event in this respect. However, Hinchcliffe (1974) highlights the local government act of 1948 as the principle proponent of distinctive change. This allowed local authorities to charge a sum of 6d (old pence), which contributed toward the cost of developing regional repertory theatres. In addition there was Arts Council sponsorship for new playwrights who focussed upon the pressing issues of contemporary society. Furthermore the appearance of the English Stage Company at the Royal Court Theatre cemented this speedy and profound change. The theatre's "angry" new dramatists were young and articulated their scorn for modern society through regional working-class accents. Arnold Wesker's Centre 42 in a radical change from the politics of London theatre used the trade unions as a vehicle in order to mobilise art and culture to the working-class populace (Laing 1986, Sinfield 1989). Indeed the traditional middle class cultural dominance of West End theatre was shifting. Only a minority of the young play-writes had the benefit of a University education. Salford's Shelagh Delaney being especially notable for failing to achieve Grammar School status. Arnold Wesker – famous for "Roots", and Harold Pinter, - particularly for "The Caretaker", both emerged from ethnic Jewish backgrounds whilst Alun Owen, John Osborne and Clive Exton all spent a number of lean years struggling as minor actors in local theatre (Ibid.: 1986, 1989).

The ethos of the Royal Court was to provide a theatre in opposition to the bourgeois values of the dominant commercial theatre of the period. Plays began to place greater emphasis upon the writer's particular perspective such as Angus Wilson's "The Mulberry Bush". However, it was John Osborne's "Look Back in Anger" which attracted most publicity and helped keep the Royal Court functioning as a business. During the period between 1956 and 1962 the plays of John Osborne became the most successful. Hence George Devine, director of the Royal Court, stressed that his theatre had proved its worth over commercial rivals. The Royal Court theatre, turned out to be a notable promoter of radical new dramatists such as Osborne, John Arden and Arnold Wesker - men who probably would not have been welcomed into commercial theatre, yet at the same time, writers whose concentration on contemporary issues captured audiences who were attracted by a more intellectually challenging form of theatre.

Also at this time, another theatrical pioneer, Joan Littlewood was producing plays by other contemporary writers such as "The Hostage" by Brendan Behan and Shelagh Delaney's "A Taste of Honey". Littlewood's Theatre Workshop was formed in 1945 and according to Hinchliffe:

> "Her belief in getting the theatre back to the people, however vague that phrase is, by the rejection of scripts and the use

of improvisation techniques and strongly directed ensemble work turns out to be more significant than "Look Back in Anger". She suggests a kind of theatre in which the producer is more important than the text, action than the word. She insisted on the spontaneous and the topical thus preventing any possibility that her kind of theatre could become a museum" (Hinchliffe 1974: 53-54).

In her production of Charles Chilton's "Oh, What a Lovely War" (1963) Littlewood exemplified this approach through the use of original documents and songs from World War One. Littlewood delineated the folly and waste of war and instead reinforced the desire for collective commitment. Littlewood frequently foregrounded contemporary concerns such as prison-life and the IRA in Brendan Behan's "The Quare Fellow," whilst "A Taste of Honey", was regarded by critic and film director Lindsay Anderson as a welcome change from "The middle-brow, middle-class vacuum of the west end," symptomatic of a bourgeois cultural identity (Hinchliffe 1974: 55).

The BBC also played a symbolic role in representing the changing national image at this time; both in relation to its programming policy and through the formation and re-affirmation of different sub-cultural identities. For example, the middle ground position which the corporation occupied during the Suez crisis angered Eden and the imperial establishment (Sked and Cook 1984, Marwick 1998). This lead to questions concerning the political and national allegiance of this institution once seen as emblematic of British imperialism under the helm of John Reith's leadership.

In the late 1950s, through the efforts of Charles Parker and Ewan McColl the BBC produced a successful series of Radio Ballads. Folk music was symbolic of the indigenous culture of working people (Laing 1986: 163-6), and the left mobilised it as a cultural emblem to cement the common myths and celebrate the heroic deeds and lives of the martyrs of the alternative British history which was in danger of being alienated and marginalised by rock'n'roll, advertising and the commercialised Pop industry.

Ewan MacColl, Peggy Seeger and Charles Parker created a collection of "Radio Ballads" between 1958-63, interspersing songs in the folk manner with the recorded speech of ordinary working people whom had previously barely been given air time before on BBC radio (Laing 1986: 162-6, Sinfield 1989, Briggs 1995, Marwick 1998). One such programme, "The Ballad of John Axon" (1958), told the true story of an engine driver killed whilst valiantly attempting to stop a runaway train. MacColl, Parker and Seeger succeeded in assuaging the BBC establishment who felt that the capitalist employers' viewpoint should also be expressed in these radio documentaries (Laing 1986). The aforementioned cultural artefacts were symbolic of an alternative national identity which attempted to articulate the heroism and social and cultural diversity of Britain's heritage.

Furthermore in a review of the first two radio ballads, "Song of a Road" and "John Axon", both produced in 1958, Trade Unionist Bill Holdsworth, congratulated MacColl for "making a great contribution to the fight against the mass pop-culture" by bringing alive "the personal dramas of our own day and age" (Holdsworth 1960 in Laing 1986: 165).

At the end of the 1950s the BBC broadcast a range of programmes concerning specific occupational subcultures, such as coal-mining and herring fishing. "The particular significance of this in the late 1950s was in the emphasis of work as the primary determinant both of lifestyle and in alternative ways of viewing the nation - a contradiction of the conventional wisdom concerning the changes wrought by affluence" (Laing 1986: 165).

Between 1958 and 1963 the contemporary state of working-class culture was articulated and analysed through a diverse compendium of BBC television programming. This ranged from political debates and party political broadcasts to current affairs. Perhaps symbolic of this was Christopher Mayhew's series <u>What is Class?</u> which featured an enthralling interview with Dennis Potter, who ruminated on the social divide between his two cultural identities as miner's son and Oxford undergraduate. In Potter's own contribution <u>Between Two Rivers</u> (June 1960) an unambiguously stated voice over was employed to condemn the corrosive effects of the new affluence on the traditional forest mining community in which Potter was raised (Laing 1986, Briggs 1995).

Examples such as these seemed characteristic of the progressive reign of Hugh Carlton-Greene, Director General of the BBC between 1960 and 1969, who pushed at the existing cultural boundaries by helping to galvanise and explore the comparatively new spheres of satirical comedy and socially stimulating drama (Ridgman 1992).

In a speech in Ottawa in November 1961 Greene stressed how important it was that the BBC be emancipated from both political and commercial pressures.

> "Nobody in Britain seriously regards the BBC these days as a servant of government, dancing to whatever tune the government calls... We are outside the business ring which largely controls the British entertainment world... The BBC has a peculiar place in national life... other things being equal, the public clearly prefers the BBC for both the lighter and the more serious sides of life" (Hugh Carlton-Greene in Briggs 1995: 324).

According to Briggs (1995) what was essentially significant about the beginning of the sixties in relation to other eras in the annuls of broadcasting was that with Greene as Director-General the BBC endeavoured to associate itself closely with the distinctive pattern of social and cultural change.

Greene had minimal involvement in programming although his regime helped create the environment in which producers and script-writers could develop and explore a new range of programme making.

However the production which Greene was most closely aligned to was a programme that perhaps embodied the counter vitality of the period.

That Was The Week That Was or (TW3), as it became known was broadcast on 24 November 1962. This production was regarded as a refreshing and contemporary satire comprising of thinly veiled attacks on the snobbery and hypocrisy of senior politicians with original songs and sketches which together pointedly criticised aspects of modern society (Goldie 1977, Briggs 1995).

TW3's audience grew rapidly reaching a maximum in April 1963, of 12 million. Views concerning this anti-establishment satirical current affairs programme were divided. "Some people liked the vitality of TW3 and the absence of cant; others objected either to smutty schoolboy jokes, or at the deepest level to what they considered "blasphemy". The performers in the programme welcomed the polarisation" (Briggs 1995: 351). TW3 offered a radical social change both from the consensual conformity of wartime cultural products as well as the middle-ground perspective of senior politicians of the period. As Briggs concludes: "Nothing bland would do. For the makers of the programme to have "againsts" as well as "fors" was a test of the effectiveness of the satire on offer" (Briggs 1995: 351).

According to Briggs (1995), Sked and Cook (1984) and Marwick (1998), there were profuse signs of national malaise when the 1960s began. Social issues concerning the effects of affluence, the decline of tradition and the heightening of the Cold War all engaged politicians, public and media alike. The educational, traditional and New Left groups expressed questions concerning the future of ageing national institutions. These ranged from the Church of England to the railways – something that Harold Macmillan was acutely mindful of when setting up The Pilkington Committee to review the future of broadcasting in September 1960 (Briggs 1995, Laing 1992).

Both the issue of competition and the comparatively new ITV companies were areas of discussion for the committee's report which in 1962 attempted to articulate the aspirations of the different groups. Consequently the Independent Television Authority's (ITA) control over the ITV companies was tightened whilst the second terrestrial channel was given to the BBC. BBC2 intended to represent the nation's social and cultural diversity through a range of programming such as regional and educational productions (Laing 1992, Briggs 1995).

Pilkington reinforced the view that the duopoly concerning the BBC and ITV signalled the emergence of competition which would surge the BBC toward a new post-war era of diverse and populist programming. The corporation made Drama the fulcrum of this policy. Apart from producing a great range of serials, from <u>Dr. Who</u> to <u>Dr. Finlay's Casebook</u>, - with the objective of securing a large widespread audience the BBC also placed great professional stall on <u>The Wednesday Play</u>, a series comprising of contemporary social dramas (Laing 1992). Neil Dunn's <u>Up the Junction</u> relating to the struggles of pregnancy and working-class life in South London's Clapham Junction was adapted for BBC television and directed by Ken Loach in 1965. Dennis Potter - another young working-class author - received a television "debut" with his political satire <u>Vote, Vote, Vote for Nigel Barton</u> (1965). However, <u>The Wednesday Plays</u>' most notable contribution was <u>Cathy Come Home</u> (1966). Written by Jeremy Sandford and sensitively directed by Ken Loach "Cathy" traces the story of a young woman amidst the affluence "boom" of contemporary Britain struggling with the twin social evils of poverty and homelessness.

The Wednesday Play was seen to symbolise the liberalism of the corporation, attracting criticism and moral condemnation which occasionally culminated in direct political attacks on the BBC. According to Whitehouse (1971) <u>The Wednesday Play</u> "roamed clumsily, even subversively, amongst the most sensitive areas of human, social and international relationships, and was quite prepared to exploit its opportunities for propaganda" (Whitehouse 1971: 73). Moreover Ridgman (1992) claims that this Christian fundamentalist perspective of the BBC as "the enemy within" was shared by the political right: "In 1989 the liberal Tory MP Julian Critchley, himself an advocate, at the end of the 1960s, for the idea of an establishment of a Broadcasting Council, attributed the lasting "hatred" of his party for the BBC not merely to the satire of <u>That Was The Week That Was</u> or just to the perceived bias of their political journalism, but to the grainy drama-documentaries which challenged the comfortable assumptions of those whom the electorate had, in its wisdom, chose to govern us". If a Tory was looking for left-wing bias at the BBC, Critchley recalls being told by Lord Swann, "he need go no further than the drama department" (Critchley cited in Ridgman 1992b: 152). Such a programme policy symbolised a significant decline in the respect given to the increasingly alienated establishment and helped mark the BBC's role in contributing toward the culture of change during this period.

Moreover, Stuart Laing (1986) reinforces the view that it was the BBC, rather than the commercially emblematic ITV[iii] which aligned itself with the restless spirit of this period - the imagined community of a new generation, free of class and cultural boundaries which had previously symbolised the tired old image of an imperial Britain. Indeed the discontented initially associated exclusively with intellectuals and the New Left had spread outwards as the satirical magazine "Private Eye" also proved to be a voice for the nation's dissenters.

Sexual immorality, was also a growing sign of moral fissures within British society during this period. The Wolfenden Report in 1957 promoted a more tolerant attitude towards what some looked upon as sexual permissiveness. On one level the Report may have condemned the increasing strain on traditional notions of the family ("the basic unit of society") by male homosexual conduct, however this did not merit marginalising homosexuality by outlawing it. Indeed the Wolfenden Committee felt that adultery, debauchery and lesbian tendencies, were just as domestically destructive (Hill 1986: 19). Hence, even though Wolfenden promoted a more understanding attitude toward the acknowledgement of different sexual orientations such as homosexual behaviour it did this within what John Hill describes as "...a general framework of moral

---

[iii] Commercial television (from 1955) was aggressively "popular" and since it was organised regionally, companies felt they should look for regional material. Through programmes such as "Coronation Street", limited versions of lower-class cultures came into public visibility (Sinfield 1989: 269).

censure, a concern with the "treatment" of homosexuality and an ideological privileging of marital heterosexuality" (Hill 1986: 19).

A combination of increasing emancipation and moderation with greater monitoring and regulation also featured Wolfenden's handling of the prostitution issue: "The guiding principle of Wolfenden was the distinction between law and morality, and the individual's right to make his/her own moral choices without legal interference as long as harm is not inflicted on another. Privacy became the key note to this principle..." claims Carol Smart (in Hill 1986: 19). Consequently Wolfenden felt justified in introducing old fashioned tougher measures, even prison, for public violations. In addition it was made easier for courts to remand offenders and order the transfer of prostitutes into the care of welfare specialists. Therefore, the Report immediately advocated overtly draconian instructions on prostitution which were then included within the Street Offences Act of 1959 whilst their proposals on homosexuality waited a further decade before being made law. Therefore, according to Hill (1986) it was the concern to continue to promote the collective traditional institutions of family and marriage, as opposed to individual sexual indulgence which permeated both Wolfendon's recommendations and consequent legislation (Ibid.: 20-1).

2.4 Conclusion

In this chapter I have analysed Britain's national identity as perceived within the post-war global arena, focussing upon the nation's role in relation to other international cultures, such as Europe, the new Commonwealth and events like Suez, because these global constructions were so influential in this period while Britain was facing both a declining and shifting position in the world. Secondly, British national identity will be examined during a period when different sources of identity, both converging and conflicting, were emerging in relation to notions of the domestic cultural community, such as economic prosperity, political crises, cultural changes and social divisions. Therefore the social and cultural revolution which impacted upon Britain during 1955-65 overturned the previously imperialist era of consolidation through a range of fundamental social, cultural and economic changes. These initiated the untying of social and cultural knots which had held together the common experiences of a nation an imagined community, related by language, shared ideas and values (Perkin 1981). The borderlines of the establishment previously impenetrable, became harder to defend, loosened through a disappearing empire and an outdated class system. In so doing I have returned to the detailed analysis I first undertook in my Theses "Realist Nights and Heritage Mornings." (2001).

The stringent social bonds which had applied to society during the era of consolidation through evangelical religion were at the same time abandoned as capital punishment was abolished and arts censorship re-evaluated and then relaxed. Moreover during this period abortion and homosexuality were made lawful, whilst sexual behaviour changed as contraceptives became more easily accessible and divorce less difficult to attain. In addition constraints on gambling and drinking were eased (Hill 1986, Richards 1997, Marwick 1998).

> "Fashions changed, changed again, changed faster and still faster: fashions in politics, in political style, in causes, in music, in popular culture, in myths, in education, in beauty, in heroes and idols, in attitudes, in responses, in work, in love and friendship, in food, in newspapers, in entertainment, in fashion. What had once lasted a generation now lasted a year, what had lasted a year lasted a month, a week, a day. There was a restlessness in the time that communicated itself everywhere and to everyone" (Levin in Sinfield 1989: 283).

Conflicting cultural identity constructions jostled for recognition within the national social vacuum vacated by establishment imperialism. British pop icons "The Beatles" and the "Rolling Stones" amongst others, were seen as cultural symbols of this new youthful and dynamic national identity. Both the middle-class discontented and higher educated young embraced and encouraged this rebellion as did the young working class. New areas of employment were emerging within the cultural fields of production. The young, mobilised and determined, unhesitatingly rejected and reassessed traditionally accepted beliefs concerning high-culture - (and its patronising authoritative identity of establishment otherness) - through "pop art, fringe theatre, underground poetry and the new respect shown to television and popular music - (Sinfield 1989: 283-4) - as "Art", "literature" and "poetry" resembled graffiti, and advertisements, comics and pop songs"... within this new cultural jungle whilst <u>all</u> combined to help illustrate the social diversity which helped comprise the fragmented jigsaw of 1960s British National Identity.

Chapter III.

Questioning National Identity - Great Britain in 1955 - 1965

3.1 Introduction

Until the early 1950s, established notions of national identity were rooted in pre-war, class-conscious certainties and subject to imperialist influences. By the middle of the decade, as the Empire declined and imperialist influence faded, a newly empowered working class began to emerge. As it collided with a weakened but still largely inflexible and class ordered hierarchy tensions arose. The imperialist establishment and the invigorated working class reacted differently to the loss of Empire subjecting British society to strain and challenging the notional national consensus thought to exist during the era of Empire. These strains and challenges helped to define changing perceptions of national identity during the late 1950s and early 1960s. This chapter will consider those tensions and the associated economic, social, cultural and political changes conveyed by the Social Realist films. During the course of this Chapter I shall again be utilising the same themes, concerns and analysis first adopted in "Realist Nights and Heritage Mornings" (2001).

Such a discussion will inevitably involve a consideration of contemporary influences including the Suez crisis, the Commonwealth, nuclear weapons, CND, and the New Left, which I will set within a sociological and historical framework. Fundamentally, I will contend that the differing responses within British society to the collapse of the Empire have determined constructions of national identity. In seeking to establish this contention, I shall analyse the nation's position in relation to "other" international cultures. The old order had survived poverty in the 1930s and war in the 40s but seemed weakened by the peace and comparative prosperity of the 1950s. I will try to explain why, when the country had "never had it so good" according to its Edwardian Premier Macmillan, the traditional imperialist establishment had failed to maintain power. Rather than reinforce its position it seemed unable to face unprecedented threat.

I will identify the significant social and cultural aspects of national identity formation during the 1955-65 period including affluence, social mobility and consumerism, imperial decline and moral change. I will highlight the increased politicisation of culture

CHAPTER III - QUESTIONING NATIONAL IDENTITY

and cultural products such as "Social Realist" media during this specified period. I will consider their representation through selected British media in terms of their social, moral and political commitment towards broader social and cultural changes within Britain and their consequences for the questioning of contemporary national identity. The chapter breaks down into four subsections. The first will deal with class, the second morality, the third questions of post imperialism and the final sub section will discuss other contributions to the culture of change such as contemporary television.

Overall, it will become apparent that as the 1950s progressed the working class in general and disaffected young men in particular, were refusing to accept pre-war imperial class order. Each would display some resistance to traditional notions of order and make some limited attempt to change his environment. However, each would return to the familiarity of an environment that was invariably provincial, industrial and dark. Significantly, there is little evidence of a collective, political or didactic response to the changes taking place within society. The reactions are of a disparate collection of individuals united by a commonality of circumstance. Equally, the films portraying these individual characters do not suggest any alternative paradigm for the society they appear to challenge.

In the first sub section I intend to consider in detail <u>Room at the Top</u>, <u>A Kind of Loving</u>, <u>Saturday Night and Sunday Morning</u>, <u>The Loneliness of The Long Distance Runner</u> and <u>Look Back in Anger</u>. I will contend that unusually in British cultural history the daily lives of the working class found representation in mainstream British media from a working class perspective. I will discuss the refusal of Arthur Seaton in <u>Saturday Night and Sunday Morning</u> to accept the preordained role in society established for his parents and the older generations of his class. I will suggest that he typified the emergent individual working class challenge to an imperial class based hierarchy and I will examine the immediate social strains that result from this challenge.

I shall then focus upon the social resistance offered by Colin Smith in <u>The Loneliness of The Long Distance Runner</u>. Also based on a novel by Alan Sillitoe, the film depicts Colin Smith as a disaffected youth. He refuses to sully his hands with paid employment because he does not want the "bosses to get all the profit" while he "slaves" his "guts out". <u>Saturday Night and Sunday Morning</u> ends with Arthur throwing a few symbolic stones at a new housing estate. <u>In The Loneliness of The Long Distance Runner</u> Colin throws away the chance of winning the race and also the relative privileges the Governor would bestow. It is significant that in an earlier scene the Governor tells Colin that he can think of no "higher honour than for a man to represent his country at the Olympic Games". During the cross cutting montage in the penultimate scenes, as the audience witness Colin deliberately losing the race the aural flashback changes the Governors words from "country" to Ruxton Towers. Colin refuses to be a representative of either his country or his institution.

I will also discuss Joe Lampton and his refusal to accept that his class should limit his ambitions. Whilst discussing Jimmy Porter and Vic Brown I will chart the extent to which some other members of the working class, were as early as the mid 1950s, detecting and rejecting rampant consumerism. I will also consider the fears they expressed about the suffocation of traditional working class values and interests by this new and shallow consumerist society. I will contrast these individuals with characters from own ranks, typified by the Rothwell women in <u>A Kind of Loving</u>, who seemed to embrace the new consumerist culture. In addition I shall analyse the extent to which the Rothwell women and Doreen in <u>Saturday Night and Sunday Morning</u> formed the core of a more modern, aspirant, materialist, upper working or lower middle class.

In the second sub section I shall examine the questioning of conventionally accepted notions of contemporary morality. In studying <u>Room at the Top</u>, <u>A Taste of Honey</u> and <u>Saturday Night and Sunday Morning</u> I will detail some of the struggles the filmmakers encountered in bringing these films to the screen. Most of the influential Social Realist films focused upon male characters carelessly impregnating their girlfriends. I shall discuss the differing ways the characters reacted to their predicament. I will attempt to delineate the extent to which the British Board of Film Censors executed its perceived duty to limit the moral arenas on film. This tendency to restrict access to the working class and limit screen recreations of contemporary morality formed a significant element in the questioning of national identity. I shall then demonstrate how changes to traditional concepts of morality now permit an audience for the sexual philandering of <u>Alfie</u>. Moreover I will then ask whether this film propounded a radical moral code for mid 1960s Britain or whether it was in some respects a re-affirmation of more traditional moral responses.

In the third sub section I will consider post imperial consequences for a questioning of national identity. The national humiliation of Suez and issues of post imperial decline were of special significance during the mid 1950s and informed, in particular, the work of John Osborne. I shall analyse <u>The Entertainer</u> and demonstrate how the film portrayed a declining national esteem by using the story of a spent and weary Music Hall as a metaphor. This film suggested that Edwardian certainty and traditional honourable forms of working class entertainment such as the Music Hall had given way to American mass culture and crass consumerism.

I will also consider Colin Smith in <u>The Loneliness of The Long Distance Runner</u>. As the only principal Social Realist character imprisoned for criminal behaviour, the film allows for a comparison of the institutions of Borstal and the public school. I will analyse the extent to which this perceived national decay affected questions of national identity. This allegory for national decline was made towards the end of the Social Realist cycle. I will also consider <u>This Sporting Life</u> and <u>Billy Liar</u>, two films which are generally regarded as concluding the cycle. Broadly in this sub section, I shall consider the extent to which British national identity was subject to redefinition following the transformation from imperial power with a particular emphasis on the working class. I will then examine the rise of the James Bond cycle and articulate how this character came to present a stylised and diluted form of British nationalism of the 1960s. In this analysis I shall endeavour to ascertain the self image of a post imperial Britain. I shall contrast Bond with the more overtly working class spy Harry Palmer and extract relevant themes.

In the final section I will analyse two contemporary television programmes, Coronation Street and Z Cars and assess the extent, degree and manner in which each may be said to have contributed to the culture of change. Coronation Street embraced the notion of the community and overtly traded in nostalgia. Z Cars appeared to acknowledge the changes taking place within society and addressed social alienation. Overall, the Chapter will assess the articulation of shifting perceptions of national identity during 1955-65.

3.2 Affluence, Consumerism and Social Mobility

Poverty scarred the 30s and war ravaged the 40s but the 1950s, by contrast, increasingly became the decade of apparent affluence, conspicuous consumption and greater social mobility. The reality was however, a nation close to bankruptcy since whatever economic criteria are applied the nation was undoubtedly richer in absolute and real terms at the turn of the XX century when the Empire was at its zenith. The Great War largely exhausted this Edwardian wealth. World War II was essentially waged on credit and transformed Britain into a world debtor. The foreign policy that prevailed until shortly before the outbreak of World War I was very consciously one of "splendid isolation" for Britain. Buttressed by a profitable and expanding Empire and protected by the most powerful Navy in the world, such disdain for international affiliation was sustainable and credible. The economic difficulties that followed the Second World War together with the comparatively sudden loss of Empire compelled on the one hand closer relations with the USA and on the other ultimate entry into the European Union. These difficulties, combined with the loss of independence that Empire underwrote would strongly and directly influence perceptions of national identity. In the Suez fiasco, for instance, Britain had to undergo a humiliating withdrawal of her troops for fear of losing the backing of the International Monetary Fund which it desperately needed. Economic dependence upon the IMF had effectively undermined the type of colonialist venture

CHAPTER III - QUESTIONING NATIONAL IDENTITY

that imperial Britain had previously felt able to mount without any real concern for international censure.

Against this international decline, there was an impression in the 1950s and 1960s of increased affluence closely allied with greater social mobility. This distinguished these decades from earlier periods. The overt relationship between affluence and apparent social mobility contradicted by a covert link between loss of Empire and economic potency created a paradox which essentially defined perceptions of national identity at this time.

For the working classes, in particular, this was a time of relative wealth. Some may have agreed with Macmillan that they had "never had it so good". Yet, when Colin Smith in The Loneliness of The Long Distance Runner (1962) refers to his father "sweating his guts out for £9 a week" as a labourer it is with cynicism and bitter irony. Colin manifestly feels that his father saw little of this prosperity. This is reinforced when Colin accompanies his mother when she arrives at his father's factory to collect her death benefits. He is remembered, somewhat condescendingly by the patrician management figure, as a "jolly good worker". Colin reminds Mrs Smith that "Dad got them out all right" when he presumably led the last strike and "got 'em a rise n' all". This evidently rather bitter strike action does not sit easily with perceptions of the period which are of relatively harmonious industrial relations. Colin disbelieves the sentiments of loss expressed by the management figure. There is little indication that Colin detects any real improvement in social mobility.

By contrast, in Jack Clayton's Room at the Top (1959) Joe Lampton, another young working class male with equally modest roots claws his way up the post war, social ladder. He hears that there is "always room at the top" for those like him. One must therefore examine why Colin is serving time in Borstal with little more than a life of recidivism ahead whereas Joe acquires all the surface trappings of wealth and social success. Which of these two fictional characters represent the "social realism" that the respective films seek to depict? It is difficult to establish any degree of commonality between Joe and Colin. The latter character appears to despise the shallow values of consumerism. In one scene he symbolically burns a pound note given to him by his mother for the assistance he has rendered in helping her to spend the death benefits paid out by his father's employer. Since he sets fire to it on the metaphorical alter of his father's bedroom it is not difficult to see this as a ritual sacrificial offering. Joe on the other hand appears to dedicate his whole existence to the pursuit of material gain.

Colin and Joe shared with many of the new wave protagonists a refusal to accept the hitherto apparently fixed and given set of social relations. The traditional-class ordered social and economic divisions within society were increasingly under question. The concept of Englishness in this respect was undergoing change, and the films of the era articulate the conditions of this change. In particular, some of the Social Realist films of the early 1960s, produced by the "Angry Generation", attempted to warn of the moral dangers threatened by the materialistic benefits of an emerging consumerist culture.

I have already observed that in <u>The Loneliness of The Long Distance Runner</u> (1962) Colin seems repulsed by the consumerist binge his mother embarks upon with the insurance on her late husband's life. Although she herself remarked bitterly to her husband's employers "it's a shame you had to wait for the poor sod to die before parting with £500" she showed a ready willingness to spend it. Equally, when Frank Machin in <u>This Sporting Life</u> (1963) creates his own opportunity for a trial with the City Rugby Club his primary concern is the size of his signing-on fee. He obstinately holds out for and is given the then huge sum of £1,000. He is lodging with Mrs Hammond and clearly owns no property of his own. Rather than purchasing a suitable car, he deliberately and ostentatiously purchases a Bentley. This vulgar celebration of his newly found economic power sits, at a surface level, uneasily with any criticism of consumerism. However, Frank is using an icon of wealth and conspicuous consumption to demonstrate his personal worth.

As we have seen from previous chapters, the wealth of the workers had substantially improved from pre-war times. Although the actions of Frank Machin were extreme, there was general evidence of increasing acquisitiveness particularly among the traditional working class. With a barrage of new products advertised within the expanding consumerist market, such as televisions and washing machines, the traditional values and in many ways the "essence" of the working class were being dramatically altered. An increase in the ownership of television sets was crucial in connecting the economics of consumerism with an emerging representational culture (Laing 1986).

After years of absolute and relative economic deprivation, one might expect the working classes to welcome this improved prosperity. Historic perceptions of their role within the nation's identity might suggest an acceptance of the increase without any underlying cultural implications. However, despite this apparent improvement as we have noted the decade also witnessed the emergence of the 'angry young men'. The reader may wonder why Jimmy Porter, who by virtue of his university degree had joined the educated elite, did not embrace full membership of the middle classes. It took considerable dedication and effort for a member of the relatively uneducated working classes to graduate. Yet, almost as soon as he perceives the threshold of the middle class he rejects both it and its bourgeois values. Contrasted with this violent revulsion is the core presence in his life of two middle class women. He chose to marry Alison the embodiment of the middle class. Furthermore, virtually the moment Alison leaves he develops a passionate relationship with Helena who only hours before had been the target for his class driven scorn and vitriol.

In 1956 film director Lindsay Anderson, at this time associated with the New Left, wrote a now famous critical manifesto – "Stand Up! Stand Up!" in *Sight and Sound* in which he called for a more socially conscious and responsible British cinema. In February of that year Anderson, Karel Reisz, and Tony Richardson amongst others organised a series of documentary screenings at the National Film Theatre. Using the title Free Cinema, they attempted to focus on specific aspects of contemporary British working class life. In the programme notes Anderson outlined Free Cinema's characteristics, claiming it was a cinema of the contemporary and reacting to:

"A British cinema still obstinately class-bound; still rejecting the stimulus of contemporary life, as well as the responsibility to criticise; still reflecting a metropolitan Southern English culture which excludes the rich diversity of tradition and personality which is the whole of Britain" (Anderson cited in Laing 1986: 114).

In addition Free Cinema was independent of the constraints of the commercial cinema and therefore was able to produce films that expressed the director's views and not primarily those of the producers. Free Cinema believed in location shooting, focusing on the lives of ordinary working people. Together with the "Angry Writers" and the Royal Court, Free Cinema represented the lives of the working class at a "particular cultural moment" in British social history. Geographic mobility and urban redevelopment fractured traditional working class communities whilst the effects of new economic prosperity emerged together with a rush of low culture mass entertainment (Hill 1985: 194). The views held by Free Cinema emanated from "preoccupations common among intellectuals in the second half of the fifties: a sympathetic interest in communities... fascination with the newly emerging youth culture... unease about the quality of leisure in urban society and respect for the traditional working class" (Lovell and Hillier 1972: 142).

Indeed <u>Every Day Except Christmas</u> (1957) much like Anderson's first film <u>Meet the Pioneers</u> (1948) illustrated the dignity of the traditional working class as well as reinforcing a sense of local and national community. <u>O Dreamland</u> (1953) revealed the increasing prevalence of mass culture in working class life.

Furthermore many of the Free Cinema directors, Anderson, Reisz and Richardson were to convey this same concern with the lives of the working class in the commercial cinema through the British Social Realist films between 1958-63. With a declared desire to wrestle with contemporary social issues, Social Realist cinema distanced itself from the bourgeois conventions and middle-class beliefs of traditional post-war British cinema. It instead endeavoured to represent the lives and struggles of factory workers, foot soldiers, Sergeant Pilots and young working-class graduates. The central figure was a young working class hero - usually a gritty northerner and nearly always male - whose confidence and vitality contrasted with the submissive and conformist working class mass (Hill 1986, Laing 1986, Sinfield 1989).

Although the majority of the working class remained compromised by economic necessity they did have, for almost certainly the first time, alternative role models in Social Realist films, young men who they might wish to emulate. This movement examined the relationship between material improvement that was undoubtedly taking place among the working class, allied to a perceived cultural loss. The films attempted to question whether material gain inevitably led to a loss of traditional culture or an undermining of morality. They identified the beginning of an internal convulsion within the working class and began charting the slow and gradual encroachments made by the bourgeois. This would in turn help create a disenfranchised underclass and an aspirant middle class *nouveau riche* associated with Thatcher's 1980s enterprise culture.

This new wave of films gives representation to increasing social and cultural fragmentation but significantly, it does not form part of any cohesive social or ideological polemic. As John Hill (1986) has noted, the emphasis in New Wave films is on the personal lives of the young working class males as opposed to their daily drudgery in the factories. For example in <u>A Kind of Loving</u> we see Vic making eyes at Ingrid (June Ritchie), a typist at the firm (Dawson and Whittakers), across the work's canteen - the talk amongst his colleagues concerns Vic's romantic interest in Ingrid. The next cut is a dissolve which takes us straight to the end of the working day several hours later, as hordes of employees (including Vic and Ingrid) are seen streaming away from the factory confines as in <u>Saturday Night and Sunday Morning</u> (1960). Later scenes supposedly within working hours continue to concentrate on the personal lives of the principal protagonist as Vic and Ingrid are seen surreptitiously exchanging private notes through the office boy, whilst in another scene Vic and Conroy argue in the drawing office over Vic's relationship with Ingrid before both end up locked in a scuffle on the floor.

Vic and Ingrid, like Arthur and Doreen in <u>Saturday Night and Sunday Morning</u> depict two strands of the working class suggesting the emergence of a social and economic pluralism within that demographic grouping. Vic's roots are traditional and respectable, personified by his father's position as a railwayman, a player in the local brass band and possessing what Laing describes as "sound common sense" (Laing 1986: 131). It is interesting to note that Vic who unlike Joe Lampton is amiable, modest and self-effacing has never considered that as a draughtsman he has achieved real success in his father's eyes. As a draughtsman, however, he is unconsciously distancing himself from his traditional, blue-collar worker father. Vic's father jokes: "white collar workers don't get tea, you want to get a day's work done before you get tea". A similarly, socially loaded but ostensibly humorous remark is made by Mr Barlow to his scholarship-boy son Ken in the first episode of <u>Coronation Street</u> (1960). In addition Vic's sister Christine had married middle-class schoolteacher David amid her working class community whilst old women candidly described her as having "done well for 'erself". Vic's father is portrayed by Wilfred Bramble as the traditional, stolid working class male. A veteran of the Somme, he is happy enough but also sufficiently aware to appreciate the nuances of factory life and to acknowledge that in his world the drawing office is significantly socially and economically distant from the factory floor.

As a Somme veteran, Mr Brown would have been born at the tail end of Queen Victoria's reign but at the height of the British Empire. He would have reached maturity in a class ordered society divided along rigid social lines with Victoria's son, King Edward VII topping the social order. Among his various hereditary titles, King Edward was also the Emperor of India. Since Benjamin Disreali had bestowed upon Queen Victoria the title Empress of India the two titles had co-existed. Great Britain therefore had as head of state a ruler whose titles reflected in equal measure that ruler's status as head of state but also as the titular leader of an Empire. In 1952 following the death of the last Emperor of India, the last Empress entered an enforced partial retirement with the artificially created title of Queen Mother.

Therefore by the late 1950s not only was the Empire unravelling at an increasing rate but the titular linkage of Monarch and Emperor had effectively been broken. The traditional pre-war class order was changing. However, it is vitally important to note that these changes were not primarily the result of a cohesive or collective politically motivated group with a clear and unified agenda for change. The changes were more attributable to the emergence of disparate groupings within society seeking a degree of liberation from the traditional imperialist class based social order. As we have noted the protagonists in the films studied differed markedly from each other and it is difficult to find very much evidence of any didactic attitude to class, consumerism or Empire.

The New Wave films tend collectively to promote the contention that affluence and consumerism had begun to permeate contemporary British life by the late 1950s. This helped create a situation in which social and cultural identities were becoming more distinctive and a reshaping of social spheres including politics, work, morality, pop culture and music were becoming more evident. However, the approach to and uses of consumerism adopted by the films varies. I have already commented upon the differing attitudes taken by Colin Smith, Joe Lampton and Frank Machin. As I have noted earlier by the late 1950s the effects of the Education Act 1944 were beginning to become apparent. This, combined with full employment, welfare capitalism and the consensus policies of the Butskellite era, helped empower the working class. Their response, as articulated in the cinema of the period, was disparate, fragmented and inherently individual.

Room at the Top (1959) presents a story surrounding the social aspirations of an ambitious and acquisitive, working class accounts clerk, Joe Lampton, in 1950s industrial Yorkshire. According to Walker (1974), the driving force of Room at the Top is the wish of Joe Lampton to obtain the values and possessions of a higher class. However, the film thematically questions whether he simply wants their "brass" or wishes to acquire all the trappings of the middle class.

"Even the note of watery-eyed remorse which Joe Lampton strikes as the limousine speeds him off from his wedding, up the hill to "the top", is ambiguous, directed less at his own lost integrity than at the loss of a mistress whom he would surely have regarded as one of the luxurious accessories legitimately available to him in his new-found social status" (Walker 1974: 45).

Whilst this may seem a harsh judgement from Alexander Walker there can be little doubt that Alice is sacrificed in favour of Joe's vaulting ambition. He directs the reader to his venal and acquisitive nature with his envious attitude towards the material evidence of local industrialist Brown's successes. Addressing work mate Charles he refers sardonically to "all those chimneys that's money, beautiful, beautiful, belching out day and night". Later he drives past Brown's sumptuous mansion and bitterly complains: "that lot drive me mad, they think they have a divine right to everything". He appears uncertain whether to nurture traditional class envy or to suppress his working class roots in order to ape and ultimately join this group he also seems to despise.

For instance when he comes to Warnley for the first time and is about to meet his future landlady, he contemplates stretching his vowels and therefore conspicuously adopting the style, mannerisms and modes of speech of the moneyed class. This putative affectation contrasts with Brown, the particular man he aspires to emulate who seems to have acquired a wife of peerless social finesse and factories "belching" money without refining his broad Yorkshire dialect. At the core of his ambition and determination to succeed lies uncertainty and confusion. This narrative theme is replicated in most of the major Social Realist films, novels and plays.

As Joe ponders his choice of accent the film deprives the middle and upper class characters, Jack Wales and George Aisgill in particular, of any redeeming features. Depicted as little more than one dimensional class caricatures they are so repellent that almost any character set in opposition to them would engender audience sympathy. This is a striking departure from the novel.

CHAPTER III - QUESTIONING NATIONAL IDENTITY

For example, upon Lampton's first meeting with Jack Wales Joe is introduced to him as a "fellow flyer from the war". However Wales has no hesitation in locating him as a Sergeant-Observer rather than an officer: "Oh, I can tell" Wales arrogantly informs Lampton in one of the most socially significant scenes of the film.

Class difference is counter-pointed over the next two scenes as Joe watches helplessly whilst Wales drives Susan away in the Lagonda. The film then cuts to Joe who is seen travelling by bus into town the next morning, representing his relative lack of social mobility (Marwick 1990). This friction is made worse as Lampton and Wales have a further altercation with Jack reminding the "sergeant" of his Distinguished Flying-Cross for war time services and glorious escape from captivity. This contrasts with Joe's reluctance to escape from a prisoner of war camp, something he describes as "an officer's privilege". Later at a formal dinner the cruel disdain and critical coldness of the upper classes is illustrated as Jack Wales rebuffs Joe's social advances toward Susan. He humiliates him through the deliberate name dropping of leading socialites and war-time officers known to Wales - who were naturally unfamiliar to Lampton's distinct class background.

These points are driven home with little attempt at subtlety or finesse. Whilst the primary dramatic purpose may have been the engendering of audience identification with an unsympathetic central character it can also be asserted that there is a further more relevant reason for their inclusion. The sneering condescension that Jack Wales has for Joe is palpably rooted in the class system but is expressed not merely in strict social terms but also through the medium of their respective wartime military ranks. Of greater apparent concern to Jack Wales was his superior position as a defender of the realm and of the Empire. Joe regarded his time as a POW as his only opportunity to study. He regarded escape as a privilege of rank not open to him. Despite the blatant and hostile attempts by Jack Wales to induce a sense of shame in Joe about his military record he fails signally. He invokes instead raging resentment, which furthers his ambitions towards Susan Brown.

The harsh and highly critical treatment of these upper and middle class characters makes another suggestion to a contemporary audience. The ambition shown by Joe is effectively dual. He wishes to abandon his working class background and acquire the material benefits of the wealthy. The proposition made by the film is that these ambitions are only valid if Joe consciously rejects a class order that is predicated upon social standing and military rank. To be complicit in this dismissal a contemporary audience must also reject an order based upon an individual's rank in the hierarchy of Empire. The character of Jack Wales reinforces the link between social positioning and Empire. Joe does not share the affinity Jack has with the RAF and with the primacy of imperial defence. By portraying Jack in such an obnoxious fashion, 1950s viewers were encouraged to detach from the imperial social order and in turn invited to consider a new basis for identity.

This is a clear portrayal of the collision between the patrician defenders of Empire such as Jack Wales and the new outwardly self-serving class climbing working class Joe. This clash is at its most striking in the scene with George Aisgill when he uses his wealth and influence, warning Joe to keep away from his wife Alice or else "I'll break you... I'll smear you both across the headlines". This exemplifies the differences in class and power between the two. It is emphasised with a high-level point-of-view shot from Aisgill looking down upon the isolated, vulnerable and confused Lampton. Joe in turn looks up from a low-level angle to the clinical and domineering Aisgill. This scene also highlights the majestic hypocrisy of Aisgill who, despite admonishing Lampton for having an affair with Alice, is himself guilty - as a serial womaniser - of being unfaithful to her.

This destruction of the upper and middle class characters helped signal to Joe Lampton his contempt for the class and social orders of Empire. At one level this reinforces traditional notions that in order for a member of the working class to break down class barriers there must be an overwhelming moral imperative. Since there is little apparent moral strength to be found in the character of Joe Lampton the justification is to be found in the immorality of his class enemies. The result suggested that it was now possible for the central character of a British film to be seen rejecting assumptions of class and his place in the social order. It is

CHAPTER III - QUESTIONING NATIONAL IDENTITY

doubtful that such a challenge to conventional thinking would have found resonance with contemporary audiences were the Empire not on the decline.

As with Joe Lampton, Arthur Seaton in Saturday Night and Sunday Morning (1960) also rails against the constraints of his class. He resents the 'gaffers' and talks of his parents as "dead from the neck up... wi' all the fight knocked out of them". Interestingly the targets for Arthur's withering scorn are the older members of his own class. When criticised by his foreman for earning more than the tool-setters he justifies it by reference to his own hard work implying that the other less well paid workers are not working as hard or as productively. Indeed he sneers at the foreman's generation and their stoical reminiscences about the "good old days". When the foreman tells Arthur he started on seven shillings a week Arthur tells him he must have "had a marvellous time starving". Arthur has a clearly defined sense of his own value and complains more than once in the film about the Income Tax he has to pay. This was at a time when considerable numbers of the working classes failed to earn enough to trouble the Inland Revenue (Laing 1986, Marwick 1998).

Arthur does not blame his parents for their passive docility stating that they "had their hash settled before the War". This together with the frequent belittling of the narrow distinctions in rank and skill that existed on the factory floor at this time indicate a refusal to accept any form of class or rank order in his life. He does not define his existence by deference to any form of hierarchy and his attitude towards authority is one of contempt. It is the attributing of his parental impotence to events before the War that significantly signal to the contemporary reader that Arthur's own identification will not be drawn from pre-war imperial notions. Further Arthur directly blames this society for his parent's condition. As Room at the Top and Saturday Night and Sunday Morning were both box office hits it seems reasonable to suppose that they struck a chord with contemporary audiences.

Unlike Joe, Arthur does not contemplate stepping outside his class and does not appear to covet even the job of foreman. Conventional advancement seems to hold little interest for him.

He considers himself his own man and talks loudly of avoiding the classic pitfalls he sees around him including marriage and mortgage. The final scene frames Arthur and Doreen walking in the fields on a hill outside the city with Arthur throwing stones at the new housing estates increasingly "advancing" on the countryside. He shows no desire to acquire the trappings of wealth but by the final scene, his anger and rage seem reduced to this somewhat impotent and childish act. Given that Arthur and Doreen are likely to live there, she reproaches him. Defiantly, he tells her "it won't be the last one I throw," suggesting more in hope than anger that he will retain some measure of independence. Arthur seems instinctively aware of the greater possibilities life must offer but seems equally unaware how to explore them.

This thematic strand is apparent in almost all of the Social Realism films and it is significant that the protagonists are frustrated by the social constraints of their own class but find little comfort in an increasingly consumerist orientated society. Arthur for instance takes little comfort in his collection of expensive suits despite their receiving Doreen's approval. The central characters refuse the constraints of narrow class based distinctions and refuse to defer to pre-war notions of order. Equally, they find little to replace them. Arthur berates his father for watching television in an almost somnolent fashion. He finds it difficult to accept that for his father television is a cerebral truncheon with which he can bludgeon his own sensibilities and enter the fantasy world created by the advertisements. This use of television contrasts however with the Rothwell women in <u>A Kind of Loving</u> (1962) who regard the medium as a realistic model for their lives. It is for them a social and cultural icon and represents a legitimate base for their aspirations. The consumer messages are avidly welcomed and perceived by them as significant social favours.

Equally, they serve no more useful purpose than to foster illusions. For the Rothwell women this is the belief that they will some day be able to emulate the lives seen on television and for Mr Seaton the fantasy of ultimate escape from working class drudgery. The effect is to create a perceived connection with a greater more glamorous and more powerful society than is immediately accessible to them. The consumer culture typified by television operates to enable a sense of belonging that was comparable to the sense of belonging felt by many to the greater and more powerful concept of Empire. Although tangible economic or social benefits of Empire were, in reality, available to few, its existence created a sense of membership of a society in which the sum exceeded the parts.

However, as we have seen, this approach to contemporary television divides the characters. Vic, in <u>A Kind of Loving</u> initially seems oblivious to the more consumerist Ingrid and the shallow aspirations and values of her mother Mrs Rothwell, a member of a new consumerist working class. However even Vic makes a manful effort to watch the plethora of quiz shows on commercial television which hold the Rothwells almost silently spellbound. The emergent divisions in working class culture pose difficult challenges for Vic. The film articulates the uneasy alliance between the older more traditional working class values and identity that Vic and his family seem to espouse and the new petit bourgeois values enthusiastically adopted by the Rothwells. The attitudes of the Rothwell household seem strikingly similar to those of Doreen and her mother. Likewise, Arthur in <u>Saturday Night and Sunday Morning</u> (1960) receives a cool welcome by Doreen's snobbish mother upon their first meeting, "he looks a bit rough if you ask me". The difference between Arthur and Vic when called upon to respond to this new and emergent culture is that Vic makes an honest effort to accommodate it whereas Arthur could not care less.

In <u>Room at the Top</u>, Joe abandons his integrity and conspicuously fails to be true to "thine own self". One particularly socially significant scene occurs in the amateur dramatics society when he mispronounces "brazier" as "brassiere" prompting contemptuous laughter from other cast members and especially Jack Wales. Joe's defiant proclamation "I am working class and proud of it" seems almost as theatrically intoned as the play he is rehearsing (Walker 1974). Although the accepted motive for Joe joining a group for which he is manifestly ill equipped to participate is to be nearer to Susan, he may also have been attempting to ape the social mores of the upper classes.

Joe's desire for Susan appears indistinguishable from his desire for wealth and material trappings. This is neatly illustrated in the scene outside the clothes shop where Joe desires to "own" Susan as we see her reflection through the shop window – much in the manner he would with an expensive consumerist item (Hill 1986). When Joe returns to the home of his uncle and aunt his sincerity is in question when asked about his designs on Susan. 'I ask you about the girl and all you do is tell me about her father's brass; you wouldn't sell yourself for a handful of silver?', his aunt asks him. 'Sure it's the girl you want, Joe, not the brass?' stresses the uncle who warns Joe that 'money marries money'. Joe replies, perhaps naively, that he sees nothing wrong in wanting both the girl and the money.

Joe's aunt and uncle here represent the traditional working class counter-pointed against a new general acquisitive consumerism characterised in the film through the personification of Joe. Their evident disdain for and disappointment with the idea that Joe could select his future wife for her dowry, at one level represents the old, nobler and somehow finer values of the traditional working class. At another, however, it also represents an unquestioning acceptance of their role in the pre-war imperial social order. This, for them is a place that is largely unfamiliar with "brass". Joe seeks to break free of the restricted ambitions, which in his eyes limit his aunt and uncle.

The willingness with which Joe seeks to embrace a world of capitalism marks his personal departure from the economic limitations that may have still bound him had the War not allowed him to qualify in the lower reaches of accountancy. The novel is set in 1947 but the period is not so clearly delineated in the film. However, the narrative is significantly influenced by the War and there are frequent references to it. In general, the attitude displayed by Joe and his working class ex-servicemen friends is one of release and an apparently voracious appetite for the consumerist trappings not available to them before. At one level the film suggests a direct relationship between the weakening of the old social order and the increased opportunity for advancement for Joe.

CHAPTER III - QUESTIONING NATIONAL IDENTITY

However this is then set in opposition to the emotional and spiritual price, which Joe must pay for his pursuit of superficial, material values which is emphasised in the film. This transforms him into a wealthy dullard. Joe's "emotionless" determination to attain material success receives an eventual comparison with work-mate Charles. Later Charles renounces his earlier ambitions for "a girl with no brothers and sisters and a nice little family business in the background" in favour of the dependable working class June and her invalid mother. This emphasises the suffering Joe must endure in order to attain his materialist goals and carefully avoids a simple celebration of opportunism. It gives cautious expression to the diminishing of the 'old' and 'decent' working class, who valued ideals before money. Any suggestion that a new acquisitive sub class is displacing them is heavily qualified. However, the box office success of the film is a matter of record and it seems reasonable to suppose that it found resonance among a working class audience.

Joe Lampton represents, in particular to a modern audience with opportunities for historical revision, an especially bold character given that his drive for success appears matched with confidence that he can achieve these ambitions. This confidence, bordering upon arrogance, approaches a belief that success of his own choosing is his entitlement. He seems to see his ruthlessly plotted seduction of Susan and the acquisition of the Brown industrial fortune as his birthright. Such an attitude was more prevalent among the aristocracy at the time. Yet, he seems equally to see Susan and her father's money as little more than consumerist commodities presented for his delectation.

It is difficult to imagine a pre-war Joe Lampton with similar attitudes. Whilst it is possible that the hardships of war produced in some survivors a heightened sense of immediacy and gave an imperative to self-gratification it is difficult to accept this as an explanation. Charles, for one, appears to espouse similar sentiments to Joe but quickly relents and "marries a girl from his own class". Joe therefore distances himself from his friends as well as his surviving family. The general characterisation of Joe did not find complete contemporary approval. Nina Hibbin claimed in the

Daily Worker in 1959 that it was a "trick to select an immature, oversexed, unprincipled climber as the man representative of the working class" (Hibbin, *Daily Worker*, January 26, 1959: 3). Since her review appeared in the 'Daily Worker', it seems reasonable to assume that Ms Hibbin wrote from a left wing stance with proletarian sympathies. However, her article somewhat misses the point. It is clear from the narrative that Joe does not typify the working class. His self-serving, money grabbing opportunism is set in clear opposition to the traditional non-material values ascribed to his family and friends. Essentially Joe Lampton personifies the opportunity for social mobility that now exists compared with the imperialist pre-war order. His success, qualified though it is with a sense of spiritual and emotional loss, is an attempt to represent a working class not repressed by the old order. Then status in society depended upon class, military rank and upon the social class of decoration awarded for distinguished conduct in combat. Awarding a Military Medal instead of a Cross is a distinction that arises from narrow and essentially imperialist divisions in society, as Teddy bitterly observes in the film.

Representations of the Second World War are significant. War films until this period had tended to portray the working class as useful and pliable tools for deployment by upper class officers. In The Dambusters (1955), the Sergeant Pilots and other working class airmen had largely background roles. They were depicted willingly sacrificing themselves for the greater glory of England and Empire. Joe Lampton was also a Sergeant Pilot but spent his time in captivity much more productively and selfishly. When reminded that his nemesis Jack Wales had escaped, he bitterly noted that being a POW was the only opportunity he would have to study for the accountancy qualification he hoped would be a passport to his economic freedom.

It is significant that when Britain and her Empire were facing imminent destruction Joe was planning his place in the brave new world he hoped would follow. He would not follow the example of the "Tommies" who came back from the First World War trenches and upon being denied the 'land fit for heroes' they were promised simply accepted the situation. The working class de-mobbed

CHAPTER III - QUESTIONING NATIONAL IDENTITY

servicemen of 1945 came to expect a little more. Churchill discovered this to his personal cost when a grateful nation threw him out of office. This significant adjustment in aspirations and change in expectations took over 10 years to find representation in mainstream media entertainment. Indeed it cannot be coincidence that Social Realist cinema emerged at a time when the Empire was noticeably unravelling. For perhaps the first time, a significant section of the mainstream film industry was attempting to explore contemporary working class realities.

Room at the Top offers a particular account of social structure and class formations, which has connections with similar contemporary accounts in political and academic analysis highlighted in earlier chapters. For example, the notion that the pre-war working class community had symbolised a set of values in conflict with the bourgeois tendencies of affluent society was explored in a variety of cultural and sociological writings during the late 1950s. The central characters are themselves marked with inherent conflict and uncertainty. Joe has qualified in accountancy but has no taste for waiting 20 years to earn "£1,000 a year and a nice semi". These indicators of middle class respectability did not satisfy his immediate ambitions. The more direct route he chose was to marry his way to the top. Yet throughout his relationship with Susan, his passport to the top, he treats her with almost a casual lack of respect especially whilst attempting to seduce her.

He bears some resemblance to Jimmy Porter. Both Joe and Jimmy seem to covet and reject in equal measure. It is not clear whether they wish to defile the personal representations of the classes they purport to despise or whether they are unsettled by their own apparent success in challenging prevailing class assumptions about education and success. They seem appalled by their own aspirations. Although Joe has little in common with Jimmy, he seems equally tormented. Their fundamental unease may be founded in their sudden, albeit deliberate, loss of their working class roots. They appear to function almost as individual pluralists struggling alone against prevalent class divisions.

A Kind of Loving is particularly adroit in the way it explores the burgeoning divisions within the working class. To the middle and ruling classes of the day the working class were simply, one homogenised social grouping. Certainly, film had made little if any attempt before to define and distinguish between this numerically dominant social grouping. Ingrid and her mother are the personification of the new working class consumerism (Hill 1986, Laing 1986). For example, the contrast in life-styles is initially illustrated after Vic first meets and then walks Ingrid back to her mother's semi-detached house complete with garage in "Cross Green... it's lovely out there" (Vic). He is then shown from a high-angle shot, running home, through allotments and cobble-stoned streets to his parent's terraced house in a grimy side street without a single car in evidence. Vic is seen to pursue the traditional working class leisure pastimes with his "mate" Geoff; the pub, the snooker hall, the "Flicks", the football on a Saturday afternoon and the dance hall on a Saturday night. Ingrid's mother, Mrs Rothwell, represents a lower-middle class snobbery reflected in her derogatory description of all manual workers as "those people". She reads about "miners earning up to £30-£40 per week", and claims that they are "holding the country to ransom".

At the same time she laments the story of a retired major having to work as a car-park attendant: "It's extraordinary for a man of his background and education". A retired major in the early 1960s would almost certainly have fought in one or possibly both the World Wars and would have presented a particularly potent symbol of Empire. In one scene Vic happily fills his time talking to the window cleaner at Mrs Rothwell's house. Later, in the same sequence, Mrs Rothwell lambasts the aforementioned worker "put some elbow grease into it man". She accuses him of being "lazy, idle, slovenly", an attitude which offends Vic's more traditional proletarian values: "you don't talk to people like that" he tells Ingrid. To those she purported to admire and 'look up to' these fine social distinctions drawn by Mrs Rothwell must have seemed largely imaginary.

Vic's high cultural tastes fore-grounded in the novel through his interest in classical music are almost completely abandoned in the film in order to emphasise the friction between traditional working class values and the emerging mass culture (Hill 1986).

Mrs Rothwell personifies this through her obsession with acquisitiveness. She buys a new carpet, bedroom furniture and curtains in the anticipation of Vic and Ingrid moving in. Later in the film Vic despairs over the succession of expensive new coats, Ingrid's mother lavishes upon her. He tells her "we're supposed to be saving up so that we can get out of this bloody hole not buying coats every ten minutes".

The interior of Ingrid's mother's modern semidetached represents the late 1950s domestic pattern of consumerism. "The products of affluence - labour saving devices, more comfortable homes, even the television set - tended to benefit working class women more than it did their husbands, who had their hobbies, allotments, sporting and drinking activities to get them out of the home. But to the young working class men affluence opened up new horizons" (Murphy 1992: 30).

In addition, Ingrid's close identification with these lower-middle class aspirations may also represent her as something akin to a commodity. This alignment is suggested during Vic's first amorous embrace with Ingrid in the cinema. This scene is played out to a string of loud commercials advertising second hand cars, foreign restaurants and "a thousand blankets at never to be repeated prices", all of which enhance the feeling that Ingrid, dressed in her finery, and smelling of strong perfume - "*Desire*, I only wear it for special occasions" - is a prize worthy of Vic's ambitions.

Thematically one might compare Vic with Joe Lampton. If we interpret Joe treating Susan as little more than a consumerist acquisition rewarding him for his upward mobility Vic may also be interpreted as treating Ingrid as a prize. He is impressed with her "class". Equally, this mildly brutish, sexist treatment of women may owe more to prevailing gender attitudes and relations. The women's virginity is strongly emphasised and it may be that Ingrid was simply a rather attractively packaged opportunity for Vic to lose his own virginity. She may have been a high-class sexual commodity Vic would buy if he had the money. He is seen gazing at pictures of naked women whilst at work and later insists on Ingrid adopting some of the sexual positions he has learned about from his erotic magazines whilst they engage in intercourse.

There is, in the film, undoubtedly a pervasive consumerist influence, which is emphasised in yet another sequence. When work-mate Conroy leaves Dawson's it follows his objection to a reprimand: "I don't want people talking to me as if I've just come off the shop-floor". He returns later (prior to Vic's row with Ingrid) with an expense account, which he uses to subsidise a pub-crawl and an expensive sports car. Conroy, unusually for the time and his age, has no children. As he somewhat ironically remarks to Vic it is the "one's with children he feels sorry for". Conroy, now free of these traditional working class chains feels he can give vent to his own ambitions.

In <u>The Loneliness of The Long Distance Runner</u> (1962) the consumerist emphasis is as equally apparent through a montage sequence showing Mrs Smith cheerfully spending the £500 she received from her husband's employers following his death. A starburst separates each scene emphasising the conspicuous nature of her consumption and deliberately giving the scenes the style and resonance of television commercials. Later, his mother forcibly reminds Colin that she owns the entire contents of their house and this gives her the right to "order" him about. She tells him not to come back until he has some money. Despite the humiliation this causes especially in front of his mother's "fancy man" he is still not inclined to look for paid employment. After reacting with hostility to Audrey he confessed that he was without paid employment because he did not see why he should "spend all mi' time slaving my guts out just for the bosses to get all the profits".

It becomes apparent later on that burglary, with all its attendant risk, is a more attractive option than the paid employment that might mean swelling corporate profits. His mother's ultimatum makes an unconvincing narrative justification for Colin to take so readily to a serious crime that carries with it the risk of almost certain custody. It does however convey the depth of Colin's antipathy to the prevailing industrial hierarchy and suggests unambiguously that youth custody is preferable to economic servitude. This confronts directly the economic consensus assumed from full employment, welfare capitalism and Butskellite policies. He is unimpressed with notions of greater equality arising from increasing national prosperity. Nothing has convinced Colin that social or economic mobility is possible for him but as with so many of the new wave films they offer no alternatives. Other than to "line them against a wall" and have them shot he proposes no solution for dealing with his perceived oppressors.

3.3 Morality in Question

The struggle for social change on screen barely reflected the ongoing conflict behind audience lines between, on the one hand, the writers and directors, and on the other, the censor. Minor concessions from the protectors of public morality were extracted line by line and often word by word. To Anthony Aldgate (1995) this was "the slow, complex and fraught process of liberalisation" (Ibid.: 84). Significant changes were however taking place within the British Board of Film Censors (BBFC). In 1958 John Trevelyan, a former school teacher and educational administrator became - as secretary of the BBFC - the cutting edge of the Board during the accelerating social and cultural changes of the 1960s.

This largely unreported and unseen contest for the hearts and minds of British viewers played a significant role in the questioning of national identity during this period. It calls for consideration when evaluating the extent to which the 'new wave' media was a manifestation and reflection of emergent social and cultural change or a vehicle driving forward the changes. Tony Richardson had little doubt where the censor stood, accusing John Trevelyan of protecting audiences from identifying with their own experiences:

> "I believe that the basis of the censor's attitude is that films must not be serious - that they must work within the limits of a formula. Over both the films that I have made, <u>Look Back in Anger</u> (1959) and <u>The Entertainer</u> (1960), Mr Trevelyan has insisted that these created problems for him - not because they themselves could possibly have corrupted anyone... but because they were too "real". Audiences it was implied, must not recognise their own world and must not relate what they see on the screens back to their social experience. It would

be too disturbing... the distance from reality is all. This is something Mr Trevelyan specifically defends". (Richardson, *Encounter*, Vol. XV, No 3, September 1960, p. 64).

Richardson found himself confronting an attitude that was both patrician and patronising. The stance taken by the Board was redolent of the fondly held establishment notion that the great mass of the nation - and in particular its workers - needed protection from reality. This regulation of the perceptions of social identities may have formed part of establishment efforts to control the working-class economically and politically. However, its most profound impact was always likely to be upon received notions of morality. The films studied highlight a general movement from communal perceptions of morality toward the individual. The portrayal of a uniform moral code is an integral part of an imperial class ordered society. Such a depiction serves to encourage and engender a specific, almost pre-determined response to any moral challenge. A nation that ultimately defines the identity of its populace by reference to its imperial might and perceived standing in world affairs requires an apparently firm and collective moral foundation. A pluralist construction of morality fundamentally undermines a response to any perceived challenge to nation and Empire.

At its zenith the British Empire ruled nearly 25% of the world's population and this could only be achieved effectively with consent and not coercion. The British had for many years fondly imagined decency and a sense of fair play as typical and almost peculiarly British characteristics. The association of Britishness with these qualities was vital in fostering and projecting internationally an imagined moral superiority providing an ethical justification for Empire. Any challenge to this moral core carried with it the risk of subverting the ethical base of Empire and of British society. The main protagonists of the Social Realist or new wave films did not practice any apparently uniform approach to questions of morality. I consider it significant, and not merely a coincidence in time, that a more diffuse cinematic portrayal of questions of morality should find a mainstream audience as the Empire unravelled. The reduction

CHAPTER III - QUESTIONING NATIONAL IDENTITY

of Empire and a lessening of emphasis on imperial priorities allows the need for a cohesive and predictable moral response to a given set of challenges to diminish. It also invites a more varied and possibly even pluralist resolution of ethical dilemmas.

Moral responses to broadly similar social circumstances are varied. Considering for instance sexual morality, the central characters in many of the films have sex outside marriage. A number are committing regular adultery. Arthur, Joe and Vic all succeed in impregnating their girlfriends and In <u>A Taste Of Honey</u>, Jo, one of the few leading female characters, becomes pregnant. Whilst unplanned pregnancy was, in the pre contraceptive era, a major and vitally important social issue it is the moral response of the protagonists that is of particular interest. They react to a personal rather than collective notion of morality. Vic arguably comes closest to a traditional moral response by, initially at least, accepting his responsibilities and settling for 'a kind of loving'. For Joe it amounts to the business opportunity he craves. Arthur sees this as little more than the price he must pay for extra-marital sex although he does make a somewhat unconvincing offer to stand by Brenda.

It is unlikely that Trevelyan consciously felt that his role was to implement any discernible moral agenda. He tended to perceive his remit to be essentially that of compromise. He attempted to absorb changing tastes whilst wrestling with the writers and directors who resented having to make creative compromises within their films. He also had to deflect criticism from the morally conservative establishment in society who were stridently opposed to any change in the censorship rules (Aldgate 1995). It is likely that this morally conservative establishment consisted of the primary defenders of Empire and perceived any dilution of film censorship as an attack on the fundamental moral assumptions underpinning the Empire.

Trevelyan began his process by allowing adult films to deal with adult themes in a responsible fashion. He stated in his autobiography:

> "In my time at the Board we worked on a general policy of treating with as much tolerance and generosity as possible

any film that seemed to us to have both quality and integrity, and of being much less tolerant of films which appeared to us to have neither of these qualifications" (Trevelyan in Murphy 1997: 174).

With hindsight, one can detect the fundamental flaws undermining such a principled attempt to achieve a compromise. Throughout the late 1950s and early 1960s accelerating social and cultural change was apparent and any efforts to deter or even diffuse this change would prove to be little more than an exercise in futility. Marwick (1990) stressed that Room at the Top's portrayal of sex and class was so stark and concentrated as to be genuinely revolutionary, and Trevelyan himself, looked upon the film as signifying a changing era within British cinema:

"In retrospect one can see that Jack Clayton's film was a milestone in the history of British films and in a way a milestone in the history of British film censorship. Up to this time the cinema with rare exceptions had presented a fantasy world; this film dealt with real people and real problems. At the time its sex scenes were regarded as sensational, and some of the critics who praised the film congratulated the Board on having had the courage to pass it. Ten years later these scenes seemed very mild and unsensational... there was no nudity or simulated copulation, but there was rather more frankness about sexual relations in the dialogue than people had been used to" (Trevelyan in Matthews 1994: 144).

According to Marwick (1990), Murphy (1992) and Walker (1974) there was greater emphasis upon sex in the film than had been apparent in the novel through an honesty and sensuality uncharacteristic of British cinema at this time. For example, in the scene on the river bank where Joe and Susan make love for the first time Susan sighs: "Oh Joe, isn't it super Joe? Wasn't it wonderful?" However, a cool and distant Joe barely acknowledges Susan's sexual pleasure. Joe's superficial feelings and cynical motivation for Susan's affection are illustrated particularly clearly

CHAPTER III - QUESTIONING NATIONAL IDENTITY

during this seduction scene. Susan questions Joe's feelings for her and asks: "how much do you love me?" with Joe responding coldly: "about a million pounds worth..." and then later on "you know what Joe wants, it's what all the Joes want".

As well as making a direct reference to sex British cinema had acknowledged that this was an enjoyable experience for both men and women. (Matthews 1994). The film was marketed as "a savage story of lust and ambition". Advertising trailers featured heavily the erotic sexual appeal of French actress Simone Signoret; "shock provoking... she was French and all woman... ten years older than Joe ... ten years more experienced" (Hollywood UK BBCTV 6/9/93).

Joe's relationship with Susan compares with the more loving and intense physical satisfaction with Alice Aisgill (Hill 1986). In one scene Joe rushes to Alice to mend her cut finger with a tenderness rarely demonstrated in the rest of the film. Just before they set out for the coast together Joe tells Alice: "I couldn't do without you, I love you" whilst in the holiday cottage Alice tells Joe that "cigarettes and drink dull you. I want these four days to be sharp and clear". In an earlier scene Alice suggests a desire for their relationship to be more permanent: "I would have liked to have truly slept with you and woken up in the morning". Alice, as her friend Eva comments "is all woman" and her sexual prowess is alluded to throughout the film, partly due to her exotic (French) sensuality and through her age and greater "experience". "You look about 18 sometimes... you are rather inexperienced" she tells Joe. George Aisgill's comments acidly upon meeting Joe, "I'm always pleased to meet one of Alice's lovers". This coupled with Joe's anger when learning of how Alice used to pose in the nude - "I can understand why men kill women like you", also serves to reinforce Alice's liberal morality.

This overt, graphic and largely unsentimental portrayal of sex had a significant impact upon contemporary audiences. Sex was as an inherently satisfying physical act and not merely limited to the need for procreation. The intense passion sex sometimes arouses is witnessed in the scenes between Alice and Joe. Sex outside the bonds and bounds of holy matrimony featured predominantly.

Interestingly it was the reduction of sex from its role as the traditional, 'natural' and ultimate physical articulation of romantic love that is most notable. The encounters between Alice and Joe do contain elements of romantic love but they do not fit the traditional template since the narrative makes it clear there are few prospects of the relationship ending in marriage. Whilst the doomed nature of this relationship may lie at the narrative core of the story Alice and Joe are both too cynical to be considered "star crossed lovers" in any Shakespearean sense.

This cynicism also corrodes and undermines any prospects Joe has of forming a romantic relationship with Susan and he regards sex with her as largely for social and financial gain. When asked directly by Susan during the garden sequence how much he loved her he valued it at a "million pounds worth". Yet, when he impregnates her, to parental horror, he is told that there is always "room at the top" for people like him. Although Joe 'pays' for this instant success in other ways the reality for a 1950s audience was the association of this instant social and career success with a wilful and flagrant breach of the then prevalent moral codes. The brief scenes with Mavis amidst the seedy back streets serve to illustrate yet a further depiction of the possible cinematic uses for sex. Plumbing the depths of self pity following the dramatic death of Alice Joe adopts the name of his loathed rival- Jack Wales- and has lurid sex with Mavis almost as a cathartic act. Given that the character of Mavis is drawn as little more than a cheap street's whore this is sex as an act of self-abasement. This sweeping challenge to conventional expectations and perceptions of sex appears almost as a narrative footnote. Joe has sex with different women for different reasons but never for romantic love or for a traditional family life. By any contemporary definition of morality, this was groundbreaking.

The film's multi layered examination of sexual morality revolves around the contrasting values within Alice and Joe's relationship. Alice functions as Joe's moral conscience and her essentially humane values are set in opposition to his shallow and material values (Marwick 1990). Criticisms of Joe's excessive ambition appear firstly in the holiday scene at the cottage. Alice accuses Joe of being

CHAPTER III - QUESTIONING NATIONAL IDENTITY

motivated by jealousy: "Joe, you've been damaging yourself as a person... you don't ever have to pretend, just have to be yourself". Later on in the same scene, Joe attempts to recite the first "to thine own self be true" passage from "Hamlet", but significantly struggles and it is Alice who finishes the quote. The theme of self returns when Joe sees Alice for the last time to tell her that he is marrying Susan. Using Susan's pregnancy as a somewhat unlikely moral justification Joe appears feckless, thoughtless and selfish. Alice is then seen as a tragic and devastated figure. "What else have I got?" Alice reproaches Joe for his moral deprivation "You have done very well for yourself, finally you've got everything you wanted, haven't you?... you just had to be yourself... with me you were yourself, only with me".

Joe's loss of his true self is in keeping according to Laing (1986) with the basic opposition between the human and the material characteristic of Braine's novel. Significantly it is the human, 'moral conscience' of Alice that is ultimately reduced to a garishly mangled corpse whilst Joe's unapologetic selfishness is now made manifest to the reader.

> "In Room at the Top the "human" (as embodied most clearly in Alice, but also in Joe's parents) is the critical element which has been refused and sacrificed" (Hill 1986: 179).

The BBFC felt that the film was an example of a good X picture because of its adult approach (Aldgate 1995). The film was recognised by the Board as representing honesty, in terms of sexuality and blunt dialogue, then unknown in British cinema. This authenticity was now more acceptable. According to Murphy (1992), although critical reaction was not wholly positive there was a consensus about the sincerity of the film. Among contemporary critics, Frank Jackson singled out the significance of the film's "sincerity" when writing in Reynold's News: "At long last a British film which is truly adult. Room at the Top has an X certificate and deserves it - not for any cheap sensationalism but because it is an unblushingly frank portrayal of intimate human relationships" (cited in Aldgate 1995: 50). This frequent reference to and use of the word sincerity suggests that, in terms of critical acclaim at least, the film was simply portraying and examining an already extant set of sexual responses. This moral climate differed markedly from pre-war British cinematic depictions. The social changes were therefore most likely already under way but were now receiving mainstream cinematic representation in Room at the Top.

Joe can be usefully contrasted with Vic Brown in Schlesinger's A Kind of Loving (1962). As noted above there exist on the surface many contextual similarities. Their girlfriends, Susan and Ingrid are virgins also in love with them. Both become pregnant and succeed in achieving marriage. Here however the paths diverge. Joe is quite prepared to marry Susan seeing her as his route to the "top". Vic however is somewhat less than ready to marry Ingrid. With his early passion largely spent, he feels repulsed by her banality and the mind numbing boredom she increasingly induces in him. When Ingrid tells him with heart wrenching sincerity that she always wanted him he replies "Well now you've got me" unable to summon even a semblance of romance.

Vic is immobilised by Ingrid's pregnancy - penniless and increasingly loveless, they are literally and metaphorically shown being cramped and oppressed together in Mrs Rothwell's semi-detached house. The lack of emotional commitment and sincerity is emphasised by their 'shotgun wedding' in a drab registry office. "If her father had been alive I doubt there would 'ave been a wedding at all" Ingrid's mother remarks pointedly and bitterly. The Registrar's official pronouncement to the congregation underscores this theme; "Matrimony should not be entered into lightly… it is a lawful and binding union between one man and one woman entered into for life at the exclusion of all others". Vic enters the union with little or no enthusiasm. The Registrar's statement also serves as an ominous portent of troubles to come. Vic and Ingrid are forced to accept the unpalatable reality of their alliance (the stresses of Ingrid's miscarriage) culminating in Vic's initial bitter departure; "perhaps yer sorry you married me" (Ingrid), "there's no perhaps about it" replies Vic.

Ultimately the film presents reconciliation as 'a kind of loving'; "Well we are married aren't we?" Vic tells Ingrid in the final scene.

CHAPTER III - QUESTIONING NATIONAL IDENTITY

The hesitancy implied the closing shots depict an incomplete resolution of Vic and Ingrid's situation. Visiting the park bench featured in an earlier scene when they engaged in their first passionate embrace, they find themselves still without a place of their own. The grey dank horizon and the long-shot of the industrial city accompanied by the sound of shunting railway wagons would seem to anchor their future in the traditional northern working-class locale. John Schlesinger felt that Vic's unquestioning acceptance of his situation encouraged sympathy, empathy and understanding and this identification underwrote the success of the film at the box office (Ibid. Hollywood UK, BBC TV, 6/9/93).

This scenario captures accurately a specific point in social and moral history. Ten years before Ingrid would probably have prized her virginity and defended it until formally engaged, if not actually married. Ten years later, and allowing for the widespread acceptance and use of contraception and legalised abortion, the pregnancy may not have arisen and would not thus have compelled the marriage. Vic, many years later in one of the subsequent novels in the trilogy, notes with bitter irony the easy availability of contraception as he finds a machine in the men's toilets. He reflects how different his life might have been had contraceptives been so simply acquired without any accompanying sense of social stigma when he met Ingrid.

The narrative theme of the film appears to consolidate traditional notions of personal responsibility for actions. Christine powerfully portrays this. Senior to Vic in age she is seen to represent Vic's "ideal girl" for marriage - as he tells his brother Jimmy early on in the film. Christine and David, respectable middle-class schoolteacher seemingly approaching middle-age, personify the model relationship of his aspirations. Notably Vic is taken aback by Christine's traditional response to his predicament and even tells her she reminds him of his mother. Richard Hoggart considered this theme of working-class morality at the time:

> "We know that the pressure to conform expresses itself in an intricate network not of ideas but of prejudices which seek to impose a rigid propriety. They gain strength from the

remains of the Puritanism which once so strongly affected the working-classes and which still rules fairly strictly a number of working-class lives, lives to some degree among those in whom can be found the wider forms of tolerance" (Hoggart 1957: 79).

If one substitutes the Puritanism mentioned by Hoggart with a social or political hegemony one can detect the underlying influence of Empire. A society based upon a numerically superior working class requires for the maintenance of order and political control a certainty of ethics, a fixed response to any given circumstances and a defined set of moral parameters. The decline of Empire loosens the co-ordinates and provides for a widening of accepted social and moral behaviour. I believe that this, as much as any diminishing of Puritanism, allowed for the changing moral climate at this time. It is however highly questionable whether the contemporary working class were particularly conscious of any significantly enhanced social or moral mobility. Conversely any audience sympathy for Vic may have derived from his general feelings of hopelessness and impotence, and frustration with his inability to escape his environment. Vic seems singularly lacking in any new moral courage.

Although Susan Brown and Ingrid were socially superior to Joe and Vic both were a little naïve and wholly inexperienced. The censors may have believed that a male character palpably prepared to have sex without firstly demonstrating traditional romantic love was more morally acceptable in early 1960s British society than a female. This would suggest that these Social Realist films acted as a "moral bridge" between the English culture prior to 1955 and the burgeoning sexual adventures beginning in 1963 when, according to Phillip Larkin, sexual intercourse began.

In <u>Saturday Night and Sunday Morning</u> (1960) Arthur Seaton also has a mistress (Brenda) whom he impregnates whilst she is married to and living with one of his work mates. This film sheds some interesting light on prevailing moral perspectives. Joe Lampton and Vic Brown had demonstrated to the reader that their sexual relationships were the key to character and narrative development. Both stories focused upon the pregnancies of the leading women and the differing consequences for the protagonists. Brenda's pregnancy seems to have far fewer moral implications and is treated in more practical terms. For example, Arthur reacts by suggesting his aunt Ada, who by virtue of having an impressive number of children, must also have disposed of a corresponding number. This story tells us much about existing social attitudes and reveals in Arthur a curious blend of misogyny and naivety. A physically and mentally exhausted Brenda later tells Arthur: "you're getting off light aren't you?" - a sentiment echoed by aunt Ada.

There are no anguished debates about the moral implications of the proposed abortion, which was illegal at the time. These scenes may have disturbed a large section of the populace. Arthur does offer to marry Brenda but convinces no one. His friend Bert seems completely undisturbed by Arthur's behaviour even when he is sleeping with Brenda and courting Doreen. He believes Arthur should untangle himself from Brenda, but that seems to be simply for practical reasons. As Rod Prince commented at the time of the film's release:

"Arthur is an amoral character, and the film does not seek to condemn him on this account; but it does seek to explain him, or rather, to get him to explain himself" (Prince, *New Left Review* No. 6, November-December 1960: 16).

This lack of moral criticism is attributed by Prince to Reisz's "direct" and straightforward directorial style. The static camera - framed at medium shot - levels greater requirements upon the actors and is the cause of the film remaining "at the level of observation" (Ibid. 1960: 17).

As well as the accent being on male sexuality, Arthur enjoys different sexual rewards from the women in his life. His most "intense sexual pleasure" comes with Brenda, as they are constantly taking risks to have intercourse - in Jack and Brenda's bedroom as well as in the woods (Hill 1986: 160). This finds representation in Brenda's vocal desire and enjoyment: "what a time we had last night." However, Arthur's seduction of Doreen is more "fear-edged", shot without dialogue (Ibid.: 160), whilst their relationship progresses in the way of a normal courtship. There are evenings at the cinema, Arthur's visits to Doreen's mother's house and romantic walks in the park. Doreen is seen as a stabilising influence drawing Arthur into marriage and conformity. In publicity trailers for the film Arthur was marketed as a "convention-smashing, working-class Don Juan" (Aldgate 1995: 132). Moreover Warwickshire County Council disapproved of the aforementioned sex scenes and demanded forty seconds of cuts. However, the distributors British Lion/Bryanston refused and the film was subsequently banned in the County, despite playing to full houses in the nearby Birmingham local authority area (Marwick 1998, Aldgate 1995, Walker 1974).

The Social Realist films were produced at a time in British social history when the boundaries of culture and morality were being questioned. The attitudes of Warwickshire County Council represented the fading moralistic tradition characteristic of the pre-war establishment which the new "live now pay later" consumer society was to slowly suffocate through greater moral, cultural and economic freedoms later articulated in such "swinging London" productions as Alfie (1965), Darling (1965) and The Knack (1965).

If Saturday Night and Sunday Morning (1960) can be said to be in any consistent manner socially thematic it is for the justification of a "good time" since all the rest was, after all, merely "propaganda". The film proved to be a particular success at the box office. Contemporary audiences may have drawn from the film a proposition that anguished moralising over sexual matters was a luxury not then available to the working class who must instead adopt ruthless and pragmatic solutions.

There is little to admire in Arthur's character although his sexual anarchy may have invoked envy in contemporary males. His offer of marriage is a token gesture and even his offer to pay for a back street abortion is a working man paying for his pleasures. This does not anguish him in the manner of a Frank Machin. Even the beating inflicted upon Arthur by Jack's Army brother is a punishment and a further price Arthur must pay. He expresses no

CHAPTER III - QUESTIONING NATIONAL IDENTITY

remorse for the betrayal that led to the beating. However, it is noticeable that from this scene Arthur starts conforming to type. He becomes engaged to Doreen and appears quite happy to marry her and buy a house in the development that will consume the hills where he played as a boy. He hurls a stone at the site - a gesture at once both combative and impotent.

Arthur does not convincingly accept that having enjoyed the freedom of a "good time" the moment has come to conform to the more traditional expectations of society. This is not a strong visual metaphor for his redemption. When considered from a traditional moral perspective it seems that having seen the error of sleeping with Brenda, and having had some contrition kicked into him, he is ready to curb his impetuosity. The adoption of working class authority figures that also represent an imperialist, establishment Army, as avenging angels is significant. This however reduces the plot to a cautionary moral tale.

Strongly emerging from a consideration of the moral implications of the major Social Realist works is the distinct lack of any moral polemic. Creating broadly similar circumstances and scripted along similar narrative structures, the films reveal their protagonists reacting to their personal moral dilemmas in disparate fashion. It is as though the weakening of an imperialist hegemony has allowed the emergence of a more pluralist response to moral challenges. This response is now a reaction to immediate personal need rather than a pre-ordained response defined by class or moral dictates.

This dichotomy of response is further illustrated by a consideration of the character of Colin Smith in <u>The Loneliness Of The Long Distance Runner</u> (1962). The film establishes at the outset his deviance from traditional notions of morality. In the voice over during the opening credits sequence Colin informs the reader that running is a tradition in his family "running away from the Police usually". That this is a family view, and not peculiarly his, is reinforced by the naked hostility his mother shows to the Police during the scene when they attend the house to interview Colin after the bakery burglary. His views are further delineated when the new housemaster at Ruxton Towers, his detention centre, is interviewing him. Asked why he was there he replies that he was "sent" because he "did not run fast enough". There is no suggestion that he wishes to acknowledge that he has wronged society.

Yet, this defiant and apparently fearless attitude is set in opposition to the beach scene with Audrey. She asks him if there have been many previous girlfriends and he looks away almost bashfully and coyly telling her "not like last night". This thinly veiled reference to the sex they had the night before is also an admission that he has just lost his virginity. This is the only scene in the film revealing real tenderness resembling any notions of traditional romantic love. Colin's relationship with Audrey appears uncomplicated, healthy and the only positive in his life. This differs sharply from most of the other major Social Realist films where the sexual relationship of the central characters is usually the prelude to their destruction. The respect Colin appears to have for his girlfriend stands in marked opposition to the suspicion, contempt and at time hatred he feels for the oppressive world of Governors, Police and employers that dictate the terms of his existence.

The relationship between Colin and Audrey lacks the tension that distinguishes the relationships of other Social Realist characters. This may be attributable to the fidelity of the relationship. The British Social Realist film confronted contemporary audiences with the reality of adultery, extra marital sex and unplanned pregnancies, demonstrating both the frequencies of these occurrences and their omnipresence in society. In A Taste of Honey (1961), as with the other Social Realist films examined, the story foregrounds an unexpected pregnancy following the teenage heroine Jo's sexual encounter with Jimmy, a black sailor. This happens at a time when Helen, Jo's self-absorbed and sluttish mother, has effectively deserted her for Peter, a company car, bungalow and a vague promise of a marginally improved existence. Jo must discard the last vestiges of childhood dependence as she is forced into a situation where she must look after herself but assume maternal responsibilities. The film is almost a study in social alienation with Jo and Helen living "on the margins of working class culture and community. They flee from bed sit to attic often failing to meet the rent along the way, and are in real danger of disappearing through

CHAPTER III - QUESTIONING NATIONAL IDENTITY

the cracks in society" (Anderson in *Encore* Vol.15, July 1958: 42-43). Jo is effectively excluded from society by her poverty and feckless mother; Jimmy by his race; and Geoff by his homosexuality. Drawn together by mutual need Jo and Geoff quickly form a proto family, which is set in stark counterpoint to the adult unit comprised of Helen and Peter. Although Peter has made an "honest woman" of Helen this does not stop his philandering. Peter plays as a drunken lecherous boor whose interests never rise above material acquisition and consumption of mass culture. In the Blackpool scenes he behaves in a raucous drunken fashion, devouring food like an animal parodied by the grotesque reflections in the hall of mirrors. The mirror reflects a man attracting little audience sympathy.

By contrast the character of Geoff is shown as a nurturing nest builder as he employs his artistic skills to transform the gaunt and squalid loft which he now shares with Jo into a more welcoming environment. The constant playing of children's songs such as "When the Big Ship Sails" combined with frequent scenes of childhood games reinforces the fact that Jo stands on the cusp of maturity. This emphasises the sudden and involuntary loss of her own childhood in almost brutal fashion. Jimmy, the black sailor whose sexual dalliance with Jo had caused her unplanned pregnancy has gone. The relationship with Jo is significant in terms of the unusual and, at the time, racially loaded black and white relationship.

This alliance of outsiders drifting at the edges of society creates for the first time in British cinema an alternative to the more easily identified family structure. The shooting of the film entirely on location against a dockside already in decline economically strengthens the sense that one is witnessing a unit with no ready-made place for it even at the very margins it occupies. Despite the best endeavours of the censor, it is clear that Geoff is gay and rendered homeless by the commission of a then illegal act of homosexuality. He has no place to go. In his words he "did not much care whether he lived or died" until he met Jo. He proposes what one must assume can only ever be a sexless marriage. He is therefore ready to sacrifice sex for a cementing of the relationship he has forged with Jo. This representation of a radical alternative to the nuclear family foreshadowed the deterioration of the traditional social unit. The relationship between Jo and Geoff although unusual seems strong, and the interdependency appears to empower both characters. Indeed their attempt at decorating Jo's loft with artistic designs, which contrast with Helen's drab and untidy run-down rooms, helps signify the establishment of an independent identity for Jo (Laing 1986, Geraghty 1997b).

Yet when Helen returns unexpectedly neither Jo nor Geoff make any real effort to defend their household and Geoff leaves almost immediately. Furthermore, despite the female-orientation of the film's narrative – exceptional for New Wave cinema – the concluding sequence features a conforming conservative ideology as Helen reclaims the domestic matriarchal space from Geoff, the homosexual and surrogate mother. The notion of family relations returns, as does motherhood – eulogised in the final sequence as a heavily pregnant Jo is visually linked with the children as they play with sparklers around a bonfire, symbolising life (Lovell 1990).

The ending of the film demonstrates ambivalence as the matriarchal family, mother and daughter are reunited at the expense of social outcast Geoff. Moreover Jo reluctantly accepts this return to more traditional concepts of social normality even as she confides to Geoff; "Its you I need, not her, even if its only the choice between two old women." However neither she nor Geoff appear able to fight for the lifestyle they have created for themselves. This suggests that the re-assertion of traditional family relations will overcome the alternative family unit created by Geoff and Jo. This alternative seems to lack the confidence to withstand the resumption of a nuclear structure even when it is as flawed and fundamentally unrewarding as the unit based around Helen and Jo.

The film portrays three aspects of society that would have fallen outside mainstream moral conventions at the time: single parenthood, inter racial sex, and homosexuality. However, the ending with Helen returning to the domestic domain, constitutes a re-assertion of traditional matriarchal mores. This failure to deliver real and lasting change is common to the Social Realism film though <u>A Taste of Honey</u> (1961) does at least suggest that

British cinema was recognising possible moral alternatives. These films portrayed their characters sensitively and addressed contemporary social issues of class and sexuality. The contemporary spectator therefore witnessed working-class characterisations such as Jo and Helen's which conveyed greater depth and sincerity than previous British cinematic representations.

This film was notably one of the few contemporary productions to approach issues of homosexuality. When considering how to deal with this portrayal of homosexuality John Trevelyan felt that although social attitudes were changing the change was gradual. According to Aldgate (1995) despite the proposals made by Wolfendon in September 1957, the partial lifting of the theatrical restrictions on portraying homosexuality in the same year, and media discussions relating to the increasing seriousness of the gay issue within society, Trevelyan seemed to agree with the opinions held by Conservative voices in parliament:

"In our circles we can talk about homosexuality, but the general public is embarrassed by the subject, so until it becomes a subject that can be mentioned without offence it will be banned" (Trevelyan cited in Aldgate 1995: 128).

In this respect the censors seemed to reflect the views propagated by the Conservative government for shelving the Wolfenden Report and preventing time for parliamentary debate of its instructions. It was the opinion of R A Butler for example that there should:

"At present a very large section of the population who strongly repudiate homosexual conduct and whose moral sense would be offended by an alteration of the law which would seem to imply approval or tolerance of what they regard as a great social evil" (Cited in Aldgate 1995: 128-9).

A year had elapsed when the Wolfenden Report was discussed in the Commons in November 1958. Its recommendations about prostitution were included in the 1959 Street Offences Act. However, legislation regarding homosexuality had to wait until

1967 for detailed parliamentary scrutiny (Aldgate 1995: 129-32, Matthews 1994: 145-6).

In this social context Trevelyan and the BBFC had difficulty in dealing with a first draft screenplay for A Taste of Honey. If one overlooks the rather patronising and condescending tone adopted by Trevelyan, two interesting points emerge. Firstly, credence is given to Tony Richardson and his assertion that the BBFC were anxious to stop films being made that actually made some attempt to depict reality. Trevelyan seemed to consider it very much within the remit of the Board to decide for and on behalf of the nation what themes were fit for public consumption. Secondly, the Board felt it was imperative to deny to the gay community of the time films with which they could immediately identify.

Yet in the same year as A Taste of Honey the Board declared Victim fit for distribution. Here the former 'idol of the Odeons' and fantasy figure for thousands of heterosexual women, Dirk Bogarde, played a gay barrister hunting a group of blackmailers who were preying on homosexuals. The Board may have been influenced by the non-sensationalist playing of the role by Bogarde, and by the fact that the actor's heroic public persona lent a moral force to his portrayal. Indeed, at the close of the story Melville Farr is pointedly seen sacrificing his career to expose the extortionists leaving his marriage in ruins. However the principal reason Victim was passed was due to the BBFC significantly influencing the film's final cut. For instance it was insisted that gay characters were portrayed as normal, hard working rounded individuals who were often to be seen with non-gay friends and not "hanging around in groups" (Aldgate 1995: 134). This re-shaping, according to the Board, was designed to "let a little light and shade into" what they described as "this very sombre world". In addition any sex was to be handled with sensitivity and any overtly emotional or sexual aspects which may have undermined the film's significance were to be cut. Furthermore, the Board felt the anti-gay perspective be given a distinctive voice in the film (Aldgate 1995: 134).

Moreover, 1960 had seen two films concerning the life of Oscar Wilde - Ken Hughes's The Trials of Oscar Wilde and

CHAPTER III - QUESTIONING NATIONAL IDENTITY

Gregory Ratoff's Oscar Wilde – both of which had been passed with few difficulties. However, significantly both films were set in the socially displaced refuge of the distant past and concerned a famous literary man portrayed as a figure of integrity, a victim of narrow-minded legal and social bigotry (Richards 1992b). The policy adopted by the BBFC for Victim of playing down any potential sensationalist aspects was extended to A Taste of Honey. Consequently, following Audrey Field's initial concerns over the casting of Geoffrey ("we don't want Geoffrey too sissy") John Trevelyan outlined his perspective in a letter to Woodfall on March 2nd 1961:

> "Geoffrey seems to be less obviously a homosexual than in the play. We would not refuse to accept him as a homosexual, but I think it would be desirable to show this by inference rather than by direct treatment, particularly since you may have in mind extensive distribution in the USA under a Code Seal. The film certainly needs to establish that Geoffrey is a person who does not make sexual demands on Jo, but this can be treated with reasonable discretion..." (Trevelyan cited in Aldgate 1995: 138).

However, an ambivalent approach was adopted by the censors with regard to the scenes which openly addressed Geoffrey's sexual orientation. For example Helen's reference to "that pansified little freak" and a child imitating Geoffrey's walk were cut due to being "unnecessarily pointed" and "rather unpleasant" (cited in Aldgate 1995: 138). However, Jo's provocative questions: "I've always wanted to know about people like you" and "I want to know what you do. I want to know why you do it...?" remained. Aldgate (1995) claimed that this inconsistency "stemmed from a classic compromise reached between film-maker and censor" (Ibid.: 138-9). However, within the cautious social environment outlined above, moral concerns characteristic of the pre-permissive society were still influential in relation to emerging progressive sensibilities. In general terms, the moral position articulated in the realist cinema of the early 1960s was still one of personal responsibility within a traditional community.

By 1963 the Social Realist movement was coming to an end nevertheless two films made that year are worthy of comment. This Sporting Life (1963) directed by Lindsay Anderson featured as its central character a tough brooding and darkly repressed miner Arthur (renamed Frank for the film) Machin. He dreamed of playing his way to fame and fortune on the rugby field. The film is a dark and disturbing piece with, at its core, the story of one man and his struggles with his inability to express his emotions. The story depicts the corrosive effect this has on his relationship with Mrs Hammond his widowed landlady and lover. Her children are fatherless and her husband killed several years earlier in a factory accident.

Frank and Mrs Hammond pay a high emotional price for whatever happiness they can find. He suspects that her lovemaking is insincere and tells her that "it feels like I'm paying for it". She wrestles with her conscience and the memory of her dead husband. In the end she rejects Frank and sends him away. Her early death prevents any prospect of reconciliation or of a conventionally 'happy ending'. The torment and anguish shown by Frank and Mrs Hammond is set against the casual but studied manner in which Mrs Weaver attempts to seduce Frank. It is clear that he would not be the first of her husband's players to receive this attention. Her approach to Frank is essentially patrician as though having sex with her is simply one of the tasks he must perform in his capacity as Club servant. It is not clear whether it is the prospect of casual male prostitution that repels Frank or a refusal to betray Mrs Hammond. The complex nature of Frank's morality would have indicated to a contemporary audience the diversity of ethical responses existing among the working class that defy simple generalisation.

This film partially owes its inclusion in the New Wave category to its use of the industrial north as the backdrop and for its gritty examination of social and sexual issues. Its significance now is possibly that it was the last film to receive the Social Realist label. Anderson seems to accept that the film was so grim that it effectively killed any market for further films of this type (Murphy 1997, Laing 1986.). Having begun by examining the real lives of

CHAPTER III - QUESTIONING NATIONAL IDENTITY

groups of working people in <u>Every Day Except Christmas</u> (1957) Anderson wished to concentrate upon the struggles of an individual. At one level it could be said that the earlier Social Realism films had finally dispelled the notion of the working class as one interchangeable amorphous mass. Films could now celebrate the contrasts that existed within the larger social grouping. However the poor box office returns for <u>This Sporting Life</u> (1963) indicated that by now the gritty reality of day to day life for the Northern working class industrial man was losing its lustre.

It is interesting to compare it with a film released at almost the same time, <u>Billy Liar</u>. Its working class credentials were established by its writing team of Keith Waterhouse and Willis Hall and by the casting of another actor from the emergent pool of contemporary working class talent, Tom Courtenay. As with many of the characters portrayed in the Social Realist films Billy Fisher dreams of escape. However in his case this is literally so and the film includes many surreal sequences when his fantasises of noble grandiosity are played out. Indecision delineates his character. At a time when breach of promise was actionable in a Civil Court Billy is engaged to two different women. This however points more to his lack of decisiveness rather than as evidence of philandering. He occupies a fantasy world in which it is perfectly possible to be engaged to different women at the same time. Significantly, when Liz offers him an opportunity to escape to 'swinging London' with her he backs down, presumably preferring life in his fantasy world than trying his luck in the real but alien world of London.

This film bridges the dark and sombre Social Realism films with the colourful, hedonistic Swinging London films that followed in the mid 1960s. It suggests that the working class had begun identifying the possibilities for escape but still preferred the reassurance of the familiar. This was the beginning of a period of frenetic change, however, and by the end of 1965 at least one working class male character was unashamedly asserting a rather different code of moral values. Directed by Lewis Gilbert, a filmmaker not noted for radicalism or realism, <u>Alfie</u> (1966) chronicles the life and loves of Alfie Elkins.

This film highlights the complexity of emergent working class morality. He is a predatory London male seemingly determined to walk through life on a carpet of willing and prostrate women. Conspicuously sexist, and with more than a hint of misogyny, Alfie relentlessly refers to his women as "it", discussing and dissecting their virtues and vices straight to camera in the monologues that form the narrative spine of the picture. At first sight Alfie seems a straightforward womaniser collecting women from all sections of society: single and married, young and old, rich and poor. He treats each one with casual scorn, disposing of them clinically when they have served their purpose or become too cloying. The first woman we see is, we are told by Alfie directly to camera, "on her way out" because she wants him to meet her husband, "I can see it coming". At this early stage we are given an insight into Alfie's personal moral code. It is permissible to sleep with other men's wives providing he does not have to meet the husbands. That way he can pretend they do not exist. Meeting them would compel him to confront the consequences of his actions and cause him disquiet. He reasons that "once I've met the husband it don't half put me off the wife I mean he could be dying on his bed but if I ain't met him I won't think about him will I?".

His sense of solidarity with his fellow working class drivers is dubious and he deviously seduces Annie away from Frank. Initially, and to allay her fears he claims friendship with Frank saying "he is a good mate" and he "would share his last cigarette with you". Once he has used this to win the trust of a girl he knows to be young, presumably innocent and, more importantly alone and therefore vulnerable, he then unsettles her by telling her that Frank would "lend you his wife". This destroys her faith and trust in Frank. This casual character assassination reveals Alfie's predatory nature and his willingness to sacrifice both his relationship with Frank and any sense of class solidarity.

Throughout the film we are introduced to Alfie's harem and the emphasis is firmly upon "what's in it for Alfie". As well as sex, he manages to have his suits dry-cleaned and his feet massaged. These little perquisites appear almost as important to Alfie as the sex. They also add to the sense that, for Alfie, women are little more than consumer goods there for his delectation. When listing their attributes and additions to his daily life he has a clinical habit of referring to them as "it" as though they were a sexually transmitted disease. Other than sex, it is difficult to see what he gives them. It is noticeable that the sex scenes are all implied or alluded to and it is far from clear whether anyone actually enjoys the encounter. More strikingly displayed are the possible adverse consequences of his moral attitude. The references to Gilda and her "little friend" who "should have arrived on the 19th" are probably coded references to her periods and are a clinical as opposed to romantic reference to sex. This deliberately ambiguous portrayal adds to the general tone of moral squalor within the film. The seediness of his rented flat contrasts sharply with his well tailored clothes and reinforces the impression that Alfie lives his life on the surface, with an equally superficial personality to match.

The character is genuinely amoral. When he is justifying his behaviour to camera his explanations are always specious and give the impression of doing nothing more than nodding to socially accepted notions of morality. He seems untroubled by his actions. Even when he has developed a relationship with his own son he is able to walk away with no more than hollow justification. As he chances upon the christening of Malcolm, he approaches the back of the church and stands staring intently at the gathering as though he is about to storm the altar and claim his rightful place at the font. Even when he seems pained overhearing Humphrey asking Malcolm "who's Daddy's boy then" he still leaves.

However as the film develops Alfie does seem to experience some form of moral awareness, hardly a palpable shift toward Christianity but more a transitory pricking of his conscience. When confronted in the next scene with the consequences of his actions in the form of a dead and bloody foetus following a back street abortion, his imperturbable façade dissolves and we see him break down. We learn later that he prayed to God possibly for the first time in his adult life. During this scene with Nat he admits to having murdered his "quite perfect" child. However, he also admits that his tears were of self-pity and not anguished remorse. He borrows £25, which we subsequently learn he uses to repay, surreptitiously to Lily for the abortion. This is perhaps the closest approximation to honour that he can manage. In this respect, the moral underpinning of the narrative is the association of actions with consequences and the premise that immoral actions have especially unpleasant consequences. He questions for the first time the purpose of his relentless pursuit of sex and wonders whether it is worth the effort.

This perhaps helps Alfie to decide to settle down with Ruby who is the oldest and probably the richest of his women. In a scene played with irony Alfie finds himself hoist by his own sexual petard because Ruby appears to have exchanged him for a younger version of himself and he is now surplus to requirements: "He's younger than you! Got it!?" She tells him coolly. Alfie seems genuinely stunned by such rejection. As he strolls alone along the moonlit South Bank of the Thames he turns to camera during the film's closing sequence and seriously asks himself "what's it all about"? This scene is significant since it shows the character living by the amoral sword and then paying the price.

Studious efforts are made throughout the film to divorce the sex Alfie has from any real or lasting glamour or romance. Most of his encounters seem little more than functional. Despite being self obsessed Alfie has little to show for it as he himself accepts at the end of the film. This may be viewed as a commentary on his chosen lifestyle. The thematic suggestion is made that a life spent in the pursuit of instant gratification is ultimately unfulfilling leaving a vague yearning for something more solid. One can also draw a much more straightforward moral inference and find a dramatic premise for the proposition that an immoral or even amoral character like Alfie will always founder. The inherent paradox in <u>Alfie</u> is that it is a film shot at the height of swinging London and is at one level a celebration of sexual profligacy. Despite or possibly because of this it is increasingly bleak. Whatever emotion Alfie arouses in his audience it is unlikely to be envy. The film is capable of interpretation as a contemporary cautionary moral tale. During the final scene when he reviews his position he decides that beauty is "what the heart hungers for". Significantly, he finds that "I ain't got my peace of mind". He admits that without this he has nothing.

CHAPTER III - QUESTIONING NATIONAL IDENTITY

The Social Realist films present to contemporary audiences a society in which questions of morality were far from straightforward and responses becoming diffuse almost to the point of plurality. The reactions of the central characters tended to be determined by individual characteristics and needs as opposed to the wider dictates of class, society or Empire. The decline of the old imperialist order allowed for the emergence of more complex and diverse moral responses suggesting that ethical dimensions of national identity were less straightforward than might previously have been imagined.

3.4 Post-War Imperial Decline

"Quite simply Jimmy Porter was venting his anger on behalf of an educated generation that wanted to see some sense of meaning and purpose injected into Englishness, now that the Empire had pushed away, and who wanted to be allowed to use their own values and talents so as to forge a new cultural and political debate. Jimmy suggests that people like him were often thought of as getting their cooking from Paris, their politics from Moscow, and their morals from Port Said" (Stead 1989: 187).

John Osborne's Look Back In Anger sent seismic shock waves through the theatre when premiered at the Royal Court in 1956. Coined by a shrewd Press Officer at the Court, the phrase "angry young men" passed into the national lexicon. This new theatrical presence served notice that discontent and disaffection existed beneath the avuncular and somewhat cosy imagined consensus of 1950s Britain. The anger expressed tended however to operate in a social and economic vacuum and there is no transaction between this rage and any recognisable polemic. Porter's vitriol and bile seem unfocused and without direction. This lack of real purpose led Taylor and Pritchard (1980) to suggest, echoing the play, that by the mid 1950s there seemed to be no good brave causes left.

The differing views developing at the time also suggest a fragmentation of society rather than the emergence of a contained plurality of opinion. There is a lack of any noticeable collective response to post war change and these colliding social views emerge as a release rather than a hegemonic movement. This release follows the decline of Empire and its concomitantly narrow class hierarchies, a decline which was accompanied by an increasing realisation that Britain was no longer a first rank world power. These themes are explored particularly in both <u>Look Back in Anger</u> (1959) and in <u>The Entertainer</u> (1960).

In both cases the decline of Music Hall is used as a metaphor for national decay and loss of Empire. In <u>Look Back in Anger</u> the indigenous art of Music Hall is personified by Ma Tanner - Jimmy's surrogate mother who provides him with the money to start his market stall - and whose late husband was a Music Hall entertainer. Ma's death reflects the passing of the form. The film makes direct reference to Music Hall with Jimmy and Cliff performing an impromptu double-act using pseudo-Music Hall gags. The rapid-fire lines which include "Where's nobody", "Someday I'm going to marry her" and "Don't be afraid to sleep with yer sweetheart just because she's better than you" pay homage to this traditional mode of entertainment.

They are also humorous, irreverent symbols of working-class culture and solidarity counter-pointed against the dull sets and narrow conformity of the home counties' centred middle-class British post-war theatre signified by Helena's new play "Forgotten Heart". "It ran two years in the West End" she tells Jimmy who cynically ridicules the play's lack of emotional depth and social thrust. "A penetrating examination of love and human relationships" he remarks sarcastically and states "the bloke who wrote that was never in a woman's bedroom."

<u>The Entertainer</u>, filmed in 1960 and directed by Tony Richardson also includes similar exchanges between Frank and Archie. The narrative focuses on the retired Edwardian Music Hall star Billy Rice and his almost equally unfashionable but less talented son Archie ("TV and radio's sauciest comic"). The new mass culture replaces the authentic culture of the Music Hall personified by Billy. A retired performer, he nostalgically re-creates the old-time atmosphere in his impromptu rendition of the patriotic

CHAPTER III - QUESTIONING NATIONAL IDENTITY

"Don't let them scrap the British Navy" in front of an enthusiastic and responsive pub audience.

This contrasts with Archie's lewd and highly disparaging send up of British patriotism. Featuring a semi-naked Britannia it includes a mock rendition of "Land of Hope and Glory" and garbled pseudo-Churchillian speeches "…some people say we're finished, some people say we're done but if we all stand by this dear old man, then the battle will be won… for this was their finest shower". Moreover Archie's humorous proclamation "I'm sure you'll agree that a man like me is the spirit of our dear old countree…" acts as an ironic counterpoint to Billy's old-world chivalry, dignity and integrity.

Billy offers to help Archie avoid jail for tax evasion by making a dramatic return to the stage, the stress of which results in his death. Archie's jokes constantly crash amidst the uncaring atmosphere around him. An almost invisible audience largely greets his hollow theatrical performances with lethargy and contempt. "Does he think he's funny?" one complains. John Osborne stressed in his introduction to the play that the Music Hall was a dying art symbolising the passing of a significant section of English culture (Osborne 1957). Billy's death back stage before attempting a comeback therefore represents the death of a traditional pre-war culture and way of life (Hill 1986: 156). Billy stands for Edwardian certainty and he cannot understand why other nations seem to be able "to do what they like to us these days" as he refers to Britain's struggles with Egypt during the Suez crisis.

In his day you simply sent the Navy to "sort 'em out" - a period he strongly evokes when he performs "Don't Let Them Scrap the British Navy" to a group of old friends. Interestingly this old Music Hall piece contains the line "We've got the men we've got the ships and we've got the water, and its just as wet as in Lord Nelson's day!" This is strikingly similar to the mid XIX Century music hall song written for the Crimean War which boldly stated that "we don't want to fight but by jingo if we do we've got the ships we've got the men we've got the money too". This helped define the notion of 'jingoism' which Billy's generation promote here. Billy sees nothing wrong in subjugation by force and shows bewilderment over the handling of the Suez crisis. This acts as a canvas, juxtaposing Britain's declining Imperial influence with the run-down Music Hall culture personified by Archie-degenerating into gross humour and TV appearances.

Archie, the principal character, is deliberately multi-layered. He delivers the ridicule of Empire that the film suggests. His act is a symbolic if unsuccessful attempt to bridge the yawning cultural gap between the traditional authentic working class leisure pursuits of Music Hall and the mass culture offered by TV and radio. In the opening sequence the camera pans to reveal passers by challenging his bill board assertion that he is a well known TV and radio personality: "he's never been on TV" derides one. Archie seems more interested in setting up a new stage show than in exploring whether or not he could find TV work. However, his advertising suggests he is aware of the impact of the new medium on his putative audience. Archie is presented as a rather seedy and cynical opportunist ready to seduce a star struck working class girl Tina in order to gain access to her parents' money in order to back his new show.

Ironically his son Michael Rice the Sergeant defender of Empire when dying for "Queen and country" is frequently mentioned on television. This is set in opposition to his father's increasingly pathetic efforts to mount his next production. The death of his son invokes the only heartfelt lament from Archie when he declares that he is "dead behind these eyes". Billy displays "old world" nobility in his desire to help his son by staging a comeback. He is warned that this may kill him and with some irony dies as he is about to go on stage. This blatantly serves as a depiction of the death of Empire. However the willingness of the stage impresario to fund a comeback for Billy is explained by his claim that there is always an audience for this type of show. Evocation and destruction are set in immediate opposition. The Edwardian certainty of Billy and his act contrasts with the sparse audiences who attend Archie's smutty performances. The film represents the disintegration of the old order and the widening cracks in the social structure that had reinforced the class and cultural certainties of imperial Britain over the preceding century. These changes were becoming increasingly

CHAPTER III - QUESTIONING NATIONAL IDENTITY

widespread. There is no suggestion of a new template for a society that is no longer defined by imperial clarity. Billy mourns this loss to the nation, Archie seeks to satirise it, and Mick dies in an altogether not too convincing attempt to defend the residue of imperial power and influence. The other characters simply want to abandon the country altogether.

The passing of Empire and the associated class ordered society became increasingly prominent, with race and ethnic concerns receiving increasing cinematic attention. Indeed in the films which examine ethnicity in the period the tendency toward a "Liberal" posture probably rather effaces the undoubted racism of the larger community. The scenes in Look Back in Anger (1959) where Jimmy champions the cause of the Indian stall-holder are significant for the construction of racial identities. The Indian, Johnny Kapur, is the victim of blatant racist discrimination and "spite" from Hurst the market's authoritarian Inspector and his fellow stall-holders. Johnny behaves with a dignity and maturity noticeably lacking in his tormentors. He tells Jimmy "I'm most interested in justice but I am not in the habit of expecting it to apply to me." This seems to provide Jimmy Porter with a "good brave cause". He is therefore somewhat dismayed when Kapur explains what made him come to this "bloody country" and discovers that he did so only to escape similar discrimination in his native India as an "untouchable". This powerfully drives home the point made in both play and film that Jimmy is something of a rebel without a cause ranting and railing against perceived oppression but with no coherent ideology. His unfocused pluralism presents only a diffuse socio-cultural alternative to the traditional imperialist culture denoted by colonialism and social exclusivity.

The film was released amidst the declining revolutionary options of the 1950s. Signified by the Hungarian uprising as well as the disastrous and inept establishment mishandling of the intelligence services this resulted in the defection to Moscow of Foreign Office spies, Burgess and Maclean. Britain's crumbling imperial status had been witnessed through independence in India, Ghana and Malaya and the national humiliation at Suez - which resulted in both political impotence, through submitting to American diplomatic and economic pressure, and military withdrawal. As Jimmy Porter watches <u>Gunga Din</u> (1939) at the cinema he shouts irreverently at the screen: "Tell her Majesty to send a gun boat", then whistles a mock military tune. A man sitting in front voices the characteristic prejudices of the imperial era which also echo the racist attitudes of the market stall-holders earlier in the film; "If you don't like this country you can get out" he tells Jimmy.

The film therefore captured a mood amongst young middle-class left-wing intellectuals who were searching for a constructive philosophy or a "good brave cause". These individuals were contemptuously rejecting the increasingly alien ways of the old establishment and were instead seeking a new idealistic identity later to be expressed for so many by the Nuclear Disarmament Movement. Financially crippled by two world wars Britain had sold many of its overseas interests to raise finance, yet despite this parlous state of affairs the nation seemed to be making every effort to carry on as before. Although the jewel - India - had gone Britain appeared anxious to hold on to the Crown and still boasted a Navy with world wide capacity. In the eyes of the world, Britain remained a major power and war films made around this time continued to emphasise the key role played by Britain in thwarting the forces of evil represented by Nazi Germany. <u>The Dambusters</u> (1955) and <u>Reach For The Sky</u> (1954) were fairly typical cinematic examples of true "stiff upper lip" stoicism.

In <u>The Entertainer</u> (1960) Billy Rice, sounding like a post-imperial John Bull, criticises Hugh Gaitskell's objections to the Suez conflict; "Those rogues in Parliament, their country's always wrong, the other's in the right". In <u>Look Back in Anger</u> (1959) Allison's father almost tearfully lamented the going down of the sun over his small piece of empire. Somewhat wistfully he tells her: "I can still recall that dirty little train steaming out of that crowded suffocating Indian station with the battalion band playing for all it was worth, I knew in my heart it was all over then, everything". Later Alison tells her father that he is angry because everything in his world had changed and Jimmy was angry because nothing in his world had. Both Jimmy and Colonel Redfern were born in the wrong era. The abrupt lack of Empire was highly significant and

CHAPTER III - QUESTIONING NATIONAL IDENTITY

mourned by both. Helena tells Jimmy this whilst they walk amidst the serene park land populated with physical reminders (statues and men old enough to have fought in the Great War) of the nation's imperial heritage. Indeed intellectually, Jimmy opposes the traditional value systems of chivalry and heroic imperialism.

In The Entertainer young characters Frank and Graham see escape as a means of fulfilling their destiny. Frank ironically describing Britain as "this cosy little corner of Europe" tells his sister Jean that she is young and poor and if she stays here will simply become "old and poor". He sees Canada as his economic salvation in much the same manner as Graham covets the African job. He, however, sees nothing ironic in returning to a continent largely colonised by Britain as a guest worker when in all probability his own background is one of imperial conquest. He identifies with the economic prospects Africa holds out and the advances he can make in his career. "Everything about this country's dead" he tells Jean; "There's nothing to keep you here but a bunch of teddy boys who ought to be put in jail". He certainly does not appear to be identifying with any imperial heritage.

When he tells Mick at the station (who is leaving to participate in the Suez affair) he is about to "up the flag, off to defend the empire" he does so with ambivalence approaching irony. Mick answers in a similar manner and adopts mock Lord Kitchener speak: "my Queen and country need me" as the camera lingers on a newspaper headline: "British ultimatum to Egypt". Scepticism over the validity of imperial conflict is suggested by Jean "If it wasn't for… people still hanging on to their livings in other people's countries, my brother wouldn't be going off to fight". This was articulated by the New Left and by writers such as John Wain, Kingsley Amis and John Osborne. This is reinforced in the film by Archie's raspberry-blowing irreverence during his on stage performances and by the hardened and cynical attitudes of two journalists who remark during Mick's memorial service: "They say they'll give him the VC", "… what will they do, send it onto him?"

This destruction of the iconography of Empire is most noticeable in The Loneliness of The Long Distance Runner when Colin Smith is offered the opportunity to run for "Ruxton Towers". The

143

Governor has previously made clear his belief that there can be no greater honour for any individual than to represent his country at the Olympic games. Colin purposely loses the race at the end despite being aware of the loss of privileges that will almost certainly follow. His decision stands in marked opposition to an earlier scene when he joined with the other inmates singing "Jerusalem" heartily. At the critical moment however, he deliberately fails to bring the "honour" sought by the Governor to Ruxton and by extension to England and Empire. This wilful refusal to conform to the expectations and wishes of the Governor suggest that for Colin the assertion of his individuality is of greater importance.

An earlier scene had tested conventional notions when the inmates of Ruxton for the first time meet opposing Public School boys from Ranleigh School. After an initial display of brief, mutual suspicion, they find much in common with each other. This locates both groups as powerless within an oppressive but decaying system. The parents of the Ranleigh Captain express their concern at the school for its seeming inability to keep his behaviour under control. These scenes reflect a social order under strain but without the competing ideology of real change.

However, 1963 was a significant year for British cinematic culture witnessing the demise of the Social Realist movement. This Sporting Life and Billy Liar were amongst the last two influential productions. The New Wave receded and was succeeded by the "man of the decade" (Walker 1974: 178) and the last hero of the British Empire, James Bond. With considerable, although probably unintentional irony, the Bond films were produced by Cubby Broccoli and Harry Saltzman whom by switching his interest and investment prowess away from the Social Realist films he had produced, virtually guaranteed their extinction. In James Bond films such as Dr No (1962), From Russia with Love (1963) and Goldfinger (1964), he produced significant box office successes.

Written by Ian Fleming throughout the 1950s and early 1960s the Bond of the novels was initially a Cold War creation. From Russia With Love (1963) was produced shortly after the Soviets had suffered international humiliation during the Cuban missile crisis. SMERSH, based upon an actual Cold War secret department

CHAPTER III - QUESTIONING NATIONAL IDENTITY

of the Russian Intelligence service, orders the killing of Bond. He is a bourgeois hedonistic and decadent symbol of western ideology and his death in disgrace will create a propaganda coup for the Soviet Union (Fleming 1961, Eco 1966). Bond defends Britain and the Free World against the official (evil) Soviet spy machine.

Essentially Bond defends the residue of Empire. Unusually he has a European ally in Kerim Bey. Described as "our man in Turkey" and depicted as a loyal British Secret Serviceman, Kerim Bey, who dies for his loyalty, is the last non-American ally that Bond will have. The overpowering and killing of Kerim Bey invites the reader to recognise in stark terms the diminution of British power and Empire and the increasing reliance upon and influence of the USA. The death of Kerim Bey is set in opposition to the life of his killer. He is Red Grant, Bond's designated assassin, an efficient, sadistic killing machine in the pay roll of SMERSH. Grant takes his orders from Colonel Grubozaboyschikov, a real-life character (Fleming 1961), and the emotionless a-sexual Rosa Klebb who is a KGB Officer working for the Soviet backed terrorist group SPECTRE. Bond's mission leads him to Turkey, which played an ambiguous role during Cold War politics as a haven for spies from both east and west, emphasising in the context of the narrative Bond's sense of isolation and vulnerability.

As outlined in chapter two, concerns about global security were at this time voiced in Britain by CND and the New Left in the light of the growing nuclear arms race. In <u>Thunderball</u> (1965) Bond's opponent, Largo, as an operative of SPECTRE, uses KGB intelligence information to steal "secret" NATO atomic bombs from a British air base in order to blackmail Britain and the USA. This cycle of films features, particularly during the international tensions of the Cold War, a general emphasis upon advanced technology. Emerging within the new age of affluence, the potential of this modern technology to both serve and more significantly destroy is particularly emphasised in the Bond series (Bennett 1977, 1992). However despite the clear Cold War associations producer Cubby Broccoli attempted to play down the overtly anti-Soviet narrative of Fleming's novels by describing the films as "not political" but merely "good old fashioned entertainment"

(Woollacott 1983b: 218). The later films omitted the direct political references of <u>From Russia with Love</u> and the novels in general. The evil forces Bond has tackled more recently tend to be inclined towards world domination rather than subjugation of the West.

Bond becomes less a servant and defender of Empire and more an action figure of international adventure. As the 1960s progress, he evolves into an ambiguous hedonist more at home with "swinging London" than the austere Cold War setting of the early novels. As Britain lost more of her Empire Bond becomes less recognisably, an imperialist and less rooted in traditional class terms. Significantly, Bond becomes more reliant upon the "classless" American agent Felix Leiter. The increasingly frequent pairing of Bond and Leiter privileges the "special relationship" that Britain, and in particular a post imperial Britain is said to have with the USA, and offers the reader some compensation for the loss of imperial influence. It also encourages a belief in the myth that Britain is able, by virtue of a virile and resourceful individual like Bond, to continue shaping international affairs.

Although Fleming's background was aristocratic very little is said about Bond's personal background and he appears to emerge fully formed. The character is well into his 30s when the adventures begin and seems to be without family or friends. This image of a man without roots is foregrounded in the films, which rarely show Bond having any sort of life outside the Service. Although he is an Officer, as a Commander he does not have a particularly senior rank and this interestingly places him just above the working class ensign or Petty Officer but below the more aristocratic Admiral class. A narrative thematic strand of the Bond character is his casual but persistent insubordination. There is an underlying suspicion that his superiors would dispose of his services were it not for the fact that he never fails. This careful placing of Bond in the military hierarchy allows identification with all ranks in society and makes Bond a man for all classes. Moreover, the casting of Scotsman Sean Connery as Bond distanced the character even further from associations with the hierarchical English class system. Although his tastes are

CHAPTER III - QUESTIONING NATIONAL IDENTITY

expensive and he drives an Aston Martin, the origins and extent of his personal wealth are obscure.

Bond defeats his enemies by using his own initiative and usually ignoring his orders. Significantly however, at critical moments he also relies upon Felix Leiter, the C.I.A and the American technical and economic assistance which, by implication, Britain and her Intelligence Services are no longer able to afford. The producers clearly anticipated the US market in paying homage to American power but the films also acknowledge that the British no longer have sufficient resources to save the world alone. Where once the nation could rely on military might and financial firepower, Britain by now needed the style and flair of individual enterprise backed by American money. This was a considerable departure from the sense of solidarity and stoicism conveyed by the war films of previous decades.

The enormous success of the Bond films invited a host of imitators and attempts to satirise the genre. Perhaps the most interesting was the cinematic emergence of Harry Palmer. If Bond is the "last hero of Empire" Palmer is the "Social Realist Spy". The Palmer trilogy share the theme expressed in the New Wave films of a protagonist trapped by his environment. Whereas Bond clearly relishes his work and the films often verge on outright fantasy Palmer hates his job and this seething, brooding resentment lies at the heart of the character. Trapped into joining the army by National Service Palmer, a working-class character, was not able to obtain the deferment that a University place would have offered his more middle class counterparts. Caught indulging in some petty theft he is coerced into joining the secret service as the alternative would be custody followed by dishonourable discharge. He operates in a more traditionally imperial environment. His commanding officers are "old school" and make no effort to hide their contempt for Palmer. His world represents a social order of condescension and patronage in which Palmer is expected to know his place. This class order is implicitly criticised in having Palmer, the "anti hero" as the film's protagonist. Criticism is more overtly expressed when the cavalry twill wearing, arch- establishment Major Dolby is exposed as a traitor who has betrayed Queen, country and Empire in <u>The Ipcress File</u> (1965).

Where the Bond films, and in particular the later productions, depict glamour, exotic locations, beautiful women and a dashing hero, Palmer inhabits a gritty, seedy and often depressing world. His flat is drab and dingy. However, like Bond, he is shown to be a gourmet cook and has a sensitive appreciation of classical music: "Who's that idiot playing the piano with his elbows?" he says upon hearing a Mozart concerto on the radio. This allows an overtly working class hero to share in the taste of a perceived superior culture.

If James Bond was a fantasy figure Harry Palmer was brutally real and would have reminded working class audiences in particular that for a foot soldier without rank or privilege life may not have really changed. Palmer's superior officer Colonel Ross is played as a loyal servant of Empire but one who is also a sneering and condescending member of the upper classes who regards Palmer with thinly veiled contempt. In the world of Harry Palmer the old order still held the reigns of power and did not seem about to release them.

3.5 Contributing to the Culture of Change

In this section, I shall draw together the significant social, cultural and imperial influences upon British society during the period 1955-65. I have articulated these in the first three sections of this chapter manifested and represented through the cinema of the period. I shall discuss these British cultural artefacts in terms of their social, moral and political commitment towards broader social and cultural changes within Britain and their consequences for the questioning of national identity during this period. In doing so I am revisiting the debates, concerns and issues first discussed in "Realist Nights and Heritage Mornings" (2001).

The Social Realist films focus upon the collision between the classes and few are located exclusively in the working class. Television, however, began to explore settings in which middle or upper class characters were of secondary dramatic and narrative importance. Having considered significant films of the period,

CHAPTER III - QUESTIONING NATIONAL IDENTITY

I would now like to examine two kinds of television response to the social and cultural changes taking place. Specifically I will discuss the ways in which Coronation Street (1960) seeks to affirm older working class values and trades on nostalgia in the face of evident change. I will compare and contrast this style of programming with the way in which Z Cars accepts the changes that have taken place and documents the consequences of those changes in terms of fragmented communities and social alienation.

The year 1955 witnessed the advent of commercial television and the BBC now faced a challenge to its former monopoly. To satisfy commercial demands the independent networks had to hit the airwaves running. Importing directly from American television in terms of both commercial strategy and programme ideas they flooded their channels with programmes that were cheap, quick and easy to make. A plethora of game shows, quiz shows and soap operas followed. That portion of the aspirant working and sunken middle class that had enthusiastically espoused consumerism would have been delighted and there was much for Mrs Rothwell and Mr Seaton to watch. Indeed the diet of advertisements needed to fund the channels helped to stimulate consumerist demands from the newly affluent working class. Granada Television was created in 1955. In 1958, the Independent Television Authority (ITA) was increasingly concerned with enforcing a policy of regional programming amongst the new commercial companies (Laing 1986). In 1960, Granada found a way to both marry commercial success and mass cultural appeal with a veneration of traditional working class life in Coronation Street.

The BBC had been experimenting with the television serial format as early as 1954 with The Grove Family. This was described as an "average suburban family" (*The Spectator*, 8 April 1955: 440) and at the same time a "peculiar exercise in Suburban narcissism" (*The Listener*, 6 January 1955: 36). It was against this middle-class emphasis that Coronation Street defined itself (Laing 1986). Devised by Tony Warren, the programme was concerned with everyday life within a northern working-class community and Warren deliberately set out to preserve a dying way of life like "flies in amber" (Warren cited in *South Bank Show*, ITV, 15 December 1995).

Derek Grainger, one of the first producers of the programme compared it with "the feebleness of attitude which tries to achieve an archetypal type of popularity by trying to create stock figures in a stock formula – Mr and Mrs Everyman from a sweetly, antiseptic, dehydrated no-class land" – characteristic of The Grove Family (Grainger cited in Weatherby, *Contrast* 1, 1961-62, 285). Instead Coronation Street's settings comprised "a street full of characters all stamped with a strongly-flavoured, doughty and impudent scepticism of the Lancastrian north" (Ibid.: 285).

By the time of its first broadcast in December 1960, bulldozers were already crushing the huddled back-to-backs and dank terraced houses evoked by Coronation Street. The process of relocating whole communities into the gleaming new tower blocks, intended by contemporary planners to cure all society's ills, had already begun. Coronation Street would evolve over time into a fairy tale of working class life depicting a solidarity and community spirit of dubious authenticity. Its tenure coincided with the onset of social change. The programme may have reminded a working class audience of a community celebrating and protecting traditionalist values that would appear to be impervious to the root and branch changes taking place in society during this period.

As Britain dismantled her Empire, the traditional social order became subject to strain and the working class values championed by Coronation Street placed under perceived threat. The decline of Empire encouraged a wish to celebrate and depict these traditional values before they were lost. The programme therefore idealised the working class values of solidarity and social cohesion amid adversity. These themes resonated within Free Cinema and had mutated into the Social Realist films and formed a cinematic background for the emergence of Coronation Street. This television serial shows a fabric of society threatened by change. It depicted an enclave of society delineated by the pub, corner shop and church hall. Its inhabitants would rarely venture beyond these borders.

Broadcasting began in 1960 and Coronation Street swiftly attracted mass audiences, critical acclaim and academic interest in almost equal measure. Representations of the middle class were originally restricted to the only apparently upwardly mobile

CHAPTER III - QUESTIONING NATIONAL IDENTITY

figure, Ken Barlow, who was criticised by his father for not knowing how to "live in his own class." In the event and despite the benefits of his University education Ken would make little real effort to leave the street and would instead simply inject the occasional perceived middle class virtue, notably the benefits of education. The street quickly established a diversity of working class characters.

The Barlows represented the 'good' Hoggartian family. According to Lovell four features of Richard Hoggart's *The Uses of Literacy* are closely aligned in Coronation Street. He detects "common sense, the lack of explicit politics and industrial work-situations, the emphasis on women and the strength of women and the nostalgic perspective" (Lovell cited in Dyer 1981: 4). Ken Barlow is Hoggart's scholarship boy. The problems that his education present to his working class father are coupled with the small-minded envy he encounters from hard-up jailbird Dennis Tanner as he offers to buy him cigarettes. "It's government money really in't it?" is the ex-prisoner's ungrateful response. The reading of certain newspapers in different households signals subtle signs of relative social aspiration: Ken's *Guardian* as opposed to Elsie's tabloid.

By contrast the dysfunctional Tanners are the archetypal 'bad' family. This detailed look at complex and occasionally conflicting moral responses was present in the opening episode of Coronation Street (9 December 1960). Elsie Tanner's married daughter Linda Cheveski makes an unexpected visit and gives Elsie the distinct and uneasy impression she has left her husband – again. Elsie asks her if she has been "doing something" she "shouldn't have … its no secret why yer dad left me". It is perfectly clear that she suspects her daughter of adultery. The significance lies in the acceptance of discovery and punishment following sexual betrayal. At this time marriage was still considered to be the most effective if not the only financial security for women, generally, and working class women in particular.

The "local gossip" figure, Ena Sharples, was in the early days played in comedic fashion adopting the style of a Music Hall performer. The actress playing Ena, Violet Carson, was an authentic veteran of these traditional working class entertainment venues. Her exchange with Florrie Lindley in the opening episode; "Are you a widow woman...?" was similar in its delivery, rhythm and rapid fire retorts from Ena to a Music Hall sketch between a comic and a straight man. John Osborne mourns and eulogises the disappearance of this traditional form of working class entertainment in his work, particularly in <u>The Entertainer</u>. It is therefore ironic that this loss is emphasised by television, a distinctly XX century medium.

An episode from 1961 shows the street holding an outing to Blackpool. The return home aboard the coach conveys all of the main street characters at the time engaging in an impromptu "sing song". Significantly the songs were all from the imperialist era of the First World War such as "It's a long way to Tipperary" and "Pack up yer Troubles in yer Old Kit bag". The younger characters appear just as familiar with the words and just as comfortable singing them as the handful of elderly characters (such as Jack Walker) an authentic war veteran. The inference available for contemporary audiences was the notion that teenagers at this time identified with the wartime roles played by their elders. <u>Coronation Street</u> attracted very large audience figures almost from inception.

Originally only the six episodes written by Warren were intended to be broadcast but its almost immediate connection with a huge section of the population guaranteed an extended run, which continues today. These very early episodes therefore invoked the warmth and humour of the Music Hall together with the community spirit and unquestioning optimistic faith shown in wartime. The programme operated overtly as a celebration of the finer qualities displayed by a working class Britain during times of great adversity.

There is also a distinct impression of autonomy in that there are very few traditional authority figures in <u>Coronation Street</u> and the programme uses the homespun philosophy of traditional common sense in the everyday interactions between its characters. Rarely do members of a higher social class subordinate the characters. This refusal to surrender a way of life would have resonated with an audience feeling threatened by the wholesale changes in society. The programme located a sense of identification with the narrowest of allegiances. Coronation Street operates according to a localised frame of reference where a person's character may depend upon the street where they live. Even those from streets just a few miles away are suspicious. Ena Sharples makes this clear when describing new arrival Florrie as "very bay window". This supports Hoggart's assertion that within working class communities there lies "a fine range of distinctions in prestige from street to street... inside the single streets there are elaborate differences of status" (Hoggart 1957: 21).

According to Weatherby:

> "Coronation Street presents our back street reality as we would prefer to see it-with all the advantages without our having to pay for them, welfare without bureaucracy. It is like getting the camaraderie of hard times without the hard times, the camaraderie of the depression with the comparative affluence of today. We forget-as Coronation Street lets us forget-so much of what we'd rather not have to face" (Weatherby 1962: 283).

Coronation Street therefore represents life as we might choose to live it, in which we can identify, if not ourselves, then our neighbours. Derek Hill expands on the theme of romanticised nostalgia. He emphasises the programme's "sense of community" during a period in post-war Britain when such "urban togetherness" was arguably vanishing in both slum clearance and a disintegrating localised working class culture (Hill 1961). This acted as an emblem of a community ethos characteristic of a pre-war Hoggartian working class. Indeed it was this imagined community constructed by television which helped to fill the role left by a vanishing way of life in an increasingly personalised and home-centred society (Braine in *The Spectator,* December 1961, 948). Granada's attempt to advertise the soap as "life in an ordinary street in an ordinary town" was reinforced by both its regional locale and the working class culture of community inter-dependency.

This nostalgia enabled a mainstream 1960s audience to connect with imperialist themes evoking memories of a pre war class ordered hierarchical society. This overt trading in nostalgia operated almost as a palliative intended to soothe the introduction of contemporary social issues and complex matters not resolved by a trip to Blackpool and a singsong. The "trip" and its implied escape from the claustrophobic constraints of the native urban and industrial environment of the characters operates as a strong motif in many forms of Social Realism of the period (Hill 1986). The trips are therefore little more than slender compensation for a lifetime of industrial servitude. The characters in Coronation Street make even fewer attempts to change their environments than the protagonists in the Social Realist films.

There is, in Coronation Street, an inevitable return to reality which is shared by the New Wave protagonists. In Room at the Top (1959) the escape to the idyllic iconography of nature, sand, and sea does not seem real but a transient moment of brief halting pleasure which will have to be paid for when Joe and Alice return to the reality of Warnley. Similarly, we witness Vic and Ingrid at the Southport coast in A Kind of Loving (1962). In Saturday Night and Sunday Morning (1960) Arthur standing high up in the battlements of Nottingham Castle "admires the lovely view" of the city below before Brenda brings him "back down to earth" with the news of her failed abortion. The urban, industrial setting is being employed here as "narrative style" - as Arthur's "spacial location, high up, overlooking the city" and its problems, acts as a "metaphor for his state of mind" (Higson 1996: 139). Arthur still claims to have 'some fight' within him and declares that he will resist the repression visited upon his working class parents. However there is little evidence for believing him. Therefore at the end of the film, whilst relaxing on a hill overlooking the city, Arthur reconciles himself to settling down with Doreen and curbing his rebellious nature. The Social Realist characters seem afraid in general that abandoning the constraints of their class would ultimately lose them their identification, integrity and authority.

Despite the declared emphasis on reproducing life in an "ordinary street" the strong and persistent element of fantasy in Coronation Street tended to present a privileged version of

CHAPTER III - QUESTIONING NATIONAL IDENTITY

working class life at the end of Empire. The focus on locality, self-sufficiency and community suggested a sub cultural grouping, freed from the constraints of Empire, now able to function in and exist in a more homogeneous fashion. Coronation Street first appeared at a time of increasing prosperity and the emergence of genuine employment mobility. Until the late 1950s Britain had been, in the words of John Osborne, a collection of nation states and each had little idea how the other lived (Laing 1986, Sinfield 1989).

Local customs, dialects and demeanour were sharply defined along with class differences. Social mobility would loosen these close community ties and this fragmentation would have a significant effect upon questions of national identity. It is significant that although Vic Brown and Arthur Seaton feel trapped by their environments they make no real effort to break free. The increasing geographic and economic mobility of the 1960s would help to create a sense of social alienation that Coronation Street attempted to resist. The most striking feature of its resistance was its close identification with place. All of the principal characters, and virtually all the action, were located within the highly localised community of a single street. Moreover and unusually for contemporary British television at this time, all the principal characters were located within one social class.

Coronation Street can be contrasted with Z Cars, produced and broadcast by the BBC for the first time in January 1962. At the core of Z Cars is a quite opposite proposition. The essence of this programme is alienation and its very rootlessness. Coronation Street can be said to be celebrating a somewhat Hoggartian, romanticised working class shared in part at least by the Social Realist films. Z Cars, which was produced during the same period, embraces a view of modern life which is fractured. Here the values of the traditional urban working class are disappearing. Set in "Newtown", which was nominally Kirkby on Merseyside, the characters in Z Cars could in fact be from any new town anywhere in the country at that time. Z Cars drew upon the story documentary tradition of the 1950s which used actors to replicate "real-life" situations. The BBC had already produced police programmes such as Robert Barr's Scotland Yard (1960), Colin Morris' Who Me? (concerned with police interrogation) and Jacks and Knaves (1961) which dealt with the Lancashire Police Force (Corner 1991).

Z Cars attempted to draw upon the experiences of the contemporary police force. According to scriptwriter Troy Kennedy Martin the programme tried to "use the cops as a key or way of getting into a whole society...a kind of documentary about people's lives". To him the "cops were incidental – they were the means of finding out about people's lives" (Kennedy Martin cited in Briggs 1979: 458, 466-7). In "Four of a Kind" Lynch was seen gambling, "Fancy" Smith womanising whilst Steele attacked his wife during a row. However in "Friday Night" Steele was seen dealing sensitively with a dying young motor-cyclist in front of an unhelpful group of locals. All the Z Cars episodes focussed on the absence of community which was simultaneously being promoted by Coronation Street. Instead this new drama focussed upon social tensions and divisions not only between police and public but also amongst the police themselves. In "Happy Families" Mrs Sargent tells her eight year-old son the police will "know what to do with the likes of you...lock you up that's what..." as she stresses to a startled Fancy Smith "... well that's what your there for isn't it...?" Later in the same episode Fancy is annoyed in the belief that John Watt has abandoned the case in order to "go out with a bird". Moreover Watt's uneasy relationship with Barlow is an ongoing story-line.

Z Cars dealt with social alienation featuring both whole and socially heterogeneous communities transplanted from the decaying tenements of an urban industrial North into modern tower blocks and housing estates lacking both social amenities and a traditional sense of community. In these new pseudo-communities it was hoped, all the social problems that had bedevilled the inner cities would disappear. What actually disappeared, however, were the thin strands of community that had in the past provided some of the social glue that had made life tolerable.

Like the Social Realist films, although unlike Coronation Street, Z Cars was a male dominated narrative. However within

CHAPTER III - QUESTIONING NATIONAL IDENTITY

this narrative, and again as in Social Realism, there is an absence of a traditional father figure – an absence which is taken up by the police. In "People's Property" which deals with juvenile crime, another constant element running through the narrative of Z Cars, Fancy Smith takes young offender Jimmy, to school, instead of his ailing, disabled father. Later Watt is described by Barlow as possessing the potential to "make a good father". Moreover Watt, when discussing the boys' delinquent actions to their headmaster blames it on the "rotten world they live in, it's not surprising that these kids steal when they can see other people knocking off property legitimately and making easy money on the right side of the law". Later he claims that "these kids have suddenly become affluent".

Affluence, as we have already seen, is a constant theme in the Social Realist films and, similarly in Z Cars, is seen to present problems, in the context of the new emergent consumer society, for the cultural morality of the working class (Laing 1991: 133-4). In "Happy Families" Fancy takes on the moral role of the absent father. He traces pornographic photographs initially found in the possession of eight year-old schoolboys back to the reptilian-mannered, "affluent" and perverted father of one of the children. This episode is concerned with what John Corner (1991) describes as the "management of sexuality" amidst the social and cultural changes taking place across British society during this period (Corner 1991: 138). As Paul Lewis stressed at the time, Z Cars represented: "A stream of unstated protest about the ugliness of life in New Town, against materialistic apathy... What emerges is a kind of dry-eyed lament for life as it is messily lived in Britain in affluent 1962" (Lewis in Contrast No. 1, 1961-2, 310). In July 1955 the BBC had first broadcast Dixon of Dock Green. Dixon was seen as an avuncular authoritarian paternalistic figure who walked his beat amidst a settled, traditional East End community. Compared with this "structure of slow, traditional ceremony" Z Cars with its "fast cutting, direct editing, video recordings and back projection" represented a contemporary reality where mobile young policemen, in panda cars "which symbolised the age of affluence" moved between the problems of different, mixed communities (Laing 1986: 177).

As with <u>Coronation Street</u> and Social Realism social authenticity was emphasised through both the northern working class locale and the regional Lancastrian knowledge of the writers; Harry Kershaw, Peter Eckersley and Tony Warren for <u>Coronation Street</u> and Allan Prior with <u>Z Cars</u>. When discussing the "alien" aspects of the north of England, southerner Troy Kennedy Martin described the new town as possessing:

> "The rawness of the Wild West. It's a man's country all right, with fights in the pub and husbands hitting wives. There's a hard brand of humour. The women have a self-contained independence... It's <u>Room at the Top</u> and <u>Saturday Night and Sunday Morning</u> country, but television hadn't caught up with it" (Kennedy Martin in Laing 1991: 140).

The Z Cars patrol a world which has lost its sense of social identification and demonstrates some of the consequences of post-war urban social planning. <u>Z Cars</u> captured a sense of isolation and social alienation which contrasted starkly with the communal cohesion shown in <u>Coronation Street</u>. Rather than celebrate the sense of freedom found in <u>Coronation Street</u>, <u>Z Cars</u> suggested social disaffection and disarray. Here the removal of the constraints of Empire and its class ordered society have induced uncertainty, alienation, and communities fractured, dispersed and divested of purpose and direction.

The key distinction between 1955/65 and earlier decades lay in the new economic empowerment experienced by the working class. During a period of reducing international influence, the relationship between increased consumerism and social mobility became more apparent. Established concepts of Englishness based around class and its associated economic and social differences were in the process of change, and some of the cultural artefacts of this period articulate the essence of this change. The "Angry Writers", The Royal Court Theatre and the work of Free Cinema represented the lives and concerns of the working class at this specific time in national social history. The new found social mobility fractured traditional working class communities as growing consumerism

CHAPTER III - QUESTIONING NATIONAL IDENTITY

dovetailed with an emergence of mass cultural entertainment, threatening an embourgeoisement of the working class way of life. Like many of the programme forms on the new commercial television, Rock'n'Roll was seen as a growing American cultural and economic influence upon British society just as Suez demonstrated the strength of America's economic power in shaping British political and military concerns. The domination of the domestic pop scene performed a similar function illustrating the enthusiasm of the British youth for American musical culture. Indeed John Osborne's Look Back in Anger (1959) and The Entertainer (1960) wrestle with this American cultural infiltration.

Many of the Free Cinema directors including Lindsay Anderson, Karel Reisz and Tony Richardson warned of the moral and cultural disadvantages threatened by the material benefits of this consumerist influence, when they produced the British Social Realist cinema between 1959-63. Social Realism distanced itself from the middle class mores and bourgeois traditions of previous post-war British cinema in articulating the struggles of northern factory workers and young working class graduates. The films focussed their narratives around a young, energetic and confident male character who generally refused to submit to social disadvantage. The "anger" voiced by these male protagonists was directed at the downtrodden conformity represented by the older, more traditional working class generation of their parents. They also railed against the moral decay of the new materialism which damaged the nobility of a "pure" established working class culture. The films acknowledged these factional frictions which were beginning to appear within the working class during this period.

Look Back in Anger (1959), Saturday Night and Sunday Morning (1960) and A Kind of Loving (1962) attempted to analyse the influence of mass culture and commercial television. They articulated a fear of increasing social and cultural fragmentation but did not propose a social or ideological alternative. Furthermore, these films tended to focus on the personal lives of the protagonists as opposed to their conditions of work within the factory. This narrative preference weakens any polemic stance the films might have taken.

The essential impact of these films was to articulate the awareness that social change was possible and that this was becoming known to the working class. The British Social Realist films attempted to chart the beginning of the fracturing of the working class into distinct social and cultural identities. This became more evident in the context of the changes brought about by an increase in prosperity within post-imperial Britain, eventually influencing a range of areas such as politics, work, popular culture and issues of morality. Room at the Top (1959) and Saturday Night and Sunday Morning (1960) variously point to the absence of morality in the middle classes and the apathy and lethargy of the older members of the working class in order to accentuate the moral imperative of the "angry young man." The protagonists are ambivalent both toward the constraints of their own class and community as well as the moral and cultural "price" of the ever increasing materialism of a society outside and beyond the dark, dank urban industrial environment.

Moreover in Room at the Top what is perhaps of most significance in the new young working class male compared to his pre-war counterpart is that ex-servicemen Lampton possesses the bloody-minded ambition and confidence to achieve. He feels, unlike the romanticised image of his World War I predecessors, that wealth and success is his entitlement and not simply a working class fantasy.

As Labour triumphed in the 1945 General Election, signalling a sea change in social expectations, Social Realism distinctively captured a section of the commercial film industry by attempting to represent contemporary working class concerns. Indeed the belief that the pre-war working class culture had embodied values and mores which contradicted the materialist aspects of the embourgeoisement process was prevalent in a range of cultural and sociological academic analyses during the late 1950s (Hoggart 1957, Sigal 1960, Williams 1961). Furthermore British commercial cinema had made little attempt until Social Realism to identify and articulate the needs of the British working class.

A consequence of the accelerating social and cultural changes during this period were intensified creative struggles between the

CHAPTER III - QUESTIONING NATIONAL IDENTITY

cinematic protectors of public morality, the BBFC, and the men behind this new cinema such as Tony Richardson. The directors of the British Social Realist films found themselves confronting an official attitude they found to be hide-bound and condescending. They accused the censors of protecting working class audiences from identifying with the struggles of their everyday lives on screen. However, BBFC Secretary, John Trevelyan endeavoured to strike a balance between placating the morally conservative establishment and assimilating the social and cultural changes of the period. Acknowledging that social and cultural attitudes were rapidly changing, the BBFC "permitted adult films with adult themes" (Aldgate 1995: 50). Room at the Top was however passed by the BBFC despite real social problems fused with a sexual honesty and intimacy which was untypical of late 1950s British cinema (Matthews 1994, Marwick 1990, Aldgate 1995). The film was the first example of British Cinema representing a virile young man using his sex appeal as a tool for social advancement, implying that this was now an acceptable way to behave. As increasing numbers of the working class questioned traditional notions about their role and place in society, so too within this general atmosphere of social change, the boundaries of morality and sexuality were beginning to widen. All of these factors combined to intensify questions about national identity. The positive reception given to some of the more influential Social Realist films by contemporary audiences amounted to at least an acknowledgement by contemporary society that social, cultural and moral change _was_ possible.

In addition, A Kind of Loving (1962) presented the unambiguous morality of working class identity as Vic unquestionably accepts "his lot" and settles down into a kind of loving with the pregnant Ingrid. Such an act of moral propriety would engender much audience sympathy, empathy, understanding and identification during this period (Schlesinger 1993). Moreover, it is also likely that large numbers of the working class would identify with the feelings of powerlessness and impotence articulated by Vic at his inability to escape from the moral obligations of his social class. The portrayal in Saturday Night and Sunday Morning of the philandering Arthur Seaton, suggests that the struggles of working class life were too arduous to be concerned with emotional sentiment and earnest moralising. The British Social Realist films were produced at a time when cultural and moral parameters were being stretched beyond pre-war definitions.

National audiences were exposed to the reality of adultery and its consequent destruction of fidelity. The media artefacts of this period represented a desire to foreground this moral behaviour and demonstrate that it may be present in all classes. It was not limited to the decadence of the privileged expressed by the Profumo scandal in 1963. In <u>A Taste of Honey</u> Social Realism explores three aspects of British society not acknowledged by mainstream cinema at this time: single parenthood, inter racial sex and homosexuality. This alignment of outsiders, seen as a proto-family struggling on the margins of society challenged the established moral values of the nuclear family. Furthermore, in both this film and <u>Victim</u> one can find a plea to treat homosexuals with compassion and understanding. In <u>The Leather Boys</u> (1964) there is not just a call for sympathy but also recognition that homosexuals were capable of romantic love and of experiencing feelings of disappointment and rejection. The emergence of diverse social and ethnic groups represented in these media artefacts helped facilitate general cultural, political and moral change in British society. Apart from the positive recommendations on homosexuality in The Wolfenden Report (1957), a plethora of social legislation emerged in the late 1960s. Abortion and homosexuality were finally legalised in 1967. Contraceptives were made easier to come by and divorce more accessible by the end of the decade.

By focussing especially upon the struggles of individuals, Social Realism articulated the factional differences which existed within the working class between old and young, the rebellious and the conformist and the traditional and the new consumerist. As the 1960s progressed cinematic representation of British society moved from the grainy Social Realism of the industrial north to a colourful, hedonistic swinging London. A period of rapid social change was closing the door on a disappearing moralistic tradition and the "live now pay later" culture of immediate gratification was increasingly taking hold. This rather challenging and new

CHAPTER III - QUESTIONING NATIONAL IDENTITY

construction of morality and national identity was articulated by <u>Darling</u>, <u>The Knack</u> and <u>Alfie</u>.

At one level <u>Alfie</u> may be seen to represent this new found moral permissiveness through its celebration of sexual liberation. However, at the end of the film it strikes a very old fashioned cautionary moral note as the young working class Alfie reflects upon the spiritual and moral hollowness of his sybaritic lifestyle. The films examined in this chapter portray the deepening cracks in the hitherto solid walls of rigid class division and also show social mobility to be more possible than before. The working classes are portrayed as real living people with a depth of character, diversity and range previously unknown in the cinema. The overall impression is of a society that is fragmenting and shifting in an uncertain evolutionary manner.

The moral tone of these films in relation to British society suggests that any change beyond the incremental will be expensive and paid for in spiritual loss, personal suffering and a return to more traditional notions of morality. Moral alternatives are explored but are seen not to succeed and significantly no radical alternative moral framework is delineated or suggested at this time.

In <u>Look Back in Anger</u> and <u>The Entertainer</u> John Osborne used the decline of the Music Hall as a national metaphor. The Music Hall is represented as a humorous irreverent symbol of working class energy and solidarity. This contrasts with the drab sets, narrow conformity and soft sentimentalism of the bourgeois Home counties based middle class post-war British theatre characterised by the Noel Coward plays and "The Mousetrap". In <u>The Entertainer</u> the traditional authentic culture of the Music Hall is being rendered obsolete by the new shrill and shallow mass culture of TV, comics and suggestive sex. Moreover Britain's declining imperial influence and national humiliation at Suez is juxtaposed with the run down Music Hall culture. The soulless performances by Archie Rice the main protagonist in <u>The Entertainer</u> are a symbolic failure connecting the increasing differences between the old and the new cultures. His act slights the defiantly optimistic and essentially imperial patriotism propounded by Billy, whose death symbolises the passing of this pre-war culture.

Billy is a metaphor for the crumbling of an old patriarchal order and the emergence of widespread fissures in the social structure which had previously cemented the Victorian and Edwardian class and cultural certainties of the nation in place. Rapid decolonisation led to increased immigration in the 1950s and meant that new ethnic groups challenged established notions of white Englishness amongst the indigenous population. However the minority of films which choose to discus the race issue such as <u>Look Back in Anger</u> and <u>Sapphire</u> tend to favour a liberal stance which serves to somewhat mask this growing racial tension within areas of society.

<u>Look Back in Anger</u> was produced in the aftermath of establishment bungling over the defection of Burgess and Maclean and as the imperial edifice tottered international impotence was brutally exposed. Suez provided John Osborne with the ammunition he needed for an acerbic examination of the contemporary sociocultural and economic condition of the nation. As the fires of revolution were cruelly crushed by the communists in Hungary the young educated left in Britain including Jimmy Porter were railing against the values of subjugation exercised by the domestic, creaking, yet privileged and class bound establishment. They sought meaning and purpose in their questioning of national identity and evaluated new constructions of Englishness. In this post-imperial climate they wished to bring their liberal humanitarian values to bear upon this new construct of national, cultural and political identity. Some symmetry can be drawn here in the new nations refusing colonialism and the working class who were challenging the established social and economic structure. <u>Look Back in Anger</u> and <u>The Entertainer</u> condemn the antiquated imperial philosophy found so wanting at Suez. Jimmy Porter rages against a class-ridden society in the hope of radical change. In <u>The Entertainer</u>, Frank and Graham can only see escape by emigration from the decrepit values of the old world Englishness to the enthusiasm and financial rewards of new, more virile nations in Canada and South Africa.

If Britain's imperial stock was seen to be in terminal decline the nation was still spending heavily on armaments amidst the

CHAPTER III - QUESTIONING NATIONAL IDENTITY

Cold War tensions of the 1960s, possessing the third largest navy in the world (Sked and Cook 1984, Marwick 1998). A popular post-war hero of British cinema in this context was James Bond a fictional character cut from imperial cloth. The Soviet Union dominated the budgets and defence strategies of Anglo-American governments. The Russians in the Bond stories were through SMERSH sponsoring the enemies that challenged Bond. He personified the democratic values of a free nation and therefore offered a different, more colourful and dynamic form of Englishness than the working class grit portrayed by Social Realism. Although Bond may be seen to symbolise the last vestiges of imperial strength he is shown to act either alone or significantly with the technical, military back-up of the American CIA. In the early 1960s President Kennedy made it clear to Harold Macmillan that Britain was to play a supporting role behind the Americans in the Cold War struggle with the communists.

The Bond obsession with weapons of mass destruction, consumer gadgetry and advanced technology emerged during a significant period of social concern. Fears were expressed by the New Left and CND about the potential moral damage and humanitarian destruction caused by the effects of growing materialism and increasing nuclear arms production respectively. However if James Bond represents a classless all action fantasy national hero, in the world occupied by spy Harry Palmer, the old English establishment order still very much holds sway. Palmer, transparently working class is coerced into serving his country in the seedy underworld of the secret service by condescending upper class superiors who both despise and treat him with conspicuous contempt.

Over the course of this chapter I have endeavoured to identify the significant social and cultural aspects of national identity formation particular to the period 1955-65 as manifested and represented in the analysis of the aforementioned media artefacts. These aspects have covered the areas of affluence, social mobility and consumerism, imperial decline, moral change, immigration and ethnic difference. I have emphasised the increased politicisation of culture and cultural products such as "Social Realist" media during this specified period. I have analysed these aspects and the ways they have been represented through the characteristics of selected British media. I have undertaken this in terms of their social, moral and political commitment towards broader social and cultural changes within Britain and their similar and different consequences for the questioning of national identity.

Chapter IV.

Great Britain: A Social, Political and Cultural Perspective 1980 – 1990

4.1 Introduction

Over the course of this chapter I intend to both highlight and analyse the key social, cultural and political events and constructs which helped to characterise and illuminate perceptions of Britain's national identity during the period 1980-1990, both domestically and within the international arena. Thatcherite constructs such as enterprise, individualism and the notion of meritocracy will be covered as well as the space these and other policies occupied within the one nation/two nation debate. Other cultural aspects of national identity such as heritage and nostalgia and their relationship to the Thatcherite ethos will also be analysed. In turn I shall be discussing the pseudo-imperial disputes and diplomatic frictions expressed through the Falklands campaign on the one hand, and relations with the USA, Europe, the Commonwealth and the Cold War on the other. In doing so I am once again articulating the same arguments and concerns I first raised in my Theses "Realist Nights and Heritage Mornings." (2001).

Following a brief background to Thatcher's rise in the "Politics of Change: Consensus to Conviction" the next three sections of this chapter, starting with "Economics and Enterprise" and "The Politics of Confrontation" represent the distinctive style of Thatcherism in the domain of economics and politics whereas Thatcherism in the domain of culture revolves around concepts of "Heritage and Nostalgia." Hence unlike the period 1955-65 where I began by discussing the international context since it was a significant driver of change, in this period much of the drive comes from within, articulated through the rise of Thatcherism so I shall therefore begin here. The three aforementioned sub sections are united by their relationship to Thatcherism, especially the notions of Heritage and Nostalgia since these are the key concepts which I wish to utilise later in the analysis of the selected media products. Within "Thatcherism: the International Context" the objective is to examine the ways in which international events and activities impinged upon Thatcherite efforts to construct a distinct British national identity in the 1980s as well as recognising some of the conflicts and tensions thrown up during this process. The overall objective of this chapter is to show the reader how particular patterns develop during the Thatcherite period in order to utilise these later when approaching the analysis of particular artefacts.

4.2 The Politics of Change: Consensus to Conviction

The year 1975 saw a significant change in the leadership of the Conservative party. Resentment and opposition to Edward Heath as Conservative Party leader was gaining momentum amongst back bench MP's because of:

- His autocratic and secretive leadership style.
- His failure to implement radical "New Right" monetarist and individual policies promised in 1970.
- His loss of three out of four general elections.

The leader of the opposition to Heath was the late Keith Joseph (subsequently Lord Joseph - the controversial apostle of a "New Conservatism" based on the monetarist economics of Friederich Von Hayek and Milton Friedman). When Heath stood for re-election in February 1975 Joseph supported Margaret Thatcher, an Education Secretary in Heath's former government.

More likely candidates from the traditional wing of the party such as William Whitelaw, James Prior and Sir Geoffrey Howe remained loyal to Heath and did not contest the first ballot. This enabled Thatcher, whose humble background of shopkeeper's daughter was in marked contrast to the upper class establishment figure of Heath, surprisingly defeated the former Prime Minister 130 to 119 in the first ballot. Totally unprepared for the rejection Heath resigned immediately as party leader and by this time it was too late to stop the momentum already gained by Thatcher's campaign and in the second ballot on the 11th of February 1975 Margaret Thatcher gained 146 out of 279 votes.

As described by Derbyshire and Derbyshire:

"In what was later to be termed the back-bench "peasants revolt" the party of Conservatism had elected the country's first female party leader and had vaulted to centre-stage a figure who was to emerge as the dominating influence on British politics during the ensuing decade" (Ibid. 1989: 64).

James Callaghan's minority Labour government was still clinging on to power at the beginning of 1979. However the year started badly for the government and then only seemed to get worse. The pay restraint policies which had been introduced three years earlier were left in ruins thanks to double disappointment. Initially, at the Labour Party Conference in October 1978 and then at the Trade Union Congress (TUC) general council one month later. Such action only served to encourage the unions to make higher wage demands. Consequently, Ford motor company workers received a 17% pay increase following nine-week strike action. This was an increase of 7% on the "ceiling" level which had been negotiated between government and TUC in July 1975. Lorry and petrol tanker drivers then followed their example - asking for a 25% pay claim. Soon a whole sequence of strikes involving municipal and health workers as well as civil servants took place between the months of January and March. Many of these strikes impinged directly on the public as refuse collection, hospital services and even the burial of corpses was disrupted. These disputes finally came to a head in March only at the expense of general pay increases of around 10%. This disturbing period in Labour relations became infamously known by many as the "winter of discontent." (Derbyshire and Derbyshire 1989). Coupled with defeat in the independence referenda in Scotland and Wales the minority government was forced into a "no-confidence" vote on 28 March which they duly lost forcing a General Election on 3 May.

The Conservative Manifesto concentrated on three main areas. Firstly, the economy. Here the reigns of inflation were to be tightened through monetarism (whereby government borrowing and spending would be constrained), sometimes through the sale of state-owned industries. Individual enterprise was fore-grounded through the reduction of taxes and "deregulation" - as was increased home ownership and the increasing opportunities for share speculation. Secondly, the conservatives set their sights on trade union reform. They targeted the Employment Protection and Trades Union and Labour Relations Acts enacted between 1974-76 - tightening dismissal and redundancy rights as well as transforming balloting and picketing methods. Thatcher also pledged increased Law and Order spending and tougher sentencing.

Labour on the other hand adopted a less ostentatious approach, attempting to convey Callaghan as a competent, avuncular figure. The government's manifesto targeted reductions in inflation and unemployment as well as increases in pensions and state benefits (Derbyshire and Derbyshire 1989).

However the damage inflicted on the party as a result of the "winter of discontent" seemed critical and the conservatives triumphed with a majority of 43. The Tories achieved a swing in the vote of 5.1%, the largest since 1945 as well as gaining 2.2 million more votes than in October 1974 (Ibid., Sked and Cook 1984).

May 1979 brought not only a new government, but a new style of politics. The 1970's days of taking the middle-ground through consensus were to be replaced by the "politics of conviction": "There are dangers in consensus; it could be an attempt to satisfy people holding no particular views about anything. It seems more important to have a philosophy and policy which because they are good appeal to sufficient people to secure a majority... no great party can survive except on the basis of firm beliefs about what it wants to do. It is not enough to have reluctant support. We want people's enthusiasm as well". (Margaret Thatcher, Conservative Party Conference, Blackpool, October 1968 cited in Riddell 1989: 8-9).

Thatcher clearly saw significant social and political questions raised by the British nation's past greatness. Condemning what she felt to be the country's recent decline and promoting potential recovery. Thatcher's vision was not merely predicated upon economics. In her final broadcast before the May 1979 election, she started to sketch an impression of a new imagined national community of potential global achievement: "somewhere ahead lies greatness for our country again. This I know in my heart. Look at Britain today and you may think that an impossible dream, but there is another Britain of thoughtful people, tantalisingly slow to act, yet marvellously determined when they do" (Riddell 1989: 7).

Behind Thatcher's election triumph of May 1979 lay "the need for renewal of our traditional craftsmanship and civic spirit; renewal at every level, and in every profession, of our old vigour, and vitality" in stressing the need for recovery of Britain's "self-confidence and self-respect" (O'Shea 1984: 24-26).

Thatcher significantly drew upon an imperial parallel:

"It will not be given to this generation of our countrymen to create a great empire. But it is given to us to demand an end to decline and to make a stand against what Churchill described as the long dismal drawling tides of drift and surrender, of wrong measurements and feeble impulses" (Ibid.).

4.3 Thatcherism: Identity Construction in the 1980s

Economics and Enterprise Culture

This new national mood was to be expressed through the belief in enterprise and individualism. As we shall see Thatcher focussed upon a range of elements. These diverse contributory elements could then be utilised by the free, individual consumer, assiduously striving for himself and his family. At the same time these contributory elements, such as the law, public and personal standards, - the family as the font of moral strength, individual responsibility and national pride were bound within an identity construction of the British people, energising "anti- statist" sentiments and desires (Ibid.).

John Corner and Sylvia Harvey (1991) distinguish key aspects of the enterprise culture. These involve the foregrounding of those people who possess abilities in seizing the initiative, are conspicuously individualistic and can motivate both themselves and others to action. Those who flourish on the dynamism of competition and the excitement of commerce - they are resourceful and positive, with the ability to construct industries, generating wealth and employment.

As Margaret Thatcher herself stated:

"We are looking for self-starters. We are looking for princes of industry, people who have fantastic ability to build things and create jobs" (Barnett 1982: 15).

Corner and Harvey go on to draw upon comparisons with Samuel Smiles "self-made men" of the mid-nineteenth century[i];

"...like their precursors they refuse the complacent certainties of the old patrician aristocratic order, they overturn the stately world in which everyone knows their place and they challenge, in the process, the rules of *noblesse oblige*. Here, the impatient rejection of paternalistic "caring", as well as the tone of pushy, meritocratic and self-serving populism, grate against the traditions of honour and service of old and aristocratic conservatism. The advocacy of self-starters, who come, as it were, "from nowhere", and make it to the top, clearly also grates against the egalitarian tradition which proposes collective provision for general human advancement" (Corner and Harvey 1991: 8).

This emphasis on appealing to the "individual" in society was looked upon by some as the principle social and political force of Thatcherism. O'Shea (1984: 20) claims Thatcherism fuses a number of discontented – "disgruntled council tenant, overtaxed businessman, discontented trade unionist - into a relative unity". This in turn implies the articulation of a unifying synthetic issue – "the ordinary individual protecting his sphere of freedom". Thrift

---

[i] S.Smiles, "Self-help with Illustrations of Conduct and Perseverance", abridged by G. Bull with an introduction by Sir Keith Joseph (1986, Harmondsworth, Penguin). In the first 1859 edition, Smiles's bible of entrepreneurialism was produced in order to devalue the impression made by the cultural critics of the industrial revolution and in turn to glory in the achievements of industrial heroes.

and "good house-keeping" were promoted instead of an economic culture of 'borrowing'. Inflation was seen as a 'moral evil' whilst the "restoration of free enterprise and profitability will follow from the restoration of 'human value' " (Ibid: 31).

> "Our capitalist system produces far higher standards of living because it believes in incentives and opportunity and because it is founded on dignity and freedom" (Margaret Thatcher, Conservative Party Conference 1975 cited in Ibid.).

However, this concentration on the individual, from one who believed there was no such thing as society, generated what some saw as selfishness, an uncaring attitude to those less fortunate, personal greed and, eventually, to corporate greed, when companies reduced employee numbers in order to enhance profits for the benefit of directors and shareholders (Quart 1993). However, despite Thatcher's advocacy of the Victorian values of thrift, moral virtue and public duty:

> "In the England of the eighties, acquisitive individualism and aggressive self-interest thrived, not Victorian domestic virtues. This belief in unlimited economic growth superseded the preservation of the past" (Ibid: 21).

Margaret Thatcher's conservative government of 1979 onwards appeared to reverse a consistent policy of increasing state intervention.

Arguably one of the principle elements of Thatcher's economic model was monetarism, - especially that propagated by US economist and Nobel Prize Winner Professor Milton Friedman. This concerned keeping a tight grip on the money supply in endeavouring to lower the rate of inflation. Mrs Thatcher, however claimed to follow the beliefs of another Nobel Laureate in Economics, Professor Fredrich Von Hayek (Sked and Cook 1984).

Hayek believed that the duty of government was not to ensure that wealth be distributed but to develop the political and economic environment in which market forces could create it. Hayek, therefore, believed that the state should only play a limited role in national economic affairs. With the help of her closest political advisor, Sir Keith Joseph, who whilst an opposition MP had founded the influential Centre for Policy Studies, Mrs Thatcher entered office in 1979 with a clear conviction with regard to the significance of market-centred economic policies. (Ibid. 1984, Derbyshire and Derbyshire 1989).

The new government's first budget underlined this commitment to monetarism through a reduction in income tax and a stated intention to decrease the money supply. However, in order to prevent releasing too much money into the market, Chancellor of the Exchequer Geoffrey Howe fused the "split rate" of VAT (8% and 12.5%) increasing it to 15%, as well as raising other hidden or "stealth" taxation. Howe cut public expenditure for the next twelve months by £1.5 billion as well as reducing government spending in other areas. Steps were taken to boost business and enterprise - numerous capital taxes were greatly reduced. In addition restrictions on earnings, prices and dividends ceased (Sked and Cook 1984: 333-4, Riddell 1989).

Howe aimed at controlling the money supply or M3, which included cash and bank accounts, both current and deposit. He did this by setting M3 within a band of 7 to 11%, having been 8 to 12 a year earlier. Both business chiefs and trade unions were to use this as a gauge during wage discussions. Similarly banks were to employ the M3 as an economic compass. As a consequence of M3 the level of prices increased (Sked and Cook 1984: 334, Ibid. 1989). Hidden taxation and withdrawal of some financial aid from nationalised industries helped to push the retail prices index up by 4%. Such price rises caused a profusion of bank loans just as government spending power had been greatly limited by its decision to lower direct taxation. Public sector workers, unhappy with the Conservative's tightening of new wage controls, went on strike therefore depleting government funds even more. Furthermore growing unemployment only added to public expenditure.

As an increase in public borrowing occurred then a growth in the money supply became inevitable. However, the government's desire to maintain this aspect of economic policy was apparent when the MLR had been increased from an initial 12% in June 1979 to a new level of 17% in the Autumn. The government also slashed another £680 million in public spending - again in order to decrease money supply (Ibid. 1984, 1989).

In March of 1980 an unrepentant Geoffrey Howe endeavoured to clarify the government's economic policy to both voters and the money markets by implementing the Medium Term Financial Strategy. MTFS was devised to create specific goals concerning fiscal growth covering several years into the future, through reducing government expenditure and even increasing taxes (Ibid.).

However, according to Sked and Cook (1984), the government's economic standing was constantly being called into question in 1980 through "...an increase in unemployment (of no less than 836,000), a rapid growth in labour costs and most of all a sharp rise in the value of the pound. This had already risen by 9.25% during the previous year and now increased by a further 12%. All these factors led to greater public and private borrowing and hence to greater monetary growth. The result was that public expenditure programmes had to be cut once more in the Autumn, a new tax was levied on North Sea oil and National insurance contributions increased for employers" (Sked and Cook 1984: 335).

It seemed that the government's restrictive monetary policies had helped contribute toward a larger economic decline than had been anticipated amongst economists. In turn the degree of the decline caused the levels of restriction on these policies to be even more severe (Macinnes 1987).

During the 1979-81 Recession Britain's Gross Domestic Product (GDP) dropped by 4.5%. Between the second financial quarter of 1979 when Thatcher took office and the first quarter of 1981, industrial production fell by 12.8% (Smith 1987). Manufacturing industry was affected hardest of all as the level of output declined by 17.5% during the same period. Average profits dropped by 50% whilst rates of redundancies and business collapses were the highest since the pre-war "Depression" as prosperity proved to be a scarce commodity. Previously prosperous areas of the country were encountering economic destruction resembling that of the 1930's. The West Midlands, was second only to the Southeast in Gross Domestic Product per head of population in the mid 1970s. However in the early 1980s, following the devastation of its manufacturing industry, it found itself the poorest region in England (Macinnes 1987).

Wage levels in manufacturing dropped by around 3% in 1980 and 1981 whereas at the same time employment in this industry fell by 21%, resulting in the loss of 1.5 million jobs between December 1979 and December 1982 (Macinnes 1987). With regard to unemployment in the nation as a whole the new government had taken on 1.2 million jobless people when entering office in June 1979. By the end of 1980, the total was over 2 million. Indeed by the Autumn of 1982 it had surged past the 3 million barrier (Riddell 1989).

As well as failing to subsidise struggling industries, the aforementioned economic policies also contributed toward reductions in social spending; especially in the areas of health, education and transport, as well as the privatisation of nationalised industries such as British Airways and subsequently the public utilities: gas, water, telecommunications and electricity in order to raise more government capital (Riddell 1989, Derbyshire and Derbyshire 1989).

A range of explanations have been proffered as to why privatisation became a key aspect of Thatcher's economic policy. Firstly, there was an ideological motivation which grew out of the Thatcher government's belief in the ways of the free market. In addition, Chancellor Sir Geoffrey Howe highlighted the problem of applying strict financial limits to the nationalised industries, which had proved much harder than had been anticipated. Another reason was that the Thatcher governments encountered trouble in attempting to lower public expenditure and taxation in proportion to the Gross Domestic Product (GDP) (Swann 1988). Furthermore scholars who have studied nationalised industry such as Richard Pryke have published some significant information. In 1981 he produced a report which presented a poor record concerning the commercial viability of nationalised industries since 1968. Pryke concluded that:

> "... Most of the industries display serious inefficiency because they do not use the minimum quantities of labour and capital to produce the goods and services that they provide... Far too many of the nationalised industries' produce at a loss. In general, the nationalised industries' performance has been third rate though with some evidence here and there of first class standards" (Pryke 1981: 257).

These conclusions along with other bleak studies concerning the condition of nationalised industries from the Monopolies and Mergers Commission were utilised by the government as evidence to back their privatisation policy. Principally, the Conservatives believed that nationalised industries failed to serve the requirements of the consumer, firstly due to the monopoly status of some, which excluded them from rigorous competition and secondly, through the lack of intense motivation and desire to tackle customer problems stemming from the complacent belief that public corporations can never go out of business (Swann 1988).

A common justification for the privatisation was that sales of shares to employees of privatised firms may then initiate strong motivation in endeavouring to improve rates of efficiency in the particular organisation concerned. Some indeed felt that privatisation was a mere element of a greater policy designed to stifle the strength of trade unions following the events of the 1974 miner's strike. Hence a privatised firm, unlike a nationalised industry, would not be able to turn to the treasury to finance wage demands (Heald 1984).

During Margaret Thatcher's first government between 1979-83 she either privatised or prepared to privatise twenty-five government owned industries, receiving £1,440 million in return. Most of these sales did not involve a complete switch in ownership. The government held on to a little under 50%. During this first period of privatisation a number of the firms which were sold off such as BP, Britoil hotels (British Rail Hotels) and transport (British Freight,

CHAPTER IV - GREAT BRITAIN

British Ports) were within spheres of business which were more suited to the day to day cut and thrust of national and international competition within the private sector (Jackson 1985).

The second phase of privatisation began with the British Telecom (BT) sell off in November 1984 which yielded nearly £4 billion for the Conservative administration. The British gas sale in 1986 resulted in even higher receipts of over £5 billion. However privatisation had now entered into a sphere of potentially limited competition. The public utilities, such as telecommunications, gas, water and electricity retained exclusive total output within their own commercial fields – signalling to all that a public monopoly had now become a private one - which necessitated additional regulation in order to stop them exploiting consumers. Consequently, several new regulatory bodies were created - such as the office of telecommunications (OFTEL), the office of gas supply (OFGAS) and (OFWAT) the water regulatory body in endeavouring to deal with this government inspired problem (Ibid.).

However, numerous criticisms have been levelled at the Thatcher government's privatisation programme. Firstly, that the free market doctrine which lies behind the values of privatisation is undermined through the very absence of true competition, something which as we have seen was especially prescient in relation to the public utilities. Secondly, the government did not work to boost competition within the "open" market and instead looked upon privatisation as little more than a lucrative government money making operation. Indeed this is perhaps not surprising given that a more intense competitive environment would have culminated in the government receiving less money through the sale of these utilities than they actually attained (Veljanovski 1987). Furthermore, there was suspicion that these enterprises were undersold. Indeed there were concerns that shares were not priced high enough and that particular individuals profited considerably at the expense of the British taxpayer. The feeling that the government had not consulted the city well on this matter, (advice which had cost them exorbitant fees), became a generally expressed one within the economic environment. Subsequent evidence was to add credence to this view especially during the time of the BT sale (Ibid. 1987).

After a decade in office, however, Thatcher's privatisation programme between 1979 and 1989 had switched more than 20% of the state economy and just under half a million jobs to the private economy. Moreover it had doubled the number of shareholders in Britain and brought nearly £23 billion in receipts to the coffers of successive Conservative Chancellors (Ibid.).

Deregulation on the Stock Exchange came about following investigations by The Office of Fair Trading which located one hundred and fifty illegal procedures by those employed in the city. However a raft of changes soon came to fruition. Broker-dealers were introduced instead of the previous broker-jobber structure. Consequently firms became agents, searching the most competitive price for a client from firms in the securities market. In 1984 stock market firms were both agent and principal, giving each greater financial freedom, particularly in relation to the potential for rapid expansion and investment. In October 1986 increased competition and flexibility in brokerage commissions, which had previously been set within a rigid system, became known as the "Big Bang" (Swann 1988). A "yuppie" (young and upwardly mobile) culture was born representing the new young and highly paid members of the "City" financial and legal services organisations (Quart 1993).

Building societies operated increasingly like banks through the creation of a more equitable competitive environment due to the Building Societies Act of 1986, which recommended a diverse variety of new financial services (Swann *et al*).

The Politics of Confrontation

However, specific areas of the state apparatus – such as the restraining features of the police and legal systems - were reinforced under Thatcher. O'Shea (1984: 22-25) describes this as a shift toward an "authoritarian populism". In 1980s Britain this was to become an imposing identity construction which operated in two ways; first in "…providing a highly condensed and complex "national-popular" identity…" (which concerns a reconstruction of British history), and secondly in Thatcher's symbolic nationalist language, "…its imagery and tone, the forms of its address…"

and its persistent themes of nation and people: "we are a practical people, we judge ideas by their results" (cited in O'Shea 1984: 23). This quote and the use of "we" emphasises an imagined British community of shared values and beliefs which Thatcher uses to help reformulate trade unionism:

> "The purpose of trade union activity is to improve... the general well-being of working people. When we look at the unions today, we ask: have they achieved their own purpose? How have they affected the lives of their members and the nation at large? This is the natural question for trade unionists to ask themselves" (Margaret Thatcher, Conservative Trade Unionists' Annual Conference, November 1979 cited in Ibid.).

The "natural question" for trade unionists in this context is therefore concerned with "the nation at large" and not their own members. Thatcher here is attempting to distance the narrow social and political significance of trade unions and their factional concerns in favour of foregrounding what members of trade unions can do for the "national interest" instead. Thatcher acknowledges that workers have separate concerns: "but we are all consumers and as consumers we want a choice" (Ibid.: 23). Nicos Poulantzas (1973) has described this process as the "isolation effect" whereby social entities (such as classes) are alienated and then split into "individuals, consumers, families - non antagonistic groups", unified within an imagined community of mutual values and beliefs. For example, the individuals who just "happen to be in trade unions" were described by Thatcher as "British people" and as O'Shea states: "it is as British people that they can be trusted with good sense, not as trade unionists" (Ibid.: 24). Therefore, "the people" in this context are not discussed in relation to issues of class struggle, but in relation to "Britishness" and notions of "national identity". This exemplifies the culturally diverse identity constructions at work within the national identity framework in Thatcher's Britain which was trade unionist at one level, and British citizen on another.

However, "British" possessed different connotations during the Thatcherite 1980s than it did when articulated by the Labour Party or by post-war Tory "wets." Under Thatcher the term "British" revived and reconstructed a historically-centred patriotism sustained by the old political right-wing and symbolic of the imperialist Victorian era of consolidation. A populist[ii] nationalism (Ibid.: 25) which as we shall see later, engendered a nostalgia for amongst other things, the "Dunkirk spirit", which had been resurrected at the time of the Falklands campaign, and a celebration of British sporting success such as during the 1980 Olympic games in Moscow. Another symbol of Thatcherite nationalism was the aspect of economic competition: "and yet while other countries in the free world have gone ahead we have stood still or even slipped back"' and "now you don't build a great nation like that, and you don't build a great people like that." (Thatcher, Scottish Conservative Party Conference, Berwick, July 1978 cited in O'Shea 1984: 25). The "greatness" which Thatcher attempted to address and symbolise within this reconstructed national identity was also emphasised through an alienation of politically opposite histories such as those of the liberal-internationalists during the 1960s.

> "We are witnessing a deliberate attack on our values, a deliberate attack on those who wish to promote merit and excellence, a deliberate attack on our heritage and our great past. And there are those who gnaw away at our national self-respect, rewriting British history as centuries of unrelieved gloom, oppression and failure - as days of hopelessness not days of hope" (M. Thatcher, Conservative Party Conference, October 1975 in O'Shea 1984: 25).

[ii] Here I am using the Ernesto Laclau definition of a Populism of the dominant classes described in O'Shea (1984), thus: "when the dominant bloc experiences a profound crisis because a new fraction seeks to impose its hegemony but is unable to do so within the existing structure of the power bloc, one solution can be a direct appeal by this fraction to the masses to develop their antagonism toward the state." (O'Shea 1984: 22).

At this time the monetarist economic alternative and the notion of free enterprise were identified as morally just and were symbols of a return to the reassurance of British heritage predicated upon "dignity and freedom". These inherent British economic values were then counter-pointed against the moral bad that is inflation and the culture of government borrowing, popular during the welfare-capitalist governments of the 1960s and 1970s. Hence the philosophy of enterprise permitted the New Right to counter a traditional understanding of rule and hierarchy as well as to replace them with new ones (Corner and Harvey 1991).

In this context Thatcher was looked upon by her allies and those on the right as directly representing the nation, and in this context, opposition as we have seen can be presented as unpatriotic and alien; representing merely sectional interests, (Jessop 1984), a reflection of the potential for fractious division as well as unification within the sphere of national identity.

This conservative-inspired national populism seemed at this time to be articulated as an imagined community of "good citizens" and "hard workers." This was counter-pointed against a contained and subordinate alternative "nation" which included not only the alienated inner cities and ethnic minorities but also much of the non-skilled working class outside the South East (Ibid., Riddell 1989). Thatcher's national populism broke with the traditional conservative "one nation" approach to the Keynsian welfare system, popular in the post-war era of consensus politics and imperial decline.

Whether in the guise of social democracy or "one nation" conservatism, the Keynsian welfare system was conveyed as an attempt to group the poor, disenfranchised and underprivileged under the banner of the national community through economic prosperity, full employment, and greater, widespread welfare benefits. In other words, cultural divisions were not suggested and all groupings were actual or conceivable members of the "one nation." However in the 1980s Thatcher's Britain presented an image of social splits throughout society. This alienation between "two nations" represented the tensions inherent in social difference. The free market sector comprised those individuals who produced commodities and services which could be sold for profit without state support whilst the weak and alienated, (the unemployed, pensioners, the disabled) also included those groups who struggled financially both in the public and private spheres (Jessop 1984, Riddell 1989).

Within these splits, regional differences were becoming more evident. Towards the end of 1986, the European Commission received government forecasts concerning employment and industry until 1990. These identified the North-east, the South-west, Wales and Northern Ireland, along with cities like Liverpool and Manchester, as areas where economic prosperity was absent and unemployment would carry on rising. Devastation and decay was how officials articulated the condition of the social infrastructure in this other alienated nation (Riddell 1989). This uneven economic picture was reflected in the 1987 election, which produced a swing to Labour in Scotland, Wales and the North of England, and left Manchester, Liverpool, Bradford, Leicester and Newcastle upon Tyne among major urban districts without a single Conservative MP. Clearly there were large sections of the nation where neither the economic advantages of Thatcherism nor admiration for the Prime Minister could be seen to travel (Ibid.).

The extreme example was the "otherness" represented by Scotland. While the Tory majority became greater within the Conservative homelands of the south, in Scotland Thatcher's standing declined rapidly. In 1987 the conservatives lost half of the constituencies which had remained in their grasp, whilst six out of seven eats elected a candidate other than conservative. It was suggested that some of Thatcher's personality traits - domineering, affected, self-righteous, as well as her characteristically overt English politeness - made the Prime Minister especially unacceptable to a nation with a strong sense of its own imagined community of national identity (by way of its legal and educational autonomy from the rest of the United Kingdom) as well as its distinctive cultural history.

The emphasis upon the "two-nations" approach consolidated this Thatcherite national populism leaving the left to articulate the discontent of the vulnerable and disenfranchised groups symbolic of the "other" nation (Ibid., Jessop 1984). This "second nation" was extremely fractious but comprised areas of disobedience, organised in relation to local concerns. A widening of both political and social views could be identified in the feminist movement and CND as well as through the forum of regional Trades Councils and local government. Steven Lukes (1984) has concluded from his study of the social and employment structures in Britain in the 1980s that:

"The distinction between manual and non-manual labour is less and less relevant... Labour or work itself, and the sphere of production, seems to be becoming less central to the identity and consciousness of workers, while consumption, especially with respect to housing and transport, has become more central to their basic interests" (Lukes 1984: 269).

The most potent political challenge to Thatcherite authority during the 1980s came from the trades unions and specifically the miners.

"When we returned to office in 1979 one very major reason was that we were elected to curb excessive trade union power - of the trade unions over government- and the abuse of trade union power *vis-a-vis* employees within trade unions. The background was that a good government had been swept out of power in 1974 by a political miner's strike, and the Labour government in the late 1970's had been firmly controlled by trade union bosses" (Kenneth Clarke, Paymaster General and Employment Minister, 11 October 1985 cited in Riddell 1989: 45).

As a consequence of past events Margaret Thatcher believed that any potential challenge by the National Union of Mineworkers (NUM) would have to be quashed by a strong government with clear convictions. When Margaret Thatcher endeavoured to speed up the pit closure programme in 1981 the NUM intimated at taking strike action which culminated in a back-down by the conservatives due to concerns over the low level of back up coal supplies which could have resulted in a similar political humiliation for Thatcher's government as that which had destroyed Edward Heath's defeated 1974 administration.

In 1982 Arthur Scargill, a Marxist and an articulate and eloquent speaker within trade union circles, was elected as president of the NUM. Concerns over a clash between unions and management escalated when Ian MacGregor, known as a formidable, uncompromising manager (especially in the USA and at British Steel) was appointed Chairman of British Coal by Thatcher in September 1983 (Riddell 1989). MacGregor's brief was to make profits for the industry during a short-term period through targeting investment in larger, more efficient mines, shutting small, less successful pits whilst encouraging older workers to take early retirement through substantial settlements. Scargill and the NUM rejected these proposals which, if implemented would result in a drop in output of 4 million tonnes in 1984-85 and the shutting down of 20 pits, meaning the loss of 20,000 jobs. On March 12th 1984 a National strike began with regional areas going on strike across the country one at a time. However, Nottinghamshire miners, whose coal fields were economic and efficient voted against the strike by 3 to 1 (Ibid.).

Unfortunately, for the miners, errors in Scargill's leadership of the campaign proved damaging to their cause. Firstly, a failure to hold a national ballot prevented the miners from gaining the full support from the whole trade union movement. Secondly, Scargill's boast that coal stocks would quickly run out never materialised, placing greater strain, frustration and anger upon the miners and their increasingly impoverished and desperate families (Kinnock in Adeney and Lloyd 1986).

Derbyshire (1989) claims that the refusal by Scargill to castigate all violence, much of it a result of the "battles" between mass pickets and large-scale policing, as well as stubbornly rejecting the closure of any struggling pits only served to limit his popularity across the nation as a whole. As a result the miners became disenchanted and divided. The Union of Democratic Mineworkers (UDM) was formed which comprised the Nottinghamshire-Derbyshire miners who had rejected the strike. Whilst leaders of other unions such as the Transport Workers and the Railwaymen gave localised backing to the strike, the majority of their members continued transporting coal to power stations and steelworks. This therefore served to aid the government in keeping the industry going together with Thatcher's extensive coal reserves. This action served to isolate the miners from most of the Union Movement, with the exception of some Dockers and Seamen. With no evidence of any forthcoming power cuts or governmental climb-down miners steadily drifted back to work in Christmas 1984 and by March 5, 1985, the remaining 50% had returned signalling the end of the dispute (Riddell 1989, Derbyshire and Derbyshire 1990).

Not only had Thatcher triumphed over the miners but such a defeat for the trade union movement as a whole was to mean significant changes in future relations between workers and management as the volume of strike action, in the years which immediately followed this dispute, plummeted to a fifty year low.

Heritage and Nostalgia

According to Corner and Harvey (1991), the notion of heritage can be represented as "sets of beliefs and values as well as a symbolic physical appearance inherited from the past" (Corner and Harvey 1991: 8).

In the early stages of the Thatcher government so-called "wet" Tories like Patrick Cormack and Norman St John Stevas vigorously promoted the National Heritage. This manifested itself in statements they made, aligning a bourgeois perception of history with the surviving physical appearance of the relics of national heritage (Wright 1984). In 1980 came the National Heritage Act. This legislation was the sum of much parliamentary discussion. Thatcher's election campaign involving the reaffirmation of a national pride and traditional values within the nation's consciousness, meant that National Heritage was increasingly being promoted as an important element of Thatcherite and indeed national culture. Discussions over the National Heritage and the steps necessary to ensure its preservation had begun during Labour's term of office. A white paper proposing reform was produced under Labour in February 1979. Consequently, cross-party consensus over the National Heritage Act was clear. St. John Stevas, a government minister and main supporter of the Act saw this as a significant time for Britain:

> "Margaret Thatcher has shown herself, in just over a year in office, to be a national leader as well as a party leader" (St John Stevas in Wright 1985: 44).

The National Heritage Act comprised two aspects: (1) It entailed the preservation of the collection of properties "defined as "The Heritage""; (2) and it also endeavoured to obtain visitation rights, of a reasonable type, in order to guarantee that "The Heritage" is available for tourist consumption. The Act adopted a three pronged approach: "(1) It eases the means whereby property can be transferred to the state in lieu of capital transfer tax and estate duty; (2) It provides indemnity to museums which might otherwise be unable to afford the cost of insuring objects loaned to other exhibitors; (3) and it establishes the National Heritage Memorial Fund" (Wright 1985: 44). During its construction in the early 1980s, The National Heritage Act represented:

> "The Thatcher government's first (and perhaps less than fully conscious) attempts to revive the spirit of the Second World War and to set up its own patriotic measure against that long drawn-out betrayal known in more polite circles as the post-war settlement" (Wright 1985: 45).

Within the voluble nationalism of the Conservative Party "war" was to be waged in peace-time. The enemies were, according to Wright (1985): "socialism and the 'overweening state'." (Ibid: 46). However, the trustees of the Fund had difficulty in defining the National Heritage in unambiguous terms, and so consequently determined to allow it to "define itself" by waiting for applications for grants to arrive:

> "We awaited requests for assistance from those who believed they had a part of the national heritage worth saving. The national heritage... is simultaneously a representation of

the development of aesthetic expression and a testimony to the role played by the nation in world history. The national heritage also includes the natural riches in Britain - the great scenic areas, the fauna and flora. Its potential for enjoyment must be maintained, its educational value for succeeding generations must be enriched and its economic value in attracting tourists to this country must be appreciated and developed. But this national heritage is constantly under threat" (First Annual Report, National Heritage Memorial Fund 1980-1 in Hewison 1987: 136-7).

The "heritage industry" as it became known[iii], gained greater credence following the National Heritage Act of 1983 which displaced responsibility for historical buildings and monuments from the Department of the Environment to the Historical Buildings and Monuments Committee for England (English Heritage). In addition the Act took away controls relating to the sale of artistic artefacts. Clause 35 of the Act enabled the forming of enterprises with the following objectives. Firstly they should be allowed to publish literature or produce films promoting heritage sites. Secondly that the sale of heritage souvenirs in England should be increased. Thirdly that related facilities such as car parks or restaurants should be constructed on or near to heritage sites (Hewison 1987, 1991b).

Museums and historical buildings became venues for entertainment. The Victoria and Albert Museum was advertised as an "ace caff with quite a nice museum attached" (Mellor 1991b: 88), while Liverpool's historic Albert Dock was reconstructed into a commercialised leisure area featuring trendy boutiques, "wine bars, art gallery, museum and television studio" (Ibid. 1991: 88-9).

The role of the national heritage also conveyed the national past as an aesthetic physical appearance. "Landscapes, monuments,

---

[iii] "Heritage Industry", the phrase emanates from Robert Hewison's powerful and influential work "The heritage industry: British culture in a climate of decline." (1987).

folkways, construction skills" and artefacts are all symbolic in the mediation of a clear, unambiguous presence of a national heritage requiring "preservation, deference and respect". (Wright 1984: 50). Furthermore a "national" understanding of the past is also emblematically conveyed through "national traditions" such as Remembrance Day, as well as "reverence for national heroes" and "the commemoration of great national events" (Wright 1984: 50).

The early stages of conservative government illustrated national identity's potential for cultural division, however, under the growing issue of heritage. This occurred through a split between a Tory traditionalism and a modernising anti-traditional monetarist philosophy which was seeking to assemble support around a programme aimed at imposing a technocratic concept of progress (Ibid.).

The modernising tendency in the Party was represented by Thatcher, Heseltine and Tebbit. Heseltine was planning ways of commercialising and repackaging the insufficiently marketed monuments preserved for the nation by the Department of the Environment (the 1983 National Heritage Act). Hence, St John Stevas, "a wet", following an early cabinet re-shuffle towards the end of 1981 was removed from the political sphere of influence, and along with Ian Gilmour was overlooked in the national heritage debate (Ibid.). With Heseltine at the helm, the Department of the Environment "privatised" its duty to historic buildings and other symbols of national heritage by creating the Historic Building and Monuments Commission for England (Hewison 1987: 101).

English Heritage under Lord Montagu, author of "How to Live in a Stately Home and Make Money", determinedly marketed the estates and country houses under its auspices to potential visitors. Symbolic of the new commercially driven, anti-traditionalist identity, English Heritage's philosophy was now geared toward the gratification of "a range of spectacular entertainment" to be found at their sites (Hewison 1987: 101).

Within this new framework, heritage not only became symbolic of a re-constructed national identity, but also emblematic of Britain's attempted economic recovery from the recession of the early 1980s. The latter can be evidenced in 1985 by a switch in the ministry overseeing Tourism from the Department of Trade and Industry to the Department of Employment. In the first report published by the House of Commons Environment Committee (1987), English Heritage came under fire for not working hard enough to attract tourism. Hence, the heritage industry began to play an increasingly significant part in the regeneration of the nation's economy. Through a combination of the annual Tourist Board publication, "English Heritage Monitor", as well as the Manpower Services Commission (MSC), "new" forms of employment were developed within this industry of nostalgia, such as... "weaving, grinding corn and living in a reconstruction of an iron age round house at Manchester museum" (Hewison 1987: 102). In 1985, more than 200 museums organised MSC programmes, resulting in 2,206 full-time jobs, with an additional 2,000 gaining work in archaeology. At the same time the development of a "Heritage Industry" within the 1980s Britain presented an absurdity to tourists and the public. In addition to traditional ideas being substituted by a belief in consumerism, museums were also becoming production outlets. A new museum was not only one of the convenient ways of re-using a disused factory or iron works. (Hewison 1987, Corner and Harvey 1991). In the early 1980s it was also regarded as a mode of job development in derelict post-industrial areas across the country, which were failing to revitalise their regional economies due to the "costs" of wealth creation. Job building in manufacturing industry in 1988 was £32,000, whilst in mechanical engineering was £300,000. However the cost of creating single employment in tourism amounted to a modest £4,000 (Lumley 1988, Corner and Harvey 1991).

Hence, throughout the 1980s the nation's industrial heritage was explored in a series of museums: re-constructed emblems of Britain's imperial workhouse. Ironbridge in Shropshire, the Black Country Museum in the former engineering heartland of the West Midlands and the Big Pit Colliery in Gwent became a working museum after closing as a working colliery. South Tyneside in Northumbria was re-christened "Catherine Cookson Country", after the famous local authoress (Hewison 1987: 95-7). Here a "replica street" was constructed to commemorate her life and work. Furthermore Robert Hewison (1987) highlights the case of the Beamish Open Air Museum:

> "Beamish is an attempt to reconstruct the life of the North East on a green field site. The 200 acres of farmland and wood are dotted with the materials of the region's past: a railway station, a town street, a row of miner's cottages, a colliery. The town street evokes an indistinct period of between the wars, at just that distance in time when memory softens and sweetens. But there is no need for personal nostalgia. Here, the displays do it for you. The effect is so complete that it is the late twentieth century visitors, not the buildings, that seem out of place" (Hewison 1987: 95).

Moreover, Hewison counterpoints Beamish with the economic decline of the North-East in general and Consett, a town ten miles from the museum, in particular. Consett in the 1900s was part of Britain's industrial dominance during the era of imperial consolidation. However by 1980 following the shutdown of its British Steel plant (the town's main employer) and the three and a half thousand redundancies which followed, the town became an emblem of Britain's post-imperial, post-industrial decline. Hence, if towns like Consett became symbols of decay and alienation for substantial sectors of the British population (the traditional working-class) then heritage became a symbol not just of a national store of myths and historical reflections but also an alternative source of employment, a national economic benefit and an emblem of the 1980s enterprise ethos (Hewison 1987: 95).

Therefore, the industrial museum movement could be argued to have been ultimately anti-industrial; as the industries decline, the heritage designers take over. Moreover, Thatcher's imagined community of a reconstructed national cultural heritage was symbolic not just of a revitalisation of the national economy but also of a rejection of an ideology also inherent in Britain's national past. For according to Wright (1984: 56-62), Heritage Britain - symbolising the national past - may indeed be exoticised as a place for tourists to visit, but in the 1980s Britain dominated by anti-traditionalist "right-wing technocrats" represented by the Thatcher government, the national past was also symbolised by the alternative working-class "heritage" of trade unions which were seen as time-worn, outdated and unpatriotic. Hence the character of this "historical" legacy, in the eyes of the New Right, was not that of a national treasure but rather an "old-fashioned" relic, an obstruction to Britain's social and political reclamation (Ibid.: 55). As Wright states: "In the 1980s Conservative Government of triumphant monetarism... the past was not just a heritage or trust in need of reluctant... costly protection. Neither was it just a convenient camouflage for preserving relations of domination under the guise of national identity and interest. It is also the oblivion which stands there as the rightful abode of all those forces which resist the "rationalisation" of social relations around market forces" (Wright 1984: 55).

Such an attitude would help to expound upon the fore-grounding of traditional social or "Victorian" values, (evident during the era of imperial consolidation), and highlighted by leading heritage scholars. Hewison in (Corner and Harvey 1991) claims that the heritage notion of Britain's history is predicated upon a reconstructed and imaginary past, as social values emerged from the imperialist era of status and subordination which heritage succeeded in maintaining and bringing forth into the 1980s.

Adrian Mellor (1991b) identifies "heritage" as an eclectic collection comprised not only of museums and historic buildings but also "country houses, national trust membership, Laura Ashley-style shopping" and historical/period television dramas such as The Jewel in the Crown (1982) and Brideshead Revisited (1981) which I shall be analysing in detail in chapter 5. (Ibid.: 98).

Mellor proffers a reason as to why, as a nation, British people during the 1980s were luxuriating in nostalgia, occupying a recreated past, seemingly unable to discern between a ratified History and a seductive version of it. The explanation, Mellor believes, is that:

"In our collective experience of national decline and communal powerlessness, we have abandoned the attempt to remake our society and have reached instead for a bottle of historical valium, dragging our kids around theme parks and heritage centres of a Saturday afternoon, remembering "the way we were when the sun never set on change from half-a-crown and you didn't have to lock the back door of your empire when you went out" (Mellor in Corner and Harvey 1991: 97).

As with the industrial museums, so with the arts which were regarded as one of the nation's major "industries":

"The arts are to British tourism what the sun is to Spain... of course we must not forget the heritage and the monarchy, which with the arts, support a tourist trade which brings in some £5,000 million". (Rees-Mogg, March 1985 in Hewison 1987: 107).

Here the arts, heritage and the monarchy were all key contributory elements to Thatcher's reconstruction of 1980s Britain. At this time the role of the Arts Council became more important in the light of the conservative government's policy of cutting public expenditure and introducing privatisation. The Arts Council, became an increasingly political body, through Right-wing influence. Norman St John Stevas, the Leader of the House was eligible for a cabinet place, the arts thus received a prominent political role in national government for the first time since Jennie Lee - who was Arts Minister under the Wilson administration, during the social and cultural upheaval of the 1960s (Ibid.: 111).

In 1982 the House of Commons Select Committee on the Arts made a series of proposals, one being that the "arts ministry" be changed to the Ministry of Arts, Heritage and Tourism headed by a Cabinet minister and comprising a broader portfolio which was to include television and radio, the British Film industry and tourism. A stronger ministry would mean a weaker Arts Council, which would lose some of its work to the regional arts associations and no longer be "the sole channel of central government funding of the performing and creative arts" (Ibid.: 114). Hence, to reinforce this assertion, in 1983 the previously discreet method whereby the arts minister would put aside monies from the total Arts Council Budget for the purpose of backing performances by the "national companies", became transparently open, through the financial support given to the Royal Opera House and the Royal Shakespeare Company.

Such selective government funding of renowned National Arts Institutions as the aforementioned helps to convey, along with notions of national heritage and the monarchy, the overall emergence of a right-wing sponsored national culture within Britain at this time.

Arts funding continued to be a national problem within Britain and by the late 1980s this country was investing fewer resources in the arts than anywhere in Western Europe. State arts funding for 1987/1988 was £399 million, a tiny fraction of maximum government spending power, which amounted to £148 billion (Ibid: 118).

However, what were the social and moral implications for the nation of such a commercially-oriented arts policy? According to Hewison (1987) an ignorant and unquestioning populace may have been the purpose of the conservative's cultural policies: "An intellectual culture is also a critical culture, which is not prepared passively to accept the decisions made on its behalf by political appointees who are answerable to no one but themselves" (Ibid.: 122).

Moreover, artistic originality was seen to be compromised by commercial gain. The larger companies, driven by financial need, had to constrain their desire to experiment and instead persevere with money-making productions. Orchestras restricted practice periods and adhered to the continuing performance of popular classics. Amongst the arts in general, at this time, levels of original production and performance dropped, whilst the line between the state-funded and privately funded sectors became increasingly blurred. The National Theatre and the Royal Shakespeare Company selected and scheduled their performances upon a strict commercial premise. Indeed the RSC's production of "Les Miserables" started with "a commercial partnership."

"Under pressure to keep their auditoria full, the National revived elaborately-set pre-war farces, the RSC applied the production techniques developed by radical theatre groups in the late 1960s - but without the radicalism. The Royal Court, one of the few theatres still committed to new and politically engaged work, looked to the United States for support. Everywhere, at this time, the scale of productions was reduced, outside the West End commercial theatre survived on "expensive hollow spectacle" (Ibid: 123).

In response to this gradual sense of creative decay produced by the destruction of subsidies the government and the Arts Council decided to encourage an increase in business sponsorship. In 1976 when The Association for Business Sponsorship of the Arts (ABSA) was formed £600,000 per annum was invested by private business in arts funding. A decade later private enterprises had ploughed around £25 to £30 million in to the arts' coffers (Ibid.). However, business funding brought more acute problems to the arts. Contemporary or radical productions which criticised the philosophy of modern society struggled to find sponsorship.

In 1986 ABSA declined to support a production of "The Resistable Rise of Arturo Ui" in Sheffield. The trades union NALGO were sponsoring the play. However because NALGO had condemned the government's privatisation ethos by placing posters around the theatre the production failed to attract private funding. Arts Minister Richard Luce backed ABSA's actions: "it would be quite unacceptable for taxpayers' money to be used to support party politics in this way" (cited in Ibid.).

In this context of Thatcherite notions of national identity the left-wing progressive arts were increasingly being seen as a threat to the heritage arts, which were regarded as "the most prestigious", and so encountered little trouble in winning funding. Therefore, it was the "national companies and orchestras and galleries" which consistently attained financial backing, aided by their ability, through the size of their operations, to actively seek out commercial help. Opera companies together with symphony orchestras were particularly adroit in this regard. Emphasis on the arts as a successful component of Thatcher's Britain was perhaps best expressed by the Arts Council publication, "A Great British Success Story", which articulated its request for more state finances in 1986/87 along the lines of a national cultural commercial portfolio, claiming the arts to be "a first-rate investment" and "a product with which we compete on equal or superior terms with the rest of the world" (Ibid.: 128).

Fred Davis (1979) highlights a growth in the nation's fascination with nostalgia as conveyed through press and broadcasting. This is acknowledged by the media's preoccupation for self-obsession as events and occasions are processed by the media, and then repeated over again. Hence the length of time between the initial occurrence and its nostalgic reflection is less and less. As we shall show in later chapters, examples of "Heritage" cinema and television become symbols of a mediated national history predicated on pastiche and nostalgia.

Consequently, the establishment of a heritage industry at this time helped to present a mode of history to the nation which smothered challenge. History was turned into heritage whereby the reality of the past coupled with its social inequalities and class-conflicts were being replaced by a seamless image, a "pastiche" which was concerned only with the successes and values of the dominant class (Hewison 1987). Donald Horn, extends this point further, claiming what was presented was a version of history which precludes social, political and cultural interpretation. Such a representation of the nation's history could be argued to be an important element within Thatcher's imaginary community of Great British nationhood.

Hence, the heritage industry at this time attempted to transfer from the past to the present the reassuring reconstruction of a strong, undivided nation (Ibid.).

4.4 Thatcherism: the International Context

The Falklands and the national past

Heritage contributed in large part to satisfying one component of Thatcher's national aspirations. The re-presentation of national identity for a post-industrial, post-imperial age. Another key emblem symbolic of a new imaginary British identity proved to be victory in the Falklands conflict of 1982. The Argentinean invasion of the islands, according to Corner and Harvey (1991), allowed Thatcher to adopt the anti-dictatorship stance and rhetoric symbolic of Winston Churchill, re-packaging the language of "freedom" articulated during the Second World War, and arguing that the "Spirit of the South Atlantic was the spirit of Britain at her best" (Thatcher in O'Shea 1984: 37). Victory in the Falklands allowed the Conservative Party to attempt a new consolidation of national identity, anchored within the kind of double moral and military success within the international arena which it had humiliatingly been with-held from twenty-five years earlier during the Suez crisis. The New Right could lay claim to rediscovering Britain's credentials as the nation which had built an empire and ruled a quarter of the globe (Corner and Harvey 1991). According to Jenkins (1987: 163) a flaw "in the position of those... who at the time were critics of the war is that they underestimated the psychological needs of the nation for a success, a success of some kind, an end to national failure and humiliation, to do something well, to win. Nostalgic knee-jerk reaction it may have been, vainglorious posturing in a post-imperial world of Super Powers, but it made people feel better not worse." Moreover, it seemed to stimulate sincere admiration around the world and, at least, grudging respect. There is a note of surprise in American Congressman Alexander Haig's account of how:

> "In a reawakening of the spirit of the Blitz that exhilarated Britain, warships were withdrawn from NATO, civilian ships, including the liner Queen Elizabeth II, were requisitioned and refitted, troops were embarked, and in an astonishingly short time a task force of over 100 ships and 28,000 men was steaming under the British ensign toward the Falklands" (Haig 1984: 265).

Moreover, according to Mrs Thatcher, the Falklands factor also contributed in the fight against railway and underground disputes as well as, according to Jenkins (1987), galvanising the country into backing the medium term financial strategy: "What has indeed happened is that now once again Britain is not prepared to be pushed around... we have instead a new-found confidence - born in the economic battles at home and tested and found true 8,000 miles away... that confidence comes from the rediscovery of ourselves, and grows with recovery of our self-respect... we have ceased to be a nation in retreat... we have instead a new-found confidence - born in the economic battles at home and tested and found true 8,000 miles away... that confidence comes from the rediscovery of ourselves, and grows with the recovery of our self-respect... Britain found herself again in the South Atlantic and will not look back from the victory she has won" (Thatcher, Speech at Cheltenham Race Course, July 3rd 1982 in Jenkins 1987: 164).

However, according to Hobsbawm (1983), one of the most significant but equally troubling lessons emanating from the Falklands was a re-evaluation of nationalism: "A sinister lesson of the Falklands is the ease with which the Thatcherites captured the patriotic upsurge which initially was in no sense confined to political conservatives, let alone to Thatcherite ones. We recall the ease with which the Union Jack could be mobilised against domestic enemies as well as foreign enemies... the photograph of the soldiers coming back on the troopships, with a banner saying "call off the rail strike". Here lies the long term significance of the Falklands in British political affairs. "It is a sign of very great danger ... it acts as a sort of compensation for the feelings of decline, demoralisation and inferiority, which most people in this country feel" (Hobsbawn in Hall and Jacques 1983: 268).

Later on Thatcher claimed that: "The lesson of the Falklands is that Britain was not changed and that this nation still has those sterling qualities which shine through our history" (Thatcher in Corner and Harvey 1991: 16). However according to Corner and Harvey (1991) these "sterling qualities" entailed the use of military firepower in brutalising colonial populations into subjugation. These "qualities" seemed to many, both within the domestic and international sphere inappropriate for a post-imperial age, articulating national identity's profound potential for cultural division. This jingoistic nationalism was to be found in certain quarters of the right wing popular press. For example in "The Sun" on 21 May 1982:

"The battle has begun. Our lads are going in ready to lay down their lives for the principles that have always made Britain great. Love of country and love of freedom" (cited in O'Shea 1984: 36).

According to Barnett (1982), Thatcherism set the terms in which the war was articulated through the media onto the public consciousness. This was greatly aided by the absence of an organised and coherent political or moral opposition toward this nationalistic tone. It was also because the "otherness" of Argentina could be characterised along base, xenophobic guidelines as "fascist" and "Dago" (O'Shea 1984: 37). This also applied to the national game, soccer, concerning the debate over whether Argentinean Ricardo Villa could play for his English club in the FA Cup final or if England or Argentina should withdraw from the World Cup. In such an atmosphere of "jingoism," doubts or misgivings relating to the Falklands conflict could be interpreted as betrayal (Ibid.).

However, it is necessary at this stage to acknowledge that the conservative administration's solid performance in the opinion polls, halfway through their first term of office, was not solely down to the victory in the Falklands. Indeed the polls themselves pointed to a resurgence of support for the government which had already started before the conflict itself with no significant rise in popularity after the war had ended (Heller 1982). However, it must equally be stated that the spectre of defeat would indeed have struck Thatcher a mortal political blow. Hence victory promoted her to a higher grade of public respect. The Falklands was an event of immense political magnitude across the globe, and not least on Thatcher's personal image. This proved to be so in Argentina itself. Shortly after the war's end, an unnamed woman in Buenos Aires informed a reporter from the "New Yorker": "Thatcher deserves a statue in white marble here on the Plaza de Mayo" (Young 1989: 65). This was because she had ended the reign of the despised military junta which was responsible for the death and abduction of thousands of people, including this woman's son. In Britain, Mrs Thatcher's opinion poll rating, which was at a low at the end of 1981, rose dramatically to 44 per cent in June 1982 (Ibid.) .

Furthermore, during the conflict Thatcher kept a high public profile in an effort to retain the confidence of the nation. When South Georgia was recaptured on 25 April, she triumphantly proclaimed outside Downing Street: "Rejoice, just rejoice!" When addressing the annual conference of the Scottish Conservative Party on 14 May, she noted: "When you've spent half your political life dealing with humdrum issues like the environment, it's exciting to have a real crisis on your hands." She framed the war in moral terms, it was a fight… "between good and evil. It went far wider than the Falklands and their 1,800 British people. It was a challenge to the West. It must be ended. It will be ended" (cited in Young 1989: 273). She received a suitably jingoistic response. The Secretary of State for Scotland, George Younger, was amazed by the scene. It was not just the high octane atmosphere generated by local Conservatives that took him by surprise but the Prime Minister's enthusiasm in taking advantage of the situation. "It reminded me of the Nuremberg Rally" he told a friend when returning to London (Ibid.). Mrs Thatcher's speech at the 1982 Conservative Party Conference also used the Falklands triumph as an emblem of the Prime Minister's patriotism: "the spirit of the South Atlantic was the spirit of Britain at her best" (Wright 1984: 37).

Patrick Wright (1984: 42-6) describes such nationalistic modes of framing or analysis as a "public thematisation," which prompts the "people" to interpret and identify with important events within the conditions of a "national… cultural… historical…identity". The tone changes, energising nostalgia, hope and prejudice. It can on occasion overtly counterpoint its "'British' sense of balance against the emotionalism, deviance, bigotry or aggression of others… 'foolish Europe' or 'bloody Argies'.

Amidst the Falklands' crisis, this public thematisation attempted to organise public thinking: "During 1982 this nationalist thematisation of British life seemed to enter the news not just as a formal characteristic of its presentation but increasingly at the level of content itself; it seemed to become so strong that it was actually capable of generating events" (Ibid.: 47). Hence, Wright claims that the "nation" became central to British political life during the 1980s. In this context, tradition is "national identity". However in this instance the "nation" is a public consciousness, "a sense of identity" which locates its strength in a number of "experiences, and which is capable of colonising and making sense of others".

On a similar theme, Williams (1983) highlights during the era of decline an apparent loss of the nation's confident social identity and its strident belief both in the contemporary and the future: which therefore makes it increasingly vulnerable to a shallow and imitative reproduction of itself. Williams explains: "It is not because the British people are excessively nationalist and self-confident that you got the observed jingoism of the Falklands episode it is because the real national self-identification and self-confidence that once existed had gone, that a certain artificial, frenetic from-the-top, imagery of a nation can be injected" (Ibid.: 10). The kind of "spectacular consumerist militarism" with which Williams identifies the Falklands war, with the epicentre of the conflict 8,000 miles away, limits the impact of war for everyone other than the luckless individuals who are there, to television reportage, nationalistic rhetoric and symbols (Ibid.).

This, therefore, merely cannot be identified with other nationalist perspectives, even of national identity. It is through the psychology of distance that this type of shallow and seamless image of the nation can be manufactured and projected – in other words an imagined community of nationalism.

In addition Williams argues that many of the negative aspects which ought to be disturbing - jingoism and public acceptance can be looked upon as fallout emerging from the increasing insecurity and fracturing of contemporary society. (Ibid: 10-12).

Two important aspects of Thatcherite patriotism prevailed at this time. Firstly, Mrs Thatcher articulated herself as the emblem of the legacy Thatcherism was attempting to reformulate; "a force for freedom - with the fires burning deep within us ready to drive forward again." She summons up Churchill: "I know you will understand the humility I feel at following in the footsteps of great men like... Winston Churchill, a man called by history to raise the name of Britain to supreme highs in the history of the free world" (Conservative Party Conference, October 1975 cited in O'Shea 1984: 27). Secondly the features and the sounds of Thatcherism were close to the nationalistic imperialism of the early 20th century, and during the era of consolidation, - a tradition clearly characterised by racism.

Hewison (1987) describes the symbolism of the Falklands as "the encapsulated heritage event; a battle for a distinctly "British" and utterly remote piece of moorland. The effect of the Falklands expedition was to strengthen Britain's inward conservatism. "We" had won. The position of the Falklands remains unchanged" (Ibid: 142).

Another event in 1982 which was to become emblematic of the nation's sea-fairing heritage was the recovery of the "Mary Rose", Henry VIII's flag ship which had sunk in 1545 off Portsmouth. The fact that the "Mary Rose" was resurrected in the year of the Falklands, according to Wright (1985) gives the event contemporary significance. The emergence of the two events before the national gaze in 1982 - and the "collective" feeling of identity initiated by it suggested a national commonality through the resurrection of the "Mary Rose" and the Falklands conflict (Ibid: 164). With regard to national identity what deemed these events historically significant was due partly to their distinctiveness but moreover according to Wright (Ibid.) "their symbolic resonance of tradition and continuity with the past". In the same way that the resurfacing of the "Mary Rose" was mediated as bringing the nation back an artefact of its historical culture – something which the country had not seen for nearly 450 years - the Falklands reaffirmed that Britain of the 1980s was still a proud, patriotic and formidable nation, with self-belief and moral certainty, with the ability, once more, to act swiftly and decisively (Thatcher, Cheltenham Speech cited in Barnett 1982: 15).

Both these events could also be described as symbols of an imaginary community of deep horizontal comradeship, the former an emblem of the era of emergence and the latter a symbolic reminder of the period of Gun-Boat diplomacy, both characteristic during the era of imperialistic consolidation.

According to Wright (1985: 179), this contemporary "sense of historical existence" creates a common collection of beliefs and values into which connections to the past can be incorporated. It is this "sense of historical existence" which explains the country's alacrity to consume the past in the romanticised conditions of national identity. In this context history is transformed into a heritage which has been misplaced and through their re-emergence events such as the "Mary Rose", the liberation of the Falkland Islands and… "the "Victorian values" of Thatcher's 1983 election campaign…" legitimise a romanticised perception of the past.

In this mythical framework the "Mary Rose" becomes a "time-capsule" - a fragment of idealised history which has borne the national essence and identity down to the present. In this sense it is "we" who ride through time and are still "there" to be discovered in the sludge of contemporary life, just as it is "we" who get betrayed or lost, even to ourselves, at the bottom of the sea." Hence the "Mary Rose" is located in a nationalistic trend concerning an undermined or endangered mode of existence of a collective sense of identity. One of these conditions is what Wright terms the "postulated purity" of an evidential form of identity. Examples of this evidence or proof of identity can be the Mary Rose, the Stonehenge or the Houses of Parliament, but could also be represented by "our" land and mode of existence as Thatcher described it during the 1983 General election (Ibid.).

The second condition of this nationalistic trend can be articulated through the anti-patriotic "Marxist socialism" which Thatcher, during the 1983 election, stated she would banish and ostracise from the nation, as "…immigrants, extraparliamentarians, invading "Argies", bureaucracy and post-war Labour reform, or the "enemy within" as Thatcher called the striking miners in 1984" (Ibid.). The third condition of this trend is war and triumph for the just – the reclamation of national pride. Like the Falklands conflict, Thatcher's 1983 election victory was waged along the lines of this nationalistic trend (Ibid: 183).

CHAPTER IV - GREAT BRITAIN

Contrasting Relations: Europe, USA and Immigration

One of the more transparent paradoxes of Thatcherite nationalism concerned its encouraging attitude to Japanese and American investment on one level, and, on the other its zealous defence of British Parliamentary sovereignty together with its old values and patronage from the perceived threat of the supra-national structure of a federal Europe (Corner and Harvey 1991). The British policy was re-affirmed by the then Conservative Party chairman Kenneth Baker who claimed: "We will not agree to Westminster being reduced to a glorified county council" (*The Guardian*, January 13, 1990: 9). Thus, the British government took a traditionalist stance toward the mechanics of political representation. Even though the common market would produce a free exchange of products which was acceptable to the New Right, common political institutions were not: The nation-state was still regarded as the principal font of political policy making. At the Fontainbleau Summit on June 25, 1984 Britain "won" a substantial reduction in its annual budget payments toward the European Community. However, according to Young (1989) and Sked and Cook (1984), Britain had also alienated many potential allies in Europe, as well as jeopardising at the expense of this narrow national insistence the opportunity for advancement in relation to other European reforms, particularly in agriculture, which stagnated the development of the community. Quite apart from being unfortunate for Europe, this nationalistic struggle, it was further argued, extended the period when Britain could be accepted together with France and Germany as one of the three leading nations of Europe (Young 1989). Here again Thatcherite national identity conceptions led to cultural division amongst politically closely aligned nations.

However, to the British government and Margaret Thatcher in particular, this could be seen as a "victory", not just against the ever imposing symbolism of a European super-state but also for the re-constructed British values of "common sense" and "fairness" (O'Shea 1984). Generally, European affairs at this time were a clear indication of Thatcher's approach to foreign policy.

This, according to Riddell (1989), concerned a series of strident nationalistic speeches representing an inherent belief, or prejudice, followed by extensive internal debate, persuasion by the Foreign Office and ultimately a negotiated policy. Thatcher looked upon the Foreign Office's apparent neutrality and desire to constantly have friendly and agreeable relations with other countries as non-nationalistic and opposed to British interests which Thatcher understood she was protecting. (Ibid, Hall and Jacques). Consequently, frictions between Whitehall and Downing Street were commonplace as Thatcher appointed her own "Foreign Affairs Adviser", at the same time as she alienated "wet" Whitehall civil servants. This view led Norman Tebbit in characteristic fashion to talk of a "ministry for foreigners".

The diversity of levels of identity construction could be seen even in the personal image of Margaret Thatcher herself. On one level she was a political leader; on another she was symbolic of Britain's international position in the 1980s. Perhaps, because she was the first female political leader of a major western power, and also due to her belligerent personal style especially evidenced during the victorious Falklands war in 1982, she became a symbol, to some, of a Britain with its national pride restored (Riddell 1989, Young 1989, Hall and Jacques 1983). Thatcher was lauded by American congressmen in 1985 and enthusiastically greeted by mass crowds, mainly comprised of adoring women when in Moscow in 1987. Mrs Thatcher could be argued to have been the principal emblem of a new strain of national identity (Riddell 1989).

The "special relationship" with the United States and in particular the close friendship between Thatcher and Reagan, permitted Britain some leeway in appearing to have rediscovered a degree of global strength and influence, though this special relationship was certainly strained by Britain's war with Argentina over the Falklands - a conflict which could have caused harm to American interests in the Southern hemisphere (Corner and Harvey 1991).

In an address given to the US congress in February 1985, Thatcher drew upon Churchill's belief in the intellectual and moral co-operation between the English-speaking peoples of the world. Thatcher respected the American philosophy of enterprise and British conservative ministers frequently travelled stateside to examine policy for regenerating the British economy especially within the areas of inner city deprivation, education and privatisation (Riddell 1989).

President Reagan saw Mrs Thatcher as an ideological ally as they struggled against communism. Such Cold War allegiance allowed Britain's voice to be heard within the oval office as well as on occasion to impinge upon US opinion, such as when Mrs Thatcher persuaded Reagan to stop the US Justice Department's judicial action against British Airways which was in turn preventing its privatisation. Perhaps the most potent example of Britain's perceived new-found influence within the relationship was the access it gained to intelligence and supplies held by the US during the Falklands war which proved crucial in the British triumph. This suggested an intimate professional relationship between the governments and military of both countries (Riddell 1989, Kavanagh 1987, Derbyshire and Derbyshire 1989).

Sir William Henderson, then the British ambassador in Washington revealed the promises by then Secretary of State Alexander Haig that the Falklands conflict would not be a repetition of Suez, when American opposition caused the British and French to pull out of the invasion and incur international embarrassment in the process (Henderson 1987). Britain would have struggled to win back the Falklands without American backing.

However, Thatcher's aspirations were called into question by critics of the "special relationship," who regarded it as too one-sided, therefore reinforcing US imperialist ambitions. For example, Reagan's arrogance in ordering an American invasion of Grenada in 1983 which was a Commonwealth country, without consulting or informing Thatcher clearly suggested that the US was (and is) of greater political and economic significance to Britain than the other way around. (Adonis and Hames 1984, Kavanagh 1987, Derbyshire and Derbyshire 1989). Furthermore the absence of information regarding Grenada was deliberate. US national interests were prioritised, a similar story to when "Star Wars", the strategic defence initiative was revealed in 1983. Later, in April 1986, the Thatcher government suffered considerable temporary hostility in Britain when alone in Europe it allowed the US Air Force to use its F-111 bases in Britain from which to bomb Tripoli in Libya. This was an act of political support for American foreign policy and also a repayment of the military co-operation given by the Americans during the Falklands conflict. However, the degree of internal British hostility meant that the bombings were only ever a "one-off." Indeed it left Thatcher open to claims from the left that she was the Americans' "poodle" and that Britain was a mere "colony" for US interests (Ibid., Jenkins 1987).

However, another examination of the claims that Mrs Thatcher's and hence Britain's influence on the world stage was significant came within the sphere of nuclear arms talks during the 1980s. The warmth of Mr Gorbachev's welcome during Thatcher's visits in 1987 and 1989 as well as the length of the meetings in Moscow indicated the notion amongst the Soviets that Mrs Thatcher exerted a limited though tangible influence over the US, especially with regard to President Reagan. Even though the British tabloid and Tory press claimed that she was articulating Western policy or behaving as a leading negotiator clearly she was not (Riddell 1989, Derbyshire and Derbyshire 1989, Young 1989).

The evidence suggesting any particular British influence over the Americans in the arms race was also examined, firstly in December 1984 over Star Wars (SDI), and then, two years later, after the Reykiavik Summit. The American promise of large SDI research work for British companies never came to fruition. This was seen as another example of the enormous inconsistency in UK/US defence contracts. Indeed this aspect was highlighted later through insufficient contracts initially promised to Britain by Boeing over the AWACS airborne early warning project.

Mrs Thatcher mediated in 1986 on behalf of Western Europe over American and Soviet negotiations concerning the potential withdrawal of particular categories of nuclear weaponry in Europe. The prospect of both a decrease in the weapons and their ultimate removal, from the American nuclear arsenal caused consternation amongst democratic European governments. This would present Soviet forces with a distinct military edge through their vast collection of conventional weapons. Mrs Thatcher, to the relief of many European leaders as well as significant American advisers, extracted concrete assurances from President Reagan. This seemed to illustrate that Thatcher and Britain were at their more influential at a time of divisions within the American government, hence her personal friendship with the President aided the Prime Minister in supporting the side which suited her preference (Kavanagh 1987, Riddell 1989, Derbyshire and Derbyshire 1989).

Within the sphere of economic trade, leading British groups grew both in the US on a grand-scale and in Europe. Among the British companies with substantial stakes in the American economy in the late 1980s were BP, BAT (Farmers Insurance), Grand Metropolitan (Pillsbury Food Group), Maxwell Communications (MacMillan), Hanson, ICI (Stanffer Chemicals), Marks and Spencer (Brooks brothers), Tate and Lyle (Staley), Blue Arrow (Manpower), and Saatchi & Saatchi. Such global economic expansion, particularly in the rich American and EC markets, increased in significance all the principal British companies (Marquand 1988).

Such economic imperialism was also illustrated by international take-overs and mergers by British firms which amounted to £8.9 billion in 1986, £11.5 billion a year later and £8.4 billion in 1988. Of these three-quarters occurred in the USA where Britain was the biggest foreign investor (Ibid.). However, foreign acquisitions of UK companies totalled a mere £2.9 billion in 1986 and £2.3 billion in 1987 by comparison.

One of the most prominent elements of the Thatcherite ethos was to reconstruct Britain's Imperial past in a contemporary setting - through the production of Britain's "Sterling Qualities" (Corner and Harvey 1991: 16). However, because these "Qualities" had concerned the use of imperial white might in killing and subjugating colonial peoples, they were surely irrelevant in a post-imperial, multiethnic society and in opposition to its multicultural aspirations (Gilroy 1987). Part of the inheritance of Britain's colonial history has been the automatic assumption of white dominance and its articulation through pervasive modes of racism. Immigrants from the Commonwealth, who made their life in Britain, were the victims of discrimination within many social spheres during the 1980s: employment, education, accommodation and policing. For example in 1985 black unemployment was nearly twice that of white (Ibid.).

In the first half of the 1980s this discrimination was belligerently defied by a sequence of violent civil disruptions which started in Brixton in April 1981, then spread in the summer to Toxteth, central Liverpool, Moss Side, Manchester, Bristol, Leicester and numerous parts of inner city London. In 1985 Handsworth in Birmingham was the centre of similar violence, where two Asians died in a burnt out shop. In Brixton, three weeks later similar violence occurred following a bungled police raid in which a middle-aged black woman was shot and seriously injured. However, arguably the most horrific scenes took place at the Broadwater Farm Estate, Tottenham, North London when another heavy-handed police raid culminated in the death of an ailing black woman Mrs Cynthia Jarrett who died having been pushed to the floor and denied medical help. In the ensuing mass riot, which continued until 4:35 am the next morning, PC Keith Blakelock was savagely hacked to death with knives and a machete, whilst out of a total of 200 police causalities, several were very seriously wounded (Marwick 1990).

The initial response of the Conservatives was to condemn these riots, and Thatcher herself had already sown the seeds of a latent racist response in a speech delivered in 1978, articulating the fear that:

"This country might be rather swamped by people with a different culture" (Walker and Walker 1987: 62).

Also in 1981 the Conservative government had past the British Nationality Act which would delineate entitlement to British citizenship and residence in the United Kingdom. This limited British citizenship with maximum residency rights to people already legally living in the UK as well as to those who had one British parent and had been registered abroad at birth. Significantly the Act also created a third category of British citizens, "British overseas citizens". These individuals were people who lived abroad but who had no familial or residential ties with Britain in recent years. In addition these people did not have rights to enter, which meant that hardly any nation would acknowledge their passports. Furthermore, in 1982 the Government endeavoured to clamp down on immigration with respect to marriages, suspecting that many of these ties entered into by immigrants were frequently ploys in order to allow young men, particularly from India and Pakistan to slip through the system. These new rules, however, hit problems in Parliament - from both left and right of the Conservative Party as well as constitutional concerns surrounding the European Convention on Human Rights. Ultimately, against the Government's wishes, the regulations were changed in 1983 in order to permit women holding British citizenship to bring their husbands or fiances from abroad. (Sked and Cook 1984; Gilroy 1987).

However, towards the end of the 1980's a more thoughtful and inclusive policy was developed along the lines of the general "populist" invitation to all people of "substance" to join the acquisitive "democracy". Thus the 1987 Conservative Election Manifesto argued:

"Immigrant communities have already shown that it is possible to play an active and influential role in the mainstream of British life without losing one's distinctive cultural traditions" (cited in Walker and Walker 1987: 65).

4.5 Conclusion

In summary, the Falklands together with the 1981 British Nationality Act conveyed a strident, macho perception of nationality and nationalism. Under Thatcher there was seldom the potential for variety; nationalism was a superior power, ruling over all other concerns. Thatcher's governments throughout the 1980s looked upon the constant sectional debates concerning class, unions, race, culture and politics, associated with the 1960s and 1970s, as time consuming and weary-some. The 1980s were to be about tough choices for the nation conveyed through the politics of conviction.

The nation, the people, the culture were at risk from Argentineans, from the immigrants of former colonies which Britain once ruled and from the Left, who believed in genuine tolerance of ethnic or cultural difference and not "assimilation". Every social, cultural, economic, racial and political aspect was articulated in terms of the "nation", the "island race" (Walker and Walker 1987, Miles and Phizacklea 1984).

During this chapter I have endeavoured to analyse the significant social, cultural and political events and constructs which contributed toward the character and perception of Britain's national identity through both a domestic and international context during the period 1980-90. I began by briefly analysing Thatcher's initial rise to power, aided by her preaching of a new politics of conviction. I then articulated how the distinctive style of Thatcherism was conveyed within the sphere of economics and politics. In addition I have attempted to detail how within the sphere of culture Thatcherism gravitated around notions of Heritage and Nostalgia, the concepts of which I shall draw upon in my later analysis of specific cultural artefacts. Indeed I have discussed how each of these aspects related to Thatcherism. With regard to the International context I have analysed the ways in which global events impacted upon Thatcherite designs in constructing a distinctive British national identity during this period, acknowledging the frictions and conflicts which were thus thrown up. My overall aim has been to demonstrate to the reader how a distinctive pattern developed during the 1980s in order to draw upon an understanding of these at a later stage when analysing the selected media products.

Chapter V.

Reclaiming National Identity - Great Britain in 1980 - 1990

5.1 Introduction

By 1979, the Conservatives had been out of office for almost twelve of the previous fifteen years. The party that returned to office that year bore little resemblance to the one led by the Edwardian figures of Harold MacMillan and Alec Douglas Home. The first female leader of a major British political party became Prime Minister and Margaret Thatcher lost little time in setting out her political aims, making no secret of the strength of her views and the extent of her ambitions. In 1975, she had addressed her party conference in these terms:

> "We are witnessing a deliberate attack on our values, a deliberate attack on those who wish to promote merit and excellence, a deliberate attack on our heritage and our great past. And there are those who gnaw away at our national self-respect, rewriting British history as centuries of unrelieved gloom, oppression and failure – as days of hopelessness not days of hope" (Margaret Thatcher cited in O'Shea 1984: 25).

This speech, delivered at the outset of her leadership, at once eulogises and mourns the loss of a 'British' history, which incorporated imperial notions of greatness. Immediately she set out to challenge contemporary perceptions of the national identity and to revisit historical assumptions of British identity and heritage, investing in them her personal ideology. This explicit reference to national heritage and implicit reference to Empire found expression at the very moment of her incarnation as party leader. It also ensures that any analysis of the heritage film will involve a closer party political perspective than the Social Realist films examined above.

Her first years in office witnessed the wholesale destruction of a traditional manufacturing base that had for decades nurtured a working class heartland. Mass unemployment became swiftly associated with Thatcherism, which emerged, almost immediately, as a distinct political dogma. Chapter 3 observes how Mrs Thatcher sought to replace traditional manufacturing jobs with newly created positions in the service sector in which tourism

CHAPTER V - RECLAIMING NATIONAL IDENTITY

would feature prominently. Mrs Thatcher would encourage the creation and development of a heritage industry and significantly the first National Heritage Act became law during her first year in office.

This period also witnessed one of the many apparent revivals of British cinema, through productions which reflected the fact that to some extent at least British films were once again competing in the international image market. Indeed the Heritage film was a major component of this revival. Heritage cinema looked away from contemporary problems and reconstructed an England in its imperialist and aristocratic finery. These productions shunned a declining industrial nation beset with divisions of class and race. The national reluctance to accept the death of imperialism and the embracing of a multiracial and multicultural society featured prominently in the Heritage film.

Invariably set in the recent past and at the zenith of Empire, Heritage Films together with a small but significant number of prestige television productions create potential for a significant sociological study. It is important to ascertain the extent to which the re-packaging and re-examination of the past resonated with contemporary issues of national identification in the 1980s. It is also important to establish the extent to which these productions gave expression to the desire for a creation of a national identity rooted in and founded upon notions of imperialism. By using a qualitative thematic analysis, I will examine the ways in which these Heritage productions articulated and represented the social, political and cultural changes within 1980s Britain. I will consider the extent to which they evoked a celebration of the visual splendour of an essentially bourgeois, pastoral and aesthetic national identity. Here I am again articulating the same themes and mode of analysis I first adopted in "Realist Nights and Heritage Mornings" (2001).

At the narrative level, most productions contain at least one central character manifesting some liberal humanist tendencies. This character often strives for a type of consensual solution to perceived problems, a personal concern largely inconsistent with the ambition and conviction of Thatcherism. For example,

Fielding is prepared to sacrifice his position for Aziz in <u>A Passage to India</u>. (1984). In <u>Another Country</u> (1984) Tommy Judd is killed fighting for his Marxist principles in Spain, whilst in <u>Maurice</u> (1987) the central character is willing to abandon wealth and privilege for the love of a working class estate worker.

Subtle and ambiguous signifiers of identity exist in the Heritage films. There are clear contemporary implications of a cinema fleeing from the present in order to seek solace in the past and recapture the perceived certainty of Empire. Many of these cases involved a journey across time, culture and class. The American born director James Ivory, his Indian producer Ismail Merchant and their frequent screenwriter Ruth Prawer Jhabvala created many of the more influential Heritage films. Their careers began with examinations of contemporary Indian situations. They progressed to adaptations of Henry James' <u>The Europeans</u> (1978) and <u>The Bostonians</u> (1982) before finally arriving, literally and creatively, in England. This distancing of the creative team's ethnicity and nationality will have influenced their interpretations of 'English' heritage and the British Empire. The 'otherness' of the production staff tended to paint the portrayals of Empire in terms and colours more recognisable to a non-English audience allowing the British reader to marvel at the spectacle of former imperial glories.

Certain films of the period were however overtly critical of Thatcherism including work by Stephen Frears, Ken Loach and Mike Leigh. These productions largely though not exclusively presented a contemporary setting. Dealing with themes of social and economic alienation and instability, they indicated shifting, fluid and interchanging national identities in an increasingly fragmented and unstable post-imperialist environment. They commented upon the prevailing Thatcherite economics of the free market, which were tending to produce high unemployment and aggravated social disquiet. The underlying tension featured in many of these films and, some such as Lindsay Anderson's <u>Britannia Hospital</u> (1982) portrayed a society so fundamentally and graphically disordered that it teetered on the brink of total anarchy. The discussion that follows is divided into a series of subsections focussed upon different themes.

CHAPTER V - RECLAIMING NATIONAL IDENTITY

In the subsection discussing questions of class I have selected as the principal case study Brideshead Revisited (1981). I shall seek to demonstrate how it presented a dominantly heritage view of national identity from the period in which it is set. By referencing across the burgeoning heritage industry, I shall show how the productions tended to present an imagined view of national identity with the more strident elements of class struggle understated if not actually undermined. I shall then examine Maurice (1987) A Room with a View (1985) and Another Country (1984) in order to demonstrate how this reconstruction has been further refined. Here I will also seek to indicate the extent to which this identity has been delineated and liberal values invested to produce a model acceptable to a contemporary audience. I have chosen Brideshead as the principal artefact because it appeared very early in the heritage cycle and the central role of the house makes it appear as a metaphor for the nation. I shall then conclude with a more brief examination of some non-heritage films of the 1980s. However in order to begin this subsection I have focussed upon a discussion of The Long Good Friday (1979). It is one of the first films of the period demonstrating some of the re-emergent nationalist strains yet also contrasts strikingly with the heritage films that follow.

In the subsection dealing with morality, I shall discuss Chariots of Fire (1981) as the principal Heritage product. This was an early, highly influential, commercially and critically successful film. Morality is a central theme of the film and the protagonists justify their personal ambition in terms of faith and religious conviction. The film therefore represents a reconstruction of morality expressed, not in liberal humanist terms, but in considerations of shallow self-interest. I shall seek to establish that this film, perhaps more than any other Heritage product, attempts to provide a contemporary audience with an ethical authority for the pursuit of self interest masquerading as moral conviction. I shall then introduce the Raj productions and examine how they purport to invest imperialism with imagined liberal humanist values. In this discussion, it will become apparent that these efforts are fraught with failure and delusion.

The Heritage film in general excludes the working class and renders their role superfluous or reduces it to one of simple servility. I will suggest therefore that 1980s British cinema largely minimised the role of the working class.

In the subsection considering the post imperialist aspect of national identity, I will again utilise <u>Chariots of Fire</u> as the principal cultural artefact but with a greater comparison with 'non Heritage' productions of the period. I will endeavour to demonstrate how <u>Chariots of Fire</u> in particular, and the Heritage film in general, purported to incorporate into a 1980s reconstruction of national identity imperialist values and ethics but softened by the imputation of largely imaginary liberal humanists values. Essentially, I shall discuss the extent to which the Heritage production sought to offer a modified version of imperial values and a reconstruction of Empire as a model for national identity at a time of social fragmentation. I shall suggest that the productions offered a superficially attractive fantasy of a society able to overcome differences of plurality and class collision by invoking the certainties and successes of Empire.

I shall then consider more closely than previously how the Heritage film compares to other films and television products of the 1980s demonstrating the extent of overt political influence. I shall also seek to outline the real life limitations placed upon any reconstructed national identity by considering issues of military security and film. In that context I shall examine in particular <u>The Ploughman's Lunch</u> (1983) and <u>Defence of the Realm</u> (1984).

In the final subsection I shall conclude by highlighting the limitations, undermining the attempts made by the Heritage films to reclaim national identity.

5.2 Class, Affluence and Social Mobility

It is generally considered amongst political commentators that the 1978-79 "Winter of Discontent" proved to be the electoral downfall for Jim Callaghan and his government in May 1979 (Jenkins 1987, Riddell 1989, Derbyshire and Derbyshire 1990). The wide ranging and persistent series of strikes by public sector workers during the final months of the Labour administration were deeply unpopular and were seen in some quarters as incontrovertible

CHAPTER V - RECLAIMING NATIONAL IDENTITY

evidence of a fundamental moral malaise blighting the nation. Mrs Thatcher frequently invoked historic examples of morality in order to recreate a version of national identity. On the steps of number 10 Downing Street flushed with success, she triumphantly quoted from Saint Francis of Assisi. Questions of national identity had become somewhat muted during the political discourse of the late 1960s and 1970s but would come to the fore through the 1980s finding expression in the Heritage Film's use of historical context.

Interestingly, however, it was a film made in 1979 and given a sombre contemporary setting that is arguably one of the first cultural illustrations of a proto Thatcherite figure. This film is also significant in that it depicted gangsters and criminals as metaphors for big business and unethical practice at the very beginning of her rule suggesting also a sinister relationship between the two. The Long Good Friday featured Harold Shand, a London mobster, who, by a combination of hard work, intimidation, violence and networking built a profitable "empire". As he said when addressing the other gang leaders in the infamous abattoir scene, "we've all had it sweet". Shand embodied the spirit of free enterprise and initiative. The plot turned upon his efforts to encourage the American Mafia to invest in his personal dockland development scheme.

He entertained the visiting Mafia figures on his yacht moored by the increasingly decaying and idle docklands and extended the lavish courtesies one expects to find in corporate hospitality suites. However, it was not enough for Shand to simply make more money. Of equal or even greater importance was his grandiloquent vision. He was helping to regenerate Britain and restore what he regarded as some much-needed national pride. In the next decade, he claimed, London would be "the capital of Europe". It is not stretching imagination to detect direct comparisons between Shand, and his development of decaying urban London, and the famous Empire builders of the 18th and 19th centuries. The site of his development lies in the heart of London's docklands and in many ways predicted the 1980s Canary Wharf project. Throughout the film, Shand exudes hubris and self-importance making speeches extolling national virtues and justifying his grand plans as serving the national interest. His sweeping vision is however persistently and ultimately fatally undermined by the IRA who are settling a score with Shand. The film portrays the IRA as deadly efficient assassins who strike mortal fear into some of Shand's own hardened gang members and into the corrupt and cynical Police Inspector on Shand's payroll.

In an early scene, an IRA assassin murders Colin, a confidante and associate of Shand. In the final scene, the same assassin drives Shand away at gunpoint – presumably to his death. Yet throughout the film the IRA is rarely seen and barely communicates with Shand and his gang. This suggests stealth, silence and lethal efficiency. Indeed this adds to the terror inspired by the IRA figures and helps invoke a sense of powerlessness and desperate vulnerability for Shand. It also goes some way to making an otherwise remorseless killer sympathetic. At this time Mrs Thatcher spoke often of the "enemy within" saying in Birmingham in April 1979 "Our defences within are vital if our nation is to prosper" (Thatcher cited in O'Shea 1984: 26). The IRA members, the enemy within, are portrayed in the film as an even greater danger than Shand and his disparate band.

Harold Shand typifies what at this time may well have been a nationally felt ambivalence towards America. Symbolically he needs the Mafia's financial backing and therefore courts them assiduously. However at the end of the film they dismiss him and rate Britain" a worse risk than Cuba ... a banana republic, a mess". Shand replies with a dogged and passionate defence of the realm stating that he is looking for someone with "a bit of the old Dunkirk spirit". In a blatant evocation of former imperial glory, he states that he wants someone who can "contribute to what England has given to the world; sophistication, culture, genius". He sneers and dismisses America's contribution to mankind as little more than "a hot dog".

The film suggests that enterprise and initiative will only succeed if the enemy within, in this case the IRA, are defeated. Furthermore, this reward can be realised without dependency upon the senior partner in our "special relationship" with

CHAPTER V - RECLAIMING NATIONAL IDENTITY

America. The Long Good Friday may therefore be presented as a cinematic depiction of diminishing national power and influence. This is articulated in terms of global and local politics – through the rejection of Shand's tainted "business" proposals by the American Mafia on one level and the increasingly violent struggle against Irish Republican nationalism on another. The end of Empire is complete as a remorseless killer delivers the eulogy. This final cinematic lament for former imperial glory comes from a man so intoxicated by his own limited power and so insular in outlook that he is incapable of acknowledging reality.

The heritage films, however conveyed very different representations of Empire and national identity from the contemporary world of The Long Good Friday. Visually celebratory, the heritage film is invariably set in the recent past and depicts the lives and the moral and social concerns of an upper class elite. Brideshead Revisited (1981) for example, concentrates on the aristocratic Flyte family in their palatial home. Academics, including Andrew Higson (1993) and John Hill (1999), have regarded the programme, as being part of the heritage school notwithstanding that it was a television production.

In October 1981 Granada TV broadcast Brideshead Revisited on national television. Political support for Mrs Thatcher had fallen dramatically and unemployment had reached a post war record of 3 million, (Corner and Harvey 1991). The mixed race ska band The Specials reached number one with "Ghost Town". The lyrics referred to "fighting in the dance halls" and to "people getting angry". The horn arrangement with its eerie haunting tones operated as an elegy for social alienation. The video showed the band driving through deserted streets. Rarely had the Number 1 in the nation's single charts so reflected contemporary social concerns. The relevance of the song was apparently confirmed by decaying investment and rising unemployment in most of the major English cities where rioting and social unrest were prevalent that summer. With such social upheaval afflicting a significant proportion of the working population, normal television expectations might suggest a major production depicting the lives of exclusively white aristocratic sybarites of the 1920s and 30s would struggle to find an audience. The production confounded any such expectations by attracting weekly viewing figures of 9 to 12.5 million. The success of the programme therefore has implications for discussions of contemporary national identity and its significant continuing fascination with questions of class and social mobility (Roddick in *Sight and Sound*, Vol. 51, No.1, Winter 1981-82, 58).

Contrasting sharply with Social Realism, Brideshead, loosely adapted by John Mortimer from the Evelyn Waugh novel, foregrounds the family of Lord and Lady Marchmain and their titled children. We view them through the medium of Charles Ryder firstly a friend of Sebastian and then the lover of Julia. Although clearly of a privileged class his specific social origins are somewhat ambiguous and it is possible that he is merely one of the upper-middle merchant classes and not a member of the aristocracy. Although he mixes freely with the Flytes he does so as a guest and, apart from the incident when Sebastian wishes to flee from his family, never offers to reciprocate the lavish hospitality he is shown at Brideshead. It is significant that the interior shots of his home usually show only a small portion of the dining room and only rarely venture into the drawing room. Since most of the scenes in the dining room are of Charles and his father occupying, in effect, a corner of the table, this restriction is dramatised.

It serves to remind us that, unlike Sebastian, who complains of the size of his family, Charles is quite alone in the world, save for his eccentric and indifferent father. Clearly, this also serves to emphasise the contrasting and almost limitless splendour and architectural magnificence of Brideshead. The frequent use of high angle shots, particularly of the "Great Hall" at Christmas time complete with resplendent fir tree, and wide angles to incorporate Brideshead's vast landscape further emphasise this point. The apparent effortlessness of Brideshead's "look" is visible in the opening establishing shot of the "Great House." In a later episode the same establishing shot of the Corinthian designed house and south parterre leads to a 180 degree pan shot sweeping to the right whilst we hear Julia and Charles discussing their future plans off screen. As the camera takes twenty seconds to pan slowly across to the couple standing by the Atlas fountain, the reader may admire the visual splendour of the landscaped garden on a bright summer's evening.

We are encouraged, also, by Charles's dialogue as he implores Julia: "Isn't this peace...what do you mean by peace if not this?" In an earlier episode as Charles and Sebastian return from a walk in the grounds, there is another magnificent wide-angle view of the house. This shot is repeated a number of times during the course of the serial, including Julia and Charles's aforementioned fountain sequence. A spectacular overhead shot of Charles and Cordelia wandering through the woods amidst the autumn leaves encourages the viewer to gaze appreciatively at the Corinthian designed Temple of the Four Winds. In yet another sequence, which no doubt left many a viewer gazing in awe at its sumptuous quality, Julia is resplendent in silver sequinned evening gown. She hurries out to the fountain to take the evening air, sequins glistening in the moonlight like jewels and as she sits by the fountain a pull-back dolly tracks Charles with greased back hair, in formal evening dress and hand-in-pocket puffing on a cigar as he nonchalantly makes his way around the fountain toward Julia imbued with cool authority. The combination of Jane Robinson's costumes and setting generates a powerfully romantic image of 1930s upper-class sophistication. The reader wallows in this luxurious sophistication and is invited to admire the elegance and style that existed at the high water mark of Empire.

It is clear throughout the production that the narrator Charles sees nothing strange in one family occupying such a sumptuous property attended by an equally vast number of servants. With the exception of Nanny Hawkins, they are located in the background: visually, dramatically and in the narrative. Beneath the chandeliers, amidst the marble halls and amongst the champagne bottles, crystal wine glasses, silver salvers and china tea cups, the servants meekly humble themselves completely to their masters and mistresses, rendering impossible any opportunity for character identification. Wilcox the butler apart, they are rarely given names and audience empathy is not encouraged. This stands in marked opposition to London Weekend's <u>Upstairs Downstairs</u> (1973) which as its title suggested relied heavily on the interplay between servant and master for its plot, dramatic drive and visual representation. This production was less than 10 years earlier and during the welfare capitalist era of consensus politics. The portrayal of the "downstairs" lower orders as developed rounded characters was "a central part of the drama and the narrative and stands in striking contrast to the virtual anonymity of their counterparts in Brideshead.

Comfort and familiarity with exotic locations are prominent in Heritage films as we witness Charles and Sebastian enjoying candle-lit dinners and taking a trip on a gondola in Venice. Many of the key scenes are played against such locations so that, for instance, when Cordelia returns from visiting Sebastian in North Africa and Charles enquires anxiously about his welfare he is standing outside the magnificent maze. Heritage films typically associate exoticism with matters of emotional gravity. Julia breaks down at the Atlas fountain and speaks of fear of eternal damnation. Charles and Sebastian appear to be at their happiest punting in idyllic Oxford and relaxing in romantic Venice. Sebastian ultimately seeks peace and salvation in a remote Tunisian monastery. This suggests a comfortable ability to discourse emotionally in a variety of settings and a class based mastery of the environment.

This provides for a sharp contrast with the use of external settings in the Social Realist films. Here the main characters are only able to find something approaching contentment when safely released from their usual, urban environments. We see Joe Lampton in Room at the Top becoming "true to himself" while enjoying a brief stay at the seaside with Alice. The scene employs a wide-angle lens with naturalistic lighting delivering an impression of a caged animal tasting freedom for the first time. There are romantic allusions as the characters run on the beach oblivious to everything but their apparent happiness. However, the scenes also play with an underlying sense of foreboding. The idyllic iconography of nature: sand, sea and the country cottage are transitory pleasures that will not overcome the inevitable return to the reality. This will destroy the illusion of happiness. Thematically the imagery conveys a sense of temporary release from these harsh urban realities that in turn

CHAPTER V - RECLAIMING NATIONAL IDENTITY

will crush the brief spiritual awakening. This return to an industrial environment is inevitable for Joe Lampton. By contrast, the Heritage film tends to give the impression that the aristocracy are inherently at ease in all environments. This familiarity flows from apparently effortless cultural, social and economic dominance. This comfortable exercise of hierarchy is resonant of the strict social structures found in a society rooted in imperialism.

The first character to suggest that Brideshead was too ostentatious and huge for one family comes in the last of the thirteen episodes from the consciously bourgeois Hooper. His question, although reasonable, is presented as an irreverent act, which inherently fails to respect the natural order of an imperial England that would have featured many such homes. Stylistically and in terms of its narrative emphasis and its settings, the production operates in dominantly heritage terms.

In Brideshead the aristocratic culture can be represented through the "nominally democratic" film and television mediums as conveying a "national cultural heritage". (Roddick, 1982: 59). Furthermore, the contemporary members of the meritocratic and professional classes relished representations of the new consumerist heritage culture of the 1980s through viewing open-air museums, national parks and real country houses. (Corner and Harvey 1991). Viewing Brideshead is rather like having a guided tour around the 18th century Castle Howard but with real actors living the parts. There is some evidence for this in the increased number of visitors to Castle Howard following the series. (Corner and Harvey 1991, Tooke and Baker in *Tourism Management* 1996, vol. 17, Part 2, p.89). In addition, visitor surveys showed that until as recently as May 1994 Brideshead Revisited was still the sole reason why many visitors had initially learned about Castle Howard. (Tooke and Baker 1996: 89). This has similarly been the case in some of the other period properties used in Heritage film making. As Tana Wollen observes:

"The old made visible gives a sign of firm anchorage in enduring values, crucial to a stable sense of identity. Made visible, the old provides a symbolic display of high culture, no matter to the viewer an exact chronology, since the well-worn objects and long-tended gardens of yesteryear lend an educated tone and bespeak discriminating good taste. While these fictions say the past has disappeared their own "quality" rests on the endurance of old values and on their displays of the kind of lifestyles for which all the accoutrements can now be bought. Their production values are as seductive as advertisements and invite the same wealth-taken-for-granted perspective as the Sunday supplements" (Wollen in Corner and Harvey 1991: 185).

It is not difficult to detect reminders of imperialism in the "old values" and "lifestyles" so admired by the 1980s social aspirant and in Brideshead's display of wealthy extravagance, which reflected this desire for socio-economic advancement. "Aloysius bears became popular with city yuppies" and wine bars in the square mile echoed to impersonations of "Sebastian's aristocratic drawl and champagne was more popular than ever" (Wollen in Corner and Harvey 1991: 183). Heritage dramas such as Brideshead gave fuel to the premise that Thatcherite entrepeneurs "could taste the flavour of old-style wealth" and display the metaphorical baubles of Empire without the traditional burdens of *noblesse oblige* or public service (Ibid: 183). Derek Granger, the producer, confidently predicted that the show would attract the "highest proportion of AB viewers ever on TV." The first edition on the 12th October 1981 drew an audience of over twelve and a half million (Granger cited in Corner and Harvey 1991: 192).

Although there does not appear to be any market research examining the social, ethnic and class construction of its audience it seems unlikely that this audience was comprised exclusively of the upper and middle classes. It must therefore be the case, given the huge number of viewers, that as early episodes of Coronation Street attracted cross class admirers, Brideshead's appeal transcended class boundaries. The appeal that this celebration of the trappings of Empire may have for a working class viewer is much harder to determine. The working class characters are located at the margins of the narrative like Nanny Hawkins. Alternatively, they are deferentially serving their masters. The general attitude to the working class is apparent in the scenes depicting the General Strike of 1924. Charles, Sebastian and the Boy Mulcaster man the emergency Fire Engines, literally and metaphorically bulldozing their way through the picket line. The use of a liveried government vehicle denotes some limited authority and the imagery is of an imperial ruling elite suppressing a peasant's revolt.

Although the plight of the Brideshead workers is one of desperation and despair, the scenes employ them merely as extras. They lose the dignity of their struggle as Charles and Sebastian visibly relish the task regarding it as sport. Whilst it might be straightforward for the newly unemployed and economically disenfranchised workers of 1981 to identify with the General Strikers this would hardly encourage identification with the production. If anything, the reader is asked to celebrate and identify with the verve and initiative shown by the central characters in putting down the strike.

Any identification with the production for a working class audience must therefore be rooted at a deeper and more symbolic level. Patrick Wright (1984) and Robert Hewison (1987) have noted frequent references to the country house as a representation of national heritage. They suggest that the inherent "prestige" of such homes and their geographical distribution across the north/south divide contribute to a sense of national identification. (Hewison 1987: 72). David Cannadine, however, gives this idea a slightly different emphasis. He suggests that concepts of a national heritage consist of "little more than a means of preserving the artefacts of an essentially elite culture by claiming in most cases most implausibly that it is everybody's" (Cannadine 1989: 259). This purported inclusiveness seeks to bind together a sense of national identity in much the same way that the Empire sought to simultaneously delineate but also transcend class divisions.

In the production the frequent use of wide angles depicting the house standing proudly in its sweeping grounds and majestic panorama suggest that it commands all in its purview, operating as a kind of national metaphor. The economic and social turmoil of the early 1980s may have created a deeply rooted need for such symbolic reassurance, such a symbol of an imagined or perceived sense of national unity resonating across class barriers. The production evoked a time of certainty and clearly delineated class divisions. The imagery conjures notions of Empire as a unifier and comforter at times of national strife. The working class characters in the production were confined to the dramatic margins but also appear to derive some security and comfort from the very apparatus of class that oppresses them. For instance Nanny Hawkins is quite obviously in retirement by virtue of her age and the complete lack of children in the house. However, she continues to reside with the family. The acceptance of the need to provide for Nanny Hawkins and, one assumes, other senior retainers is consistent with more traditional notions of the one nation Tory philosophy. Thatcherism would have compelled her to make her own provision and the responsibility of the Flyte family would end with her retirement. The life long security Nanny Hawkins enjoys may be her reward for the life long service she has given the family.

Dominating both the production and the novel is a pervasive sense of loss and we are invited to mourn the passing of more ordered, certain and presumably better times. With the notable exception of the scenes depicting the General Strike of 1924 there is an acceptance of this class based society by the characters. The implication is that the feeling of loss is consensual. This is well documented in both narrative and visual terms. The final scenes where Charles in uniform inspects Brideshead now used as a wartime barracks convey his sense of desolation. Rather than sharing the sentiments expressed by Hooper that such an enormous house was somewhat extravagant for one family he seems to regard his fellow Officers and men as barbarians at the gate.

The programme generally conveys Waugh's sense of loss and the entire production is an elegy. All the principal characters suffer loss. The production closes with Charles describing himself as "homeless, childless, middle-aged and loveless". Sebastian has lost his German lover Kurt to the Reich and seems now to be waiting for death. Bridey loses his birthright for marrying Beryl whose name "couldn't be found in Debrett's" and according to Julia was "common". Cordelia "a plain spinster" must lead a single life "full of good works". Julia seems destined to spend the remainder

CHAPTER V - RECLAIMING NATIONAL IDENTITY

of her life struggling with her Catholic guilt and trying to revive her faith in God. The suffering also conveys a degree of inevitability as though the central characters are powerless to prevent their decline. Bridey makes no secret of his disapproval of Charles and Julia living "in sin". It is Bridey who discovers that Rex is divorced and has a wife still living. However when he reveals this news, which devastates his mother Lady Marchmain, his emotional frigidity prevents him from comforting her and he is reduced to gently holding open the door for her as she leaves the room.

Brideshead is a celebration of the class certainties of the pre-war era, a nostalgic evocation of a bourgeois national past indicative of the service orientated Thatcherite heritage industry as a whole during the 1980s. It communicates, both visually and through Charles Ryder, some sense of regret at the passing of such times. In Thatcher's Britain it re-presented and relocated the aristocratic "country house values" of "serenity, family continuity and apparently harmony of environmental and human relationships," within the social anxieties and sentiments of 1980s Britain (Corner and Harvey 1991: 52).

This sense of a declining old world order contrasts with the apparent rise in fortune of the only two characters who may be construed in Thatcherite terms and whose portrayal attracts only limited sympathy. They comprise the lecturer Mr Samgrass and the man who marries Julia, Rex Mottram. Rex is a wealthy self-made businessman who we are led to believe has achieved success by his enterprise and initiative. He is a prominent Minister often heard on the radio attacking Hitler. For all his material and political success however he is described by Julia as being "a little bit of a man".

Mr Samgrass wishes to ingratiate himself with Lady Marchmain and suggests a foreign holiday for educational purposes. They hope that it will prove therapeutic for Sebastian and curb his excessive drinking. On their return Mr Samgrass proudly shows the picture stills he has taken until Cordelia complains that they are nearly all of him. It then transpires that Sebastian made his own Faustian pact with Mr Samgrass by suggesting they split the generous allowance made by Lady Marchmain for the trip.

Sebastian would take half and presumably drink it. Mr Samgrass would retain the remainder and use it to finance his own travels.

The interjection of these self serving and upwardly mobile characters contrasts with the loss of old world values represented by the Flytes. The viewer is able to participate in the sense of loss that follows the decline of these values. The production effectively presents an inherently class structured society sanitised by the removal of any apparent class struggle or serious attempt to challenge this order, and invites the contemporary audience to engage and identify with this dominantly bourgeois analysis of the period. At a practical level this is illustrated by the increased interest in Castle Howard and other similar properties discussed above. Such direct activity coupled with the televised celebration of the period may well stimulate more than mere feelings of loss or a desire to revisit the past. This points the way to a reconstruction of national identity from the class based certainty of former more glorious times. Such reconstruction would however crucially omit any significant reference to class challenges or social unrest. Struggles with conscience increasingly preoccupy the central characters in Brideshead and become more pronounced as the production evolves, adding a liberal humanist veneer to what is essentially celebratory nostalgia.

This partial re-invocation of liberal and humanist ideals within a highly class-conscious society can also be seen at work in Maurice (1987). Andrew Higson (1993) argues that under the guise of nostalgia and heritage, films such as Maurice operate as a safe critique of "contemporary anxieties and fantasies of national identity, sexuality, class and power" (Higson in Friedman 1993: 118). The inclusion of liberal humanist elements to some extent protects the heritage film from complete association with the more iniquitous aspects of the period it celebrates. The essential injustices are held at a safe distance allowing a contemporary audience to safely revisit the past and draw from it themes of national identity for current consumption.

Maurice differs from other heritage films through foregrounding the working class under-gamekeeper Alec Scudder. We witness the public school educated and middle class Maurice Hall engaged in an unsatisfactory affair with suspiciously intellectual and upper class Clive. Eventually Maurice seems to abandon his position of wealth and influence for a committed relationship with Alec suggesting the triumph of liberal humanist values. Yet in common with the heritage film in general the dramatic narrative and the mise-en-scene work against each other. In the opinion of Higson the very strength of the visual splendour freezes the film in time and prevents contemporary discourse. "The pastoral of the films therefore invents a new golden age, one that the novels depict as already tainted and unstable" (Ibid.:122). Forster's social critique of the false imitative values of suburban middle class Englishness therefore become lost in the portrayal of the Edwardian era as "almost involuntarily an object of veneration" (Hollinghurst 1987: 1225).

Higson finds that "the strength of the pastiche ...imprisons the qualities of the past, holding them in place as something to be gazed at from a reverential distance, and refusing the possibility of a dialogue with the present... images of permanence and cultural fluidity, and the ironies of the Forsterian voice" (Higson 1993: 119). Therefore, according to Higson any resonance for a contemporary audience is distanced in time. It becomes embedded in dominantly historic terms thus limiting contemporary discourse. However, it is in my opinion the very fact of the imprisoning that is significant. The historical fantasy performs a particular function in the context of 1980s aspirations. Few members of even the hard right would have wished to re-create the slums, grinding poverty, ill health and early death that was the reality for most of Britain during the Victorian and Edwardian periods. The Empire was sustained through large numbers of workers, in the colonies and in Britain, who were forced to exist on subsistence wages. It is the very "reverential distance" Higson refers to that allows for the pretence and artifice that affected much of 1980s society.

Although the values the reader is asked to recreate are already tarnished and illusory the imperial fantasy is unaffected. The film operates to insert liberal values to eradicate the tarnishing and thus render the period presented an acceptable model for reconstruction by contemporary audiences. This will remain so where the dramatic premise of the film does not suggest egalitarianism. Alec is not intended to be a social equal and on the first occasion when he has sex with Maurice he calls him "Sir". At moments of such intimacy one might not expect to find such barriers but the adherence to social rank and order takes precedence. Hill (1999: 90) finds that "...the film seems uneasy with how to show the physical desires of its characters and invests the earlier scenes of tentative physical contact with much greater charge than the scenes of actual love making". He goes on to find that the "heritage film prefers decorum and restraint to the uninhibited expression of libidinal desires and in a sense upholds the very uprightness against which many of the characters are in protest".

Concerns with liberal humanist values also influenced considerations of culture and high art in the heritage film. Although A Room with a View, (1985) not unusually for a film taken from an E.M. Forster novel, does feature certain moments of homo-eroticism, such as in the bathing sequence involving George, Freddy and the Reverend Beebe it is largely a romantic love story played as light comedy. The film is a poised, gently mocking, affectionate comedy of manners set in photogenic period and geography where the characters are presented with a veneer of affection and light satire through which more important social issues are addressed.

The class distinctions are narrow. The slight disparagement accorded to the Emersons appears to derive not from their lack of wealth but from its genesis in "trade". The Empire was historically closely associated with trade. India was essentially colonised by the East India Company who controlled much of the country before the British Government became formally involved. Accordingly, defence or celebration of Empire must also implicitly defend the mercantile classes. Therefore, in Mr Emerson we can find traces of liberal and humanitarian ideals. He makes a mockery of the comments made by the Reverend "Remember the facts about this church...how it was built by faith in the full fervour of medievalism". Emerson replies by stating "built by faith indeed, it simply means the workers weren't paid properly". There are frequent barbed social references to the Emersons as "these people". Remarks such as these distance the Emersons in the minds of the audience from the Honeychurches who appear to be of a higher social order. This may however have amounted to little more than owning an older house.

This vital distinction between inherited wealth and recently acquired wealth is emphasised. The Emersons appear to have earned their money during the lifetime of Mr Emerson and presumably by "honest endeavour". They are members of the upwardly mobile mercantile middle class of the Edwardian era. Contemporary audiences may well see in the Emersons a reflection or even personification of the aspirant meritocracy championed by Mrs Thatcher and the New Right. Furthermore, since Mr Emerson is evidently invested with liberal humanist qualities, the 1980s spectator may well have perceived this as a cinematic endorsement of the rising meritocracy of the 1980s. Consequently, the narrative may be read as a defence of this contemporary class. Against such an interpretation, we must recall that In "The Challenge of our Time" Forster stresses the Victorian liberal's belief in the values of philanthropy, intellectual curiosity and freedom of speech. Indeed Forster created settings and characters in order to convey his disdain for the upwardly mobile middle class of his day. It is therefore significant that this 1980s version of his novel does not share that view in the case of the Emersons.

The narrative criticism implicit in the novel is set in opposition to the visual celebration of the period. The audience would have noted vivid recreations of the Edwardian décor, the period costumes, the Honeychurch's country mansion and the beautiful sprawling landscapes of rural Surrey and Tuscany. However the mise-en-scene can be deconstructed in a slightly different way. Setting is a means by which film-makers can visually locate crosscurrents between the past and the present. There are connections between the Edwardian era and the Thatcher years in terms of the common presence of ostentatious architecture, decor and clothing. Obsession with appearance and excess constitute the locus of criticism in both periods. However, the Thatcherite distaste for the overtly intellectual is conveyed through the portrayal of the social climbing pretentious and ostentatious Cecil Vyse. Since Cecil displays the vulgar materialism that has been associated with the

Thatcherite new right further ambiguity arises. The film is anxious to distance itself from Cecil who is portrayed in high camp fashion. Although he is manifestly highly 'cultured', he cloaks himself with this to protect him from the vulgarity of the lower orders. His admiration of beauty and fine art leads George to advise Lucy that she should choose him over Cecil because Cecil simply wants to own her "for a possession like a painting or an ivory box. Something to own and display, he doesn't want you to be real and to think and to live, he doesn't love you".

The film does not however reject as invalid a fascination with high art and it is equally anxious to impress upon the audience its own concern with art which it seems to expect to be reciprocated by the audience. The text assumes familiarity with the "Niccola Da Tolentino at the Battle of San Romano" by Paulo Uccello which occupies the entire frame during the sequence at the National Gallery. Furthermore the travelogue-like narrative continuity constantly focuses upon aspects of architectural heritage elements. In Florence there are shots of historical grandeur such as the splendid interior of the Franciscan church of Santa Croce and the equestran statue of Cosimo de Medici by Giambologna. A pull-back dolly reveals Lucy walking across the Piazza della Signoria to expose the period and heritage authenticity. The film's evident concern to articulate its own good taste and desire to establish impeccable cultural credentials obscures the social criticism that Forster, writing in the Edwardian era, wished to make. This is a sentimental recollection of a golden Edwardian era bathed in dappled sunlight. It obscures Forster's inclination for finding solace in Victorian Liberalism.

The 1980s cinematic representation conveys an almost complete inversion of the Emersons from the original Forster novel into the liberal humanists who carry the narrative attack upon vulgarity and crass materialism. Their interest in the arts is a part of their honest vitality. Equally however the viewer may simply see an essentially visual celebration of the "last great age of the English haute bourgeoisie" (Craig 1991: 10). Cairns Craig contends that contemporary relevance is limited: "If these were films whose content was as much today as yesterday, their translation into our

CHAPTER V - RECLAIMING NATIONAL IDENTITY

own time would challenge us with the modernity of issues raised. But they never do..." (Craig in *Sight and Sound* Vol.1, Issue 2, June 1991: 12).

1980s British cinema also witnessed more realist, contemporary productions with contemporary settings making observations about the role class played in topical examinations of national identity. These films did not subscribe to the bourgeois heritage reconstruction. They offered instead a more individual analysis and included a range of differing views. In High Hopes (1988) directed by Mike Leigh the film makes its points about national identification openly and immediately. Leigh uses the patronising and condescending Tory couple who live next door to Cyril's working class mother as poisonous comic figures designed to ridicule Thatcherite social snobbery and gentrification. (Hill 1999). This film sees little common ground between the classes and does not find any actual or reconstructed sense of national unity. Identities are marked in stark and divisive class terms.

The fusion of party politics and national identity would become starker during the 1980s and issues of national identity would become expressed in class terms through certain films and television programmes. Some of these productions echoed the Social Realism films of twenty years before. One of the common features was the tendency to focus upon working class characters set against their urban environment. In High Hopes the working class characters do not engage in traditional, hard manual labour in an industrial town and Cyril works as a motorcycle messenger. However, his low status combined with well paid but dangerous work is reminiscent of some aspects of traditional working class employment. The work is depicted as innately honest and noble and is contrasted with the absurd pretensions of their upwardly mobile neighbours. Comparisons can be made with the landed class in Brideshead. The sympathetic portrayal of the Flytes is contrasted with the depiction of the newly rich and socially aspirant in High Hopes.

The desire to acquire the rituals and ceremonies of style is seen as pretentious and witless. Despite their aspirations Rupert and his wife are compelled to live cheek by jowl with the elderly

Mrs Bender who rents her property. The pursuit of upper class trappings by the middle class can be seen as bourgeois artifice and not the visual representation of recaptured national pride. There is a scene when Latitia asks her neighbour if her house has retained "all its original features". Mrs Bender stares blankly failing to comprehend the significance of the question. The ritualised excess portrayed in <u>Brideshead</u> appeared to have relevance for the characters and was to some extent talismanic. It provided a central core around which their lives revolved. <u>High Hopes</u> compares the arid pursuit of wealth and privilege of the yuppie couple with the dignity and compassion of the neighbouring working class couple. This suggests that the pursuit of wealth and privilege in the 1980s is wholly selfish and the material trappings including "original features" will not recreate the class or style they appear to wish to copy. The aspirant couple in <u>High Hopes</u> are caricatures of pretence and bourgeois artifice whose desire for advancement is coloured by their wish to adopt the mores and mannerisms of an imagined aristocratic past. The fantasy or illusion is presented as of greater substance than the reality. Provided the trappings of aristocracy and Empire are apparent then reality matters little.

Peter Greenaway's <u>The Cook, The Thief, His Wife and Her Lover</u> (1989) is outwardly more politically prescient in its use of allegory to attack the "spirit of the gaudy, yobocratic eighties" (Adair quoted in Hill 1999: 162). Greenaway explained that rampant consumerism was personified by the Thief, Albert Spica who is "a man who is thoroughly despicable in every part of his character. He has no redeeming features and is consumed by self-interest and greed" (Ibid.). However it is this very lack of any redeeming feature that tends to support John Hill when he argues that "the anti-Thatcherite allegory only stretches so far". He goes on to assert that "the condensation of the various forces at work in Thatcherism into the monstrous figure of Spica offers a relatively crude reduction of Thatcherism to naked appetite" (Hill 1999: 163).

The film draws stark comparisons between the unvarnished vulgarity of the thief with the cultural interests of the lover, the commitment of the cook and the more spiritual desires of the wife.

CHAPTER V - RECLAIMING NATIONAL IDENTITY

The criticism of the Thatcherite 1980s therefore becomes similar to High Hopes in terms of taste and cultural credentials. (Hill 1999: 163). Richard Dyer suggests "one response to Thatcherism was to identify it with the rise of a newly affluent working class steeped in neither the middle class sense of public service or the older Tory *noblesse oblige*" (Dyer 1997: 196). This, by implication acknowledges the reduction or even extinction of the traditional working class. What is apparent from The Cook and also High Hopes is the lack of any realistic, optimistic or practical solution to the vulgarity and degraded ethics that the films suggest occupies the core of Thatcherism. It is virtually impossible to infer any social vision that will successfully challenge or simply contain the rise of the rampant consumerism and greed deplored by these films.

This provides for a limited comparison with the Social Realist films. Most of the influential Realist films including Room at the Top and Saturday Night Sunday Morning and A Kind of Loving charted the rise of consumerism and the deterioration of traditional working class values. One calls to mind the Rothwell women in A Kind of Loving. The films also depicted the sense of frustration felt by the protagonists. Shown to be trapped in their essentially urban industrialised environments they were not offered an escape and for Arthur Seaton and Vic Brown no realistic alternative life styles were proposed. Joe Lampton was seen to escape his working class background but at the costs of personal happiness and self worth. In The Cook we see the eponymous chef frustrated that he is not properly valued as an "artist" and whose "good food" is largely unnoticed. Georgina feels suffocated by "the big house" she lives in and derives little comfort from the "beautiful things" her husband buys for her (Hill 1999: 163). Although both characters retaliate towards the end of the production, the "spider woman imagery" undermines the impact. (Ibid: 165). Furthermore, no alternative mode of existence or social framework is offered.

The Cook and High Hopes both depict the ravages of unchecked consumer driven avarice and the cultural barbarism of Thatcherism. The Cook is so preoccupied with charting this "cultural vandalism" that it seems unwilling or unable to contemplate a restoration of the values it promotes (Hill 1999: 163). This contrasts with the reconstruction found in the heritage film. The inclusion of high art and impeccable cultural credentials were of particular significance in A Room with a View. Cultural references permeate most of the influential heritage productions suggesting the importance and relevance of culture to any reconstructed sense of national identity.

Britannia Hospital (1982) took an even bleaker, almost apocalyptic view of contemporary society depicting a complete disintegration of any notion of a national community and any shared sense of identity. The director Lindsay Anderson began his film career in 1957 with Every Day Except Christmas which set out to explore the values of community and kinship amongst the working class in post war Britain. In Britannia Hospital he finds these mutual national values replaced by animosity, self interest and chaos. Little moral distinction is made between the various classes and social groupings. Management and workforce alike are seen as venal, anarchic and utterly self serving.

Staff at the hospital are callous and indifferent, drinking tea and playing cards while patients die. Telephones fail, bombs explode and bodies appear. The focus of its scathing satire is all encompassing and as Andrew Sarris notes there is "no one to root for and not much hope" (1983: 41). The film can be viewed in right wing terms portraying intransigent unions and industrial chaos. Equally forceful is its attack upon managerial failings in the face of such workers' power which panders further to right-wing discontent concerning the politics of "consensus" – despised by Thatcher (Hill 1999: 141).

The degree of despair that pervades the film and the absence of any alternative social or economic solution leads to an ideological vacuum which by definition creates the need for a new ideology. In 1982 Mrs Thatcher and the New Right were on hand to offer policy solutions for all of society's perceived ills. Britannia Hospital can be read in Thatcherite terms. The film may be seen as a depiction of the complete dissolution of any sense of national community but also an attack upon the consensual values and politics that had presided over such a collapse of communality.

Writing about <u>The Cook, The Thief, His Wife and Her Lover</u> John Hill found that in attacking Thatcherism the "state of the nation" film remains "locked within the discourse (they) opposed, unable to give convincing voice to an alternative social imaginary". (Hill 1999: 164). This failure of these films to present a new social vision would perhaps allow the heritage film greater scope for presenting its reconstructed version of a national past as a model for contemporary consumption. Compared to the bleakness, decay and hopelessness of national disorder offered by <u>Britannia Hospital</u> the heritage model would become rather more reassuring to 1980s audiences.

5.3 Morality

Politicians usually approach issues of morality with caution. This reluctance stems from fear of exposure as hypocrites and from a simple unwillingness to interfere with religious doctrine, which has traditionally been the fountain of guidance for issues of morality. The 1980s differed in having a Prime Minister committed to incorporating themes of morality into politics. She even sought to specify the precise version of morality that she felt most aligned with, that of the Victorian era, and tried to lead both the nation and its morality away from excessive social liberalism. This permissiveness had, in her opinion, tainted the two preceding decades. She attributed much of this apparent decay and sapping of the national moral fibre to the Labour made or Labour sponsored legislation of the 1960s. Her beliefs were deeply rooted and propounded with total conviction allowing no room for doubt or debate. Complex ethical issues became matters of simple moral certainty.

Thus, according to Mrs Thatcher, the increase in crime could be laid at the door of Sydney Silverman and his Bill to abolish hanging in the mid 1960s. She deplored what she considered contemporary sexual recklessness and its consequent explosion in the numbers of single parent families. This and the spread of sexually transmitted diseases owed much to the increased availability of contraception and later abortion legislation in 1967. The relentless rise in divorce began, according to the modern forces of conservatism, with the reforming legislation of 1969. This consensual, social legislation did not find favour with Mrs Thatcher. Her core values embraced an unshakeable belief in the power of the individual and in the inalienable right of the individual to pursue personal goals with scant regard for considerations of consensus. Conduct that might otherwise appear selfish became morally justified individualism. Individual aspiration became closely associated with notions of excellence initiative and enterprise. Mrs Thatcher consistently lauded these attributes throughout the 1980s.

Issues of morality have been prevalent features in films since the very inception of cinema and the changing state of cinematic morality operates as a periodic barometer of national consciousness. The heritage film in particular re-packaged and re-presented the past with relevance for the contemporary and gave representation to some aspects of the Thatcher creed which I shall seek to demonstrate in this subsection. I will discuss the moral justification of the pursuit of individual glory as depicted in <u>Chariots of Fire</u> (1981). This promotion of the supremacy of the individual implicitly suggested a rejection of more traditional and consensus sources of strength and in particular organised orthodox religion. As the 1980s became increasingly a decade of material and social aspiration traditionally ordered religion and theology decreased in importance. This reduction finds representation in <u>Brideshead Revisited</u> 1981, which I analyse in some detail below. First broadcast in 1981 it appeared on national television during the early years of a Thatcher government which propounded the service of self interests which stands in opposition to traditional religious notions of self sacrifice. A strong theme of Thatcherism was self reliance and the avoidance of dependence. Most if not all recognised form of theological worship contain at their core notions of faith and surrender. The individual places his trust in his perception of God or higher power and accepts that there are certain matters beyond his control.

Such acceptance and surrender does not easily comply with the central tenets of Thatcherism and its gospels of initiative and individual self-reliance. <u>Brideshead</u> depicts the increasing impotence of traditional religion at a time of emergent celebrations of self. Similarly a postulation of the personal must also implicitly reject or diminish notions of liberalism and humanism. They too contain at their core ethical constraints, which urge a restriction of the personal in favour of the greater or common good, and do not co-exist with Thatcherite notions of individualism.

I discuss at some lengths the 'Raj' productions of <u>A Passage To India</u> and <u>Jewel In The Crown</u> in this context. I suggest that these artefacts function in such a way as to proffer the social values of liberalism and humanism. These ethical values are considered within an overall framework that is essentially imperialist and are used to distract attention from some of the more overtly unjust consequences of imperialism. They are however, ultimately seen as values that are ineffective, archaic and with little relevance for contemporary society. The political centre of the 1980s was occupied by the 'new right', which displayed little enthusiasm for traditional middle class values of duty and public service. In the new imperialist society of the 1980s there would be little credit attaching to such outmoded ideals.

<u>Chariots of Fire (1981)</u> is an early and highly influential heritage film which takes as its narrative core matters of moral certainty. It focuses upon the striving of its twin central characters Harold Abrahams and Eric Liddell for success at the 1924 Olympic Games. Based loosely upon their real lives it shows their progress from local heroes to international achievement as gold medallists in their respective disciplines. At the core of the film is their desire to win. Abrahams tells the college master he wants to win for "my family, my college and my country". However, a further dynamic of the film is their apparent will to win for their respective faiths. Liddell tells his sister "God has made me fast Jenny and when I run I feel his pleasure". Abrahams, the son of a Lithuanian Jew, sees a Christian England with Anglo Saxon "corridors of power" guarded with "jealousy and venom". He proposes to "take them on, all of them one by one" and to "run them off their feet".

As a Jew and a China born Scot Abrahams and Liddell represent outsiders in 1920s English society. This distancing in ethnic, nationalist, religious and class terms contrasts with the aristocratic amateur Lord Lindsay. This character is founded loosely on the real life Lord Burleigh and seems to run purely for pleasure. There is no sense of moral purpose or deeply held religious conviction in Lindsay and he runs because he enjoys it and because he too is good. In the production, he appears as the consensual character content to occupy the moral middle ground. In reality it was Burleigh and not Abrahams who successfully completed the first "college dash" but significantly the film shows him being narrowly beaten by Abrahams. The real Abrahams did not compete.

Liddell refuses to race on a Sunday, because of his religious beliefs, and the combined efforts of the Prince of Wales and the high powered Olympic Committee fails to persuade him otherwise. However Lord Lindsay saves the day with a true gesture of *noblesse oblige* – Liddell could take his place in the 400 metres run on a weekday. This appears to be a grand aristocratic gesture possibly motivated by Old World paternalism. The motive is not an overwhelming desire to win or a moral compulsion and this relative lack of ambition stands in some contrast with Abrahams and Liddell.

To create this specific structuring of moral relationships it was necessary to separate and reduce the relatively unimportant character of Lord Lindsay by giving him the minor medal. This emphasises the success of the comparatively unprivileged Abrahams and Liddell. The spectator may find that Lindsay lost because he lacked the spirit, conviction and drive present only in the morally certain and ideologically pure, a view which resonated with contemporary Thatcherite beliefs. Eric Liddell's Minister and religious overseer tells him that it is his sacred duty to put his many gifts to good use "Eric you can praise the Lord by peeling a spud, if you peel it to perfection. Don't compromise, compromise is the language of the devil. Run in God's name and let the world stand in wonder." In terms of an absolute refusal to compromise, this was fundamental to Thatcherite philosophy.

Liddell's commitment is never questioned or threatened in the production and echoes the refusal of the contemporary New Right to question its own particular moral certainties. He is prepared to defy the entire British establishment including the Prince of Wales in his refusal to compromise and run on "the Sabbath". His personal desire to run ranked a clear second to his religious convictions. He remembers gently admonishing two young boys for playing football on "the Sabbath day". In a memorable scene, he addresses a small rain drenched group of spectators who stay behind after one of his races to hear him speak. He has won and wonders where the power to "win the race" comes from. He tells his listeners that it "comes from within". He then symbolically strikes his heart and as he does so the sun slowly appears underlining the essential truth of his beliefs. A contemporary reader may have found echoes of Thatcherism in this scene. Not in the fundamentalism of the religion but because she often spoke of the primacy of the individual and of Victorian values of self-reliance and initiative. Indeed simple moral certainty which in this case is present in an enterprising individual will provide an unbeatable force and sweep all before it.

However he also needs the support of his various Church Missions and asks his sister to look after the small Highlands Mission while he concentrates on his athletics. He then tells her that he believes God has made him for China and, we assume, a missionary. Despite this apparent concern for God and the mission, the building itself is rarely fore-grounded in the film. In one scene it appears virtually deserted and neglected. The only significant narrative reference to China is in the postscript which tells us only that he had died there. In this way the film privileges the authority of the individual over more organised forms of religious expression. The frequent references to faith and traditional and almost consciously old fashioned worship may reflect efforts to insert liberal humanist values into this otherwise driven and somewhat self centred individual. He is so concerned with his own agenda that he will disregard a personal request from his future King. This is justified in the narrative in terms of moral or religious faith rather than the act of selfishness it might otherwise appear to be.

This emphasis on individual achievement forms the narrative core of the film. British imperial heritage relies heavily upon stirring tales of individuals, Clive in India, Rhodes in South Africa and Captain Cook in Australia. The ethical simplicity of Liddell and Abrahams recalls the moral certainty driving the builders of the Empire and implicitly credits imperialism with a moral component. Although Abrahams wants to run "Christian England" off its feet and thus elevate his Jewish faith his apparently ardent Jewishness somehow fails to convince. When first entertaining Sybil he lectures her at length about the hardships of being a Jew and then after initial hesitation proceeds to eat the pigs trotters he has ordered amid scenes of genial hilarity. A refusal to eat pork is usually considered a central tenet of the Jewish faith yet Abrahams is able to transform it into a joke. He complains of suffering at the hands of Christians but it is difficult to detect any real evidence of this.

The only discrimination Abrahams seems to suffer is minor. Carter feels it amounts to little more than "the wry condescension of a couple of ageing dons" (Ibid: 14). Abrahams appears rich and can afford his own coach. He seems to have many friends. There is no suggestion that his selection for the British Olympic team would be at risk. He has "set up shop in one of the finest Universities in the land". He is an active member of the Gilbert and Sullivan Society and even held a commission in the Kings Army. Religion apart, he is virtually a complete member of the establishment that he seeks to "run off their feet". It is difficult to perceive his religious suffering as significantly more than a dramatic device employed to justify his unwavering ambition. The character wears his Jewish identity as a shield and his imagined oppression is a convenient moral Trojan horse hiding his vaulting ambition. He justifies his pursuit of personal advancement by invoking the imagined defence of his faith.

The strength Abrahams derives from his convictions enables him to challenge directly the prevailing ethos of his own University. As they entertain him to dinner, the Masters of Trinity and Caius reminds Abrahams that Cambridge games "create character, foster courage, honesty and leadership but most of all an unassailable spirit of loyalty, comradeship and mutual responsibility." Loyalty and mutual responsibility imply compromise, team spirit and the general subordination of personal ambition to the common objective. This was counter-Thatcherism and not noticeably prominent

CHAPTER V - RECLAIMING NATIONAL IDENTITY

in the production's interpretation of Harold Abrahams. The Master told him: "You are the elite and therefore expected to behave as such; your approach is a little too plebeian."

Abrahams would have none of this and in his view, their outlook was archaic. He tells them forcefully: "You yearn for victory just as I do but achieved with the apparent effortlessness of the Gods. Yours are the values of the prep school playground. I believe in the pursuit of excellence and I'll carry the future with me". He arrogantly tramples over any Corinthian traditions still prevailing at a 1920s Cambridge. He has little patience with those who would deny him victory or restrict the means of achieving such victory. There can be little doubt of his utter determination to win. When he meets his future coach Massabini he tells him directly "I want that Olympic medal but can't get it on my own". As a professional and a member of an ethnic minority, Italian-Arab Massabini is also visibly an outsider. Although Massabini feels that as the coach he "does the asking" Abrahams is not discouraged from asking. Eventually believing he can give him "an extra two yards", Massabini agrees to work for Abrahams in flagrant disregard of any amateur code of ethics. The phrase "pursuit of excellence" used by Abrahams seems oddly out of place in an upper class 1920s Britain and has a much greater 1980s resonance amidst the growing Thatcherite philosophy of free enterprise.

According to Carter this ruthless pursuit can be detected in both of the main characters. Abrahams' adopts a "professional attitude" in developing his running technique alone. He isolates himself from Sybil and his friends. He studies closely newsreel footage of his main rivals Paddock and Schultz from the U.S.A. and of course Eric Liddell. These scenes recognise the increasing importance internationally of the U.S.A and acknowledge the shifting relationship between the two nations. Later Abrahams is deeply melancholic and seethes with bitterness after losing to Liddell. With similar determination, we witness Liddell pounding over rugged highlands and energy sapping sand as he hands over the running of the mission to his sister Jenny so he can focus on his race. There is his astonishing "back from the brink" victory against the French resulting in a near seizure as he is carried from the track. His health may also be secondary to the pursuit of glory. Both men have a personal trainer distancing them from the other British runners. Both appear to possess a "win at all costs" attitude. (Carter 1982: 14-16).

This self-interest resonates with a Thatcherite morality and the justification she found within the culture of enterprise. A central tenet of the Thatcherite belief system is that riches and success earned are a just reward for enterprise, endeavour, initiative and above all merit. Abrahams and Liddell are depicted clearly earning their gold medals. These industrious efforts on the part of Liddell and Abrahams contrast sharply with the languid Lord Lindsay. Memorably we see Lindsay train by hurtling over hurdles bearing a full champagne glass placed carefully on each by his Butler. This sweeping pan shot also encompasses his magnificent country estate and tells us immediately that Lindsay is both rich and eccentric. Since Lindsay will presumably drink the champagne after training his slightly hedonistic lifestyle is distanced from the Spartan and abstemious regime adopted by Abrahams and Liddell.

A less marked thematic strand of the film is the subtle undermining of liberal humanist values particularly in the narrative. Early in the film, the Master of Caius addresses the freshmen talking about former students slaughtered only months before in the Great War. He urges his audience to take up their hopes

"and now by tragic necessity their dreams have become yours. Let me exalt you: examine yourselves, let each of you discover where your true chance of greatness lies. For their sakes, for the sake of your college and your country seize this chance, rejoice in it and let no power or persuasion deter you in your task".

This eloquent plea is coloured by the traditional liberalism of personal sacrifice for the greater good, in this case of College and country. It says nothing about the greater glory of the individual. In the only scene where Abrahams expresses any doubts about the sanctity of his mission he states that Aubrey has "secret contentment" deriving from his bravery, kindness and compassion and that this makes Aubrey his "most complete man". Aubrey is ready to "burst his heart" for England but he is never a front runner in the film, literally, metaphorically or dramatically. By distancing him from the core of the film's narrative the Old World liberal values he seems to represent are somehow diminished and rendered impotent. He seems to be not so much contented but limp, ineffectual and weak. He stands in some contrast to the vital, vigorous and virile figure of Abrahams who promises to "take the future" with him. This future will include the ambition and perceived moral certainties of Empire but carefully adapted to allow for the changes imposed by modernity.

The scene showing Liddell standing up to the British Olympic Committee and the Prince of Wales reduces the very values he espouses. The Duke of Sutherland tells Lord Birkenhead that Liddell is "a true man of principle and a true athlete. His speed is a mere extension of his life, its force. We sought to sever his running from himself. For his country's sake. No sake is worth that Effe, least of all a guilty national pride". This recognition of Liddell's "life force" and the acknowledgement of its significance is made when the problem has been safely and neatly resolved by Lindsay's sacrifice. The direct conflict between principle and politics is removed at the point of impact. This compromise becomes possible only because Lindsay in an act of *noblesse oblige* gives up his place for Liddell in matters of athletics as he did for Abrahams and the affections of Sybil in matters of love (Carter 1982: 16). Liddell is therefore able to avoid any conflict between his religious views and his earthly ambitions thanks to Lord Lindsay.

In invoking British history, the heritage film paid considerable attention to the recently surrendered Empire and in particular to India, its most glittering possession. The subjugation of a subcontinent is a topic that is almost impossible to address without some consideration of ethics and ethnicity. A Passage to India (1984) adapted a 1920s Forster novel with a period setting. The sun had yet to set upon the Empire and the shadows of post war partition had not yet disfigured India. Dyer, writing in 1993, considered the production primarily liberal in orientation and welcome for it. In the face of Thatcherism and the nation's political shift to the right he felt that the left should no longer regard liberalism as something to "condemn out of hand as weak, equivocating, untheorised, unmaterialist and of course bourgeois" (Dyer, 1993: 137). He felt that the left "needed all the liberals they could get".

This view is not however shared by Higson who saw in the Heritage Film in general, and A Passage to India in particular, "the ambivalence of nostalgia". Higson (1993: 124). He described it as an "imperialist fantasy of national identity" and

"a conservative response to a collective, post imperialist anxiety. Retreating from the social, political and economic crises of the present, it strives to recapture an image of national identity as pure, untainted, complete and in place."

It charted "the corrupt and decadent last days of imperialist power, a period when that power was already coming under attack, the pure identity becoming tainted and the culture in decline" (Ibid). This return to an imperial past allowed for a reconstruction of a time of social clarity and apparent moral certainty. Definitions of identity are sharper and less problematic when rooted in a clear hegemonic structure and would have had greater appeal at a time of social disorder and class confusion.

Therefore, for Higson, the thematic impact lies in the "decay" and destruction corroding an imperfect society such as the Raj. A society wishing to retain a clear and unambiguous identity must guard against such infiltration from impure agents of corruption. This film was made just 3 years after the notorious Nationality Act of 1981 had abolished the centuries old law granting British citizenship as a right of birth. In one of her early speeches, Mrs Thatcher warned of a Britain "swamped" by immigrants who would presumably poison the well of pure nationalism. There existed at this time a marked political inclination to seek out a return to the recent familiarity and superiority of Empire. Didactically one can detect an intention to adapt this as a template for a contemporary society but suitably modified by the removal of the more unacceptable aspects.

In any search for evidence of the liberal humanist values Dyer claims for A Passage to India the viewer would have to consider the sympathetic white liberal characters portrayed in the film. Essentially, there are three; the women Mrs Moore, Adela and the teacher Fielding. Liberal values appear to be most deeply rooted in

CHAPTER V - RECLAIMING NATIONAL IDENTITY

Fielding. When told by Turton that he "cannot run with the hare and hunt with the hounds" he resigns from the Club and by symbolic implication severs his association with the Raj. Turton has no doubt that the races must be segregated observing that "I've had 25 years experience of this country and I've never known but disaster result when English and Indians attempt to be intimate." This reminds one of Mrs Turton's earlier remark to Mrs Moore, claiming that the reason the British and the Indians don't socialise is because "East is East Mrs Moore, it's a question of culture."

Fielding states openly his willingness to sacrifice his position and leave India, if Aziz is convicted of raping Adela. Yet Fielding's motives are never entirely clear. Fielding marries at the end of the film and Aziz talks fondly of his dead wife. Both men would therefore appear to be heterosexual. However most of the action takes place after Aziz has been widowed and before Fielding meets his wife and consequently the emotional interplay is between two single men. There are strong homo-erotic currents running through their relationship. When they meet Fielding is naked behind the glass wall of his shower. Later Fielding visits the sick Aziz and puts him to bed. In one of the closing scenes Fielding visits Aziz who applies eye make up almost as though he were a young girl making herself pretty for a visit from her older man friend. As Higson notes throughout the Heritage Films "...there is a continual insistence on the pleasures of the male body" (Higson 1993: 125). The reader may speculate that the true basis of the friendship between Aziz and Fielding was rooted in frustrated homosexual desire at least on the part of Fielding thus providing his true motive. In short the apparent liberal motives imputed to Fielding may have been at least partly fraudulent, a mask for his homosexual feelings for Aziz. The uncertainty attaching to his motives tend to undermine the liberal credentials of the production.

Fielding's threat to leave India suggests that he was also placing at risk the welfare of the students of his College. This conflicts with the sense of public duty traditionally associated with liberalism and middle class perceptions of national identity. A willingness to promote personal or individual happiness at the expense of any perceived public or social responsibility was consistent with the emphasis upon the individual placed by Mrs Thatcher. It was not consistent with the notions of "self sacrifice, restraint, duty and the stiff upper lip"... identified by Richards (1997: 169) as formerly a key element in national character. If the interest shown by Fielding in Aziz is perhaps in part romantic this would equate to a pursuit of "personal happiness" thereby tainting with selfishness the purity of any liberal humanist values attributed to Fielding.

Adela makes the rape accusation which forces Aziz to trial but withdraws these at the last moment, freeing Aziz. She is aware she will be banished from the Raj and compelled to return to England. This may also appear to be an example of liberal self sacrifice. However, Aziz is not actually acquitted after trial. Pym (1985: 101) felt that in the novel Forster left the matter "tantalisingly open," and Dyer believes that Aziz "may indeed have made love to Adela" but with her consent (1993: 138). If Adela did willingly make love to Aziz, as the film permits us to infer, she may have concocted the allegation from fear, shame and regret. Her last minute retraction would save her character from complete hypocrisy and humiliation. The invention of such a serious allegation however would substantially impugn her liberal status. If she chose to have sex with Aziz she too may have been attempting to pursue personal happiness.

These characters function as a concession to a guilty white nationalism softening the blunter edges of colonialism and helping the contemporary spectator to distance himself from the excesses of the Raj. This reduction of the harsher realities of Empire allows a contemporary reconstruction of imperialism as a base for national identity. The liberal views expressed are limited to questioning colonial treatment of the subjected Indian people. At no point do they challenge the ethics of colonialism and question the fundamental occupation of another country. They accept the imperial presence in much the same manner as Turton. The liberalism is confined to the treatment of individual Indians who by virtue of this individual attention are privileged. There is no examination of the more fundamental moral question about imperialism and therefore effectively diminished resistance to an imaginary recreation.

Furthermore, within so many of the Heritage films, political critique flounders in the face of stunning visual celebration of the very object of the criticism. The narrative intent of the grand garden party scene is presumably to criticise the patronising and dismissive way that the ruling white elite treated the locals. We see the Indians either ignored or humoured like animals in a zoo with their sole purpose to provide amusement for their white captors. The incongruity of an Indian brass band struggling to play "Tea for Two" a quintessentially English popular song of the 1920s does not offend the liberal sensibilities. They struggle with the splendour of the official residence and the glories of an Indian Summer. The refined gentility distracts and seduces the viewer, softening the narrative edge the scene might otherwise possess.

India also formed the setting for a major "quality" television production made a year earlier and which may be included in the heritage cycle; Jewel in the Crown. (1983). Based on the Paul Scott novels known as "The Raj Quartet" Jewel in the Crown is set in 1942. The production finds imperial power threatened from the "enemy within" in the form of increasingly vocal demands for Indian independence. Furthermore, an alien imperialist, Japan, whose armed forces were approaching the East Indian frontiers, also endangers the Raj.

In common with A Passage to India the production foregrounds white women characters. During the opening ten episodes Daphne Manners and Sarah Layton provide the characters and unfolding events with a sense of perspective. The central authority figure however, Ronald Merrick is male and capable of ambiguous interpretation. He is a racist and ambitious policeman who is dismissive of liberalism. He brutally rapes and tortures Hari Kumar. Merrick is lower middle-class grammar school and consequently different from the aristocratic memsahibs. He has risen through Police ranks by merit and effort and in this sense may be construed as the production's only Thatcherite figure. Class origins distance him from the other white characters. They consider him "not quite our sort". Merrick's unsympathetic portrayal constitutes a veiled attack on Thatcherism.

Indian born Kumar has received a classical English education and is a man trapped in a cultural void. Birth and ethnicity prevent him from being truly "English" but his unmistakeable English accent and education keep him equally distant from his fellow Indians. Jealousy aggravates the hostility between Kumar and Merrick when it becomes clear that both display a romantic and sexual interest in Daphne Manners. Their clash brings into sharper focus the general breakdown into disorder across the Raj. In Chariots of Fire there is a perceived clarity of moral objective, which provides the dynamic driving the production and contrasts significantly with Jewel in the Crown which represents moral lethargy and impotence coupled with strong symbolic images of powerlessness. Daphne and Sarah through an enquiring conscience identified as "traditionally feminine" are the fiercest critics of the Raj. (Hill 1999: 110). Yet this is noticeably limited to the treatment of individual Indians and does not challenge the fundamental precept of imperialism any more than A Passage to India. Their concern is with conventions of colonial dominance rather than its central moral premise. The liberal humanist edge blunts at the point of impact and there is no polemic or critique of the fundamental concept of imperialism. In a manner similar to a Passage to India the effect is to privilege an imaginary version of imperialism as a desired foundation for national identity.

There are liberal humanist alliances through interracial sexual relationships between Daphne and Hari and the attempts by Sarah to liase with Ahmed. These may represent the coming together of two nations as equals. There are also suggestions made by the ambiguous relationship between Aziz and Adela. John Hill sees these as a "sexual metaphor" representing relations between the cultures of "East and West". (1999: 110). Yet any moral force is almost at once diluted if not destroyed when Merrick rapes Hari and Daphne's death renders her powerless to help Hari. Dyer (1997) suggested British women such as Daphne Manners and Sarah Layton accomplished enough to undermine the Empire by their mere existence.

"The British withdrew because they have failed and they have failed because of their women, who have weakened the fabric

CHAPTER V - RECLAIMING NATIONAL IDENTITY

of empire with both their sexuality and their questioning of the enterprise. They may not have caused the evils of India but they are the reason why the British can no longer keep the lid on the box...those who try to do something fail, go mad or create havoc" (Dyer 1997: 199).

Both Jewel in the Crown and A Passage to India allow the reader to impute broadly liberal humanist values to the central white Englishwomen. If his analysis is correct Dyer appears to be postulating a subtler and almost subversive, function for these values. He suggests that by simply questioning the enterprise they may fatally undermine its moral foundation and accelerate it's demise. This may overstate the case. In Jewel in the Crown the repetition of the "white women's mantra," "there's nothing I can do" is a genuine expression of impotence. (Dyer 1997: 187). These restrictions appear to lead to disaster for the characters. Daphne Manners in Jewel in the Crown and Mrs Moore in A Passage to India die before they are able to assist their Indian men friends. Barbie Bachelor and Susan Layton each suffer a nervous breakdown in Jewel in the Crown and in A Passage to India Adela suffers ostracism and possible rape.

These characters do not succeed in affecting any significant positive change in their environments. The advocates of moral certainty may consider them to have insufficient moral force. Their suffering may have appeared to a contemporary audience as a form of liberal self-sacrifice. The party political extremism of the early 1980s coupled with the destruction of a more consensual society created a climate in which many, traditionally liberal may have experienced some level of moral anguish and frustration. Like the women in Jewel in the Crown they too may have felt "there's nothing I can do". These liberal influences would help to distance contemporary audiences from the more brutal excesses of the Raj. This would ease acceptance of a revisited or reconstructed version of an imperial past as a valid element in modern national identity.

5.4 Englishness, Nationalism and the Imperial Heritage

> "The Stock Exchange will be pulled down, the horse plough will give way to the tractor, the country houses will be turned into children's holiday camps, the Eton and Harrow match will be forgotten, but England will still be England, an everlasting animal stretching into the future and the past, and, like all living things, having the power to change out of recognition and yet remain the same" (George Orwell cited in Auty and Roddick 1984: 104).

Orwell clearly considered Englishness constant, capable of adapting to extraneous political changes, but essentially an "everlasting animal". He wrote at the high watermark of imperialism when Empire appeared unassailable. By the 1980s, England and Britain had changed "out of recognition". Also by the 1980s Britain had as Prime Minister a politician who made little secret of her wish to restore some of this imperial lustre to a Britain apparently weary and terminally on the wane. This subsection will examine the cinematic voices of this period including those for and against the Thatcherite project to reconstruct a distinctive English identity. This project was inherently rooted in the kind of moral values discussed above which promoted jingoistic nationalism and a celebration of the apparent and real imperial heritage.

Whatever opinion one may have of Mrs Thatcher and her tenure in office there can be little doubt that she "captured the public imagination as no other British politician has since Winston Churchill". (Friedman 1993: xiv). She frequently cited Churchill, and by referring to him as "Winston" with vulgar familiarity sought to imply personal friendship and mutual political beliefs. The comparison Friedman makes would almost certainly have received her approval. He also states that British cinema has "excited little scholarly and commercial interest over the years except for the brief flurry of attention during the late Fifties and early Sixties, the so called Free Cinema movement" (Ibid. 1993: xii). He further finds that this "was not the case with British film

CHAPTER V - RECLAIMING NATIONAL IDENTITY

during the Thatcher era. On a commercial level both <u>Chariots of Fire</u> and <u>Ghandi</u> swept the Oscar competition". (Ibid. 1993:xii). He then refers to the now famous outburst of braggadocio from Colin Welland, the screenwriter of <u>Chariots of Fire</u>, "The British are coming" (Ibid. 1993:xii). Such nationalist fervour seems a little ironic coming as it does from an essentially left wing iconoclast from the 1960s. Hailing a successful new Oscar winning film as the "saviour of the British film industry" is of course nothing new and has been happening at regular intervals. In particular since Alexander Korda "saved" British cinema with his production of <u>The Private Life of Henry VIII</u> in 1933.

Where the 1980s differed was in the extent to which Mrs Thatcher's vision of a renewed national pride informed and challenged contemporary cinema. Speaking in Cheltenham in 1982 she told her audience of supporters that "the people who thought that Britain was no longer the nation that had built an Empire and ruled a quarter of the world. Well they were wrong" (Rushdie 1991: 131). This speech immediately followed the triumphant ending of the Falklands War and was delivered whilst the Oscar winning <u>Chariots of Fire</u> was playing nationally. The film presents, in united triumph, the athletes Eric Liddell, Harold Abrahams and Lord Lindsay: a China born Scot, a Jew of Lithuanian extraction and an English aristocrat. Made at a time of accelerating decline of traditional manufacturing in the industrial working class heartlands of the North, Scotland and Wales the early 1980s also saw a greater concentration of wealth in the South East. A Scot, Jew and an English aristocrat all competing under the same flag conjures up an imagined community comprising diverse ethnic elements which made for a somewhat contrived, if unified, image of national identity. This celluloid healing of cultural divisions appeared when brooding class and racial differences were leading to mass demonstrations and inner city rioting.

The timing was fortuitous. The Cold War had warmed up following the Soviet invasion of Afghanistan and taking their lead from the U.S.A some nations boycotted the 1980 Olympic Games in Moscow. Anxious to maintain the "special relationship" with the Americans at all times Mrs Thatcher pressed the British

Olympic organisation to follow suit but the issue was compromised. The British athletes would compete but as individuals and without any overt display of "guilty national pride". It would prove strangely fitting that the prestigious 100 metres sprint title, so prominent in <u>Chariots of Fire</u> was awarded to a British athlete for the first time since Abrahams. The winner would prove to be the Scot Alan Wells.

The film received a general release very shortly before the outbreak of the Falklands War in 1982. One may detect in the scenes showing the Olympic squad setting sail for Paris an invocation of the Dunkirk spirit. It was possible to compare these scenes with the sight of troops setting off for the Falklands accompanied by tearful goodbyes from the dockside crowds and the dramatic shots of the white cliffs of Dover. This also finds expression in Aubrey's nationalist sentiments in a letter to his family: "We're here for Britain and we know it. There's not a chap amongst us who isn't willing to burst his heart for all we've left behind."

Traditionally of course, pro-British sentiments have depended on antagonism from a variety of "foreigners", and there are numerous instances in the film. When Lord Birkenhead talks to Liddell in private about the Scotsman's reluctance to race on a Sunday he says that the French "do owe us something. They're not a very principled lot the frogs but when faced with a stand like yours I might get through". Such xenophobic rhetoric was in tune with Thatcherite opposition to the federalist aspirations of the EEC and the prospect of higher spending on a closer European political and economic union. She insisted that Britain receive its full budget rebate and this stand helped to ensure that future relations and negotiations between Britain and some of its European partners would be fraught with suspicion.

Later during Liddell's meeting with the Olympic Committee in Paris, Francophobia is again prevalent. Britain cannot possibly go "cap in hand to the frogs" in order to rearrange Liddell's Sunday heat. Therefore and somewhat pointedly, the Prince of Wales tells him it is a "simple matter of national dignity Liddell, being a patriot I'm sure you'll understand". Liddell is then heavily pressed into compromising his beliefs so that he may run on a Sunday and accommodate the demands "of the nation". This is evidently more morally acceptable to the Committee than appealing to "the frogs". This scene makes it palpably clear that Liddell will not compromise. There are echoes of Mrs Thatcher and her now famous "this lady's not for turning" speech in 1983 (Jenkins 1987), even though Mrs Thatcher would probably have preferred Liddell to have chosen the demands "of the nation" over his faith.

Eventually the Committee accepts his stance and the Duke of Sutherland tells Birkenhead that Liddell is a

"true man of principle and a true athlete. His "speed is a mere extension of his life, its force and we sought to sever his running from himself for his country's sake, no sake is worth that Effe, least of all a guilty national pride".

This may be the only scene that questions the supremacy of "national pride." It represents a token acknowledgement of a liberal humanist concern that "national pride" had some 6 years earlier resulted in the carnage of trench warfare. However it may suggest that national pride is great enough even to accommodate a highly principled stand made by an individual.

The alleged lack of principle on the part of "the frogs" matches a more subtle attack on American ethics. British and American psychology is distinguished and the difference between the teams articulated in their training routines. The Americans, during a montage sequence, are portrayed as robotic or palpably technological (professional) – through their aggressive training methods accompanied by dissonant synthesised music. The British, in contrast, adopt a more relaxed, (amateur) approach as they are framed in slow motion training seemingly effortlessly running along the beech to the score of Vangelis's now famous music. This contrast in approaches between the two nations is reinforced by Lord Birkenhead as he comments to an American journalist: "The Americans have prepared seriously, some would say too seriously in order to gain success but we feel we may in our unsophisticated way have their match". There is also Lord Lindsay and his Corinthian, eccentric and slightly bohemian habit of jumping over hurdles topped with full champagne glasses. This illustrates the "cast care aside" attitude he reveals to Sybil in an earlier discussion. These scenes suggest a degree of antipathy towards American attitudes.

This situation comes to a dramatic conclusion as Abrahams, and Paddock the American champion enter the stadium together. Apparent differences in national character appear between the two men. The Englishman, dressed in a plain white bathrobe with head slightly bowed, appears "quietly determined". Paddock on the other hand ostentatiously acknowledges the cheers of the crowd, as the American fans chant his name. He glories in being the "star" athlete – complete with sunglasses. As Jim Collins suggests this comparison within a 1920s setting has greater significance when considered within a 1980s context:

> "The overwhelming nostalgia is for a time when Britain was not the 'weak sister' of the United States, when it could still triumph over the superpower at its own game" (Collins 1989: 94).

The film highlights the dedication to training and success demonstrated by Abrahams and Liddell but is equally anxious to emphasise the essentially individual nature of this endeavour. We rarely see Abrahams or Liddell training with the rest of the team, which contrasts with the intensive group sessions undertaken by the Americans. We therefore have a celebration of all the qualities that have traditionally made Britain "great". Abrahams and Liddell as individuals display total commitment yet the national team avoids the uniform, and implicitly unimaginative or mechanical, routines employed by the Americans. We see the Olympic committee refusing to grovel to "the frogs" and thanks to the *noblesse oblige* displayed by the aristocratic Lindsay, Liddell is able to race and win without compromising his principles. We also have Abrahams' "most complete man," Aubrey, happy simply to be there and "burst his heart" for Britain. Ultimately Liddell, Abrahams and Lindsay are victorious under the national flag, an image suggesting that the national spirit is "tolerant" and sufficiently welcoming to be able to integrate ethnic and cultural diversity. Chariots of Fire celebrates British nationalist fervour at its most ostentatious.

Morally distant from the unscrupulous and European French, Britain is strategically superior to the robotic and obsessively professional Americans. An initial appeal by the Master of Caius to strive for the common good and honour the dead of the First World War slides seamlessly into a celebration of three disparate individuals. However, by uniting them under the flag we have themes of tolerance and inclusion woven into the nationalist fabric.

Essential to any revival of nationalist values in 1980s cinema were reconstituted perceptions of the imperial heritage. The centre of Empire was unquestionably India and colonial India featured extensively in 1980s British cinema and television concentrating on the later period of the Raj. The productions raise issues of contemporary national identity and considering the Jewel in the Crown (1983) and A Passage to India (1984), the immediate impression is of celebration and a lavish use of colour and exotic settings. This contrasted with the monochrome slate of contemporary England suggested a spectacular imperial past now reduced to functional modernism.

A Passage to India begins with Adela purchasing tickets for the trip to India she is about to take with Mrs Moore. She literally steps out of the rain into the shipping office with posters advertising the natural beauty of India. This highlights the grey, drab English weather she will shortly forsake. There is already a sense of loss even if it is only for greater travel opportunity. Shortly after their arrival at Bombay, they witness the return of the Viceroy. The quayside swells with loyal Indians in British uniforms and the Viceroy is piped ashore onto the regal red carpet amid much pomp, ceremony and military music. Despite this quasi Royal greeting from the apparently sincerely voiced crowd of locals the Viceroy and his wife stare imperiously ahead and refuse to acknowledge the reception. This scene establishes rank and hierarchy clearly defining the ruling elite. However, it also implies criticism of the structure by illustrating so vividly the arrogant disdain illustrated by the imperial couple. This visual rebuke may operate as an attempt to distance the production from the worst of the imperial excesses. However, it largely fails, and the impression is of a petulant and indulged despot who personifies British rule.

The Viceroy governs the Raj for and on behalf of the Empire. The racial hegemony is clear. This clarity and stark division of power articulates a reclamation of the self-ordained right of the imperial white Englishman to rule the Indian.

At Chandrapore there are further ceremonials to greet the Viceroy upon his arrival. Formally attired local dignitaries form a line in order to "receive" the Viceroy and the Collector. Having briefly welcomed his mother and Adela at the station Ronnie dashes off to meet the Viceroy: "We had to welcome the great man back". Irritated by this imperialistic paean Mrs Moore replies sardonically "I had no idea he was so important". The flourish of colour, brass bands and celebration of the British stands in opposition to the representation of Indians and their ramshackle, dusty railway station. A wild monkey who curiously surveys the alien ritual from the top of the tin roof completes the scene.

The style and manner of rule may be fit for debate but not the fundamental legitimacy of the Raj. Visual celebration of the finery of Empire is constant throughout the film. Deliberate narrative efforts to undermine the right of the British to rule India are largely mute. The sequence involving the grand garden party given by the Collector at his official residence exemplifies this. Held at the behest of Mrs Moore and Adela who have expressed a desire to mix socially with some of the natives, the scene ignores or patronises the Indians depicting them as animal exhibits at the zoo. Even when Mrs Turton mangles the local Urdu dialect, the Indian response is one of embarrassment and polite amusement rather than annoyance. The tenor generally is one of acceptance and tolerance of the British for their foibles and eccentricities rather than a resentment of their presence, suggesting maturity and greater sophistication on the part of the Indians.

There must however be at least an element of authenticity in the passive acceptance depicted in these scenes. It would have been a practical impossibility for Britain to administer an Empire, which included a nation as geographically huge and as populous as India, without at least a degree of consensus and consent from the subject people. The Raj productions and the Heritage films in general seemed to some extent to mount a search for this Holy

CHAPTER V - RECLAIMING NATIONAL IDENTITY

Grail of submissiveness. They embark upon a quest to redefine and rediscover this consensus for adoption as a basis for a contemporary national identity. Therefore, any attempt to provide a liberal or humanist critique of the validity of British rule is largely absent from the production. It does not noticeably surface until the trial of Aziz but by now the audience is increasingly sure of Aziz's innocence and he is now an acceptable and qualified focus for Indian nationalism. Dyer (1993: 137) finds that any lingering doubt expressed by Forster in his original novel is marginalised in the film. This, he says, is partly due to the fact that "the two good and truthful characters Mrs Moore and Fielding believe in him so steadfastly while all manner of blimpish buffoons condemn him". Therefore, at his trial, the production may safely foreground the supporters chanting "free Aziz" because we are becoming more sure of his innocence. The reader may feel that these protests are simply to campaign for the release of an innocent man and do not necessarily call into question the fundamental British right to try such a man. However British justice is seen to prevail and Aziz is released. In an ambiguous scene, the Indians outside the Court are dressed as monkeys. The depiction of the natives in this way may undermine their moral authority but also serves to remind the audience of the essential gulf between the two cultures. Equally they may be seen to be parodying British justice which is literally making monkeys out of them.

The trial scenes did present opportunities for the articulation of a liberal humanist critique of imperial ethics. The opportunity was largely lost. The audience may have anticipated an essentially corrupt trial. Mrs Moore, a likely witness for the defence, has gone home without reference to Aziz or his legal team. Ronny, the Chief Magistrate, correctly stands down because of his relationship with the complaining party. Adela makes him "an interested party ". He has delegated the conduct of the trial to his assistant Das who he says "is a good man". The reader is entitled to infer that "good" means ensuring that the 'correct', guilty, verdict is entered. When Aziz discovers the absence of Mrs Moore he protests and alleges injustice. Dramatically Adela retracts her complaint, the prosecution case very publicly collapses leading directly to the release of

Aziz. The opportunity for an examination of a possible abuse of imperial power passes. This evasion weakens any liberal criticism of the Raj and if anything serves only to vindicate the operation of British justice in colonial India.

Earlier in the film we see Aziz and his friend knocked off their bicycles by the Collector's car speeding through the market, signalling the first stirrings of anti British sentiment. These are however impotently discharged in the form of wry observations about the effect of India on the British and the corruption of MacBryde. A "good fellow when he first came out but all Englishmen are the same after two years". This elicits the reply from Ali: "Women are worse, they change after six months". This theme is not enlarged by the production and we do not find out precisely how, why or in what way this change occurs. There is therefore no dramatic or narrative exploration of the possible corrosive or corrupting effects of colonialism. The "good fellow" MacBryde appears to have become a bigot and at the trial states quite boldly that "The darker races are attracted to the fairer but not the other way around". We do not really discover whether he is intrinsically racist, whether it was inevitable in a man in his position, or whether he developed this attitude in India. Instead, we must accept the situation and hope that justice and fairness will prevail and that the liberal humanitarian Fielding will redress this prejudicial imbalance.

Indian nationalist feeling is therefore largely restricted to the trial, where it has been reduced to an overly emotional display of support for one man. The reunion of Aziz and Fielding at the end of the film may be a metaphor for the coming together of two nations as equals but this appears a little contrived. The director David Lean subsequently felt that he should have ended the film well before this point (Dyer 1993: 139). The nature of the relationship between Fielding and Aziz has changed since the trial. Until then the two men seemed to enjoy a friendship based upon personal respect. For Aziz however, the trial has sharpened or awakened nationalist feeling and he now regards Fielding as another member of the oppressive white ruling class. This remains so despite the considerable personal sacrifice Fielding made on his behalf. An authentic liberal humanist critique of the Raj would have acknowledged that following the recognition of his nationalist feelings it will no longer be possible for Aziz to return to his former relationship with Fielding. Now that Aziz has been freed it will be necessary for his country, India, to be restored to independence before a true friendship with Fielding, based upon equality, can resume. The finale of the film bears the artifice of an archetypal Hollywood "happy ending".

A Passage to India operates to reclaim notions of imperial supremacy reflecting a natural hegemonic order. The sharper edges have however, been tempered with the application of a certain liberalism. The almost constant visual blaze of colour and pageantry serves as a lament for the years when one third of the atlas was pink. When and where resistance surfaced it could be defused with "British justice" and the timely self sacrifice of one or two strongly moral minded individuals. Throughout the film, racial conflict is reduced and the overall effect is of palliative and a soothing diversion from racial divisions whether in the Raj or 1980s Britain. Andrew Higson found A Passage to India to be an "imperialist fantasy of national identity", a film which "can be seen as a conservative response to a collective, post imperial anxiety" (1993: 123).

It is illuminating to compare the film with the lavish television production Jewel in the Crown (1983). Set in wartime 1942 Jewel in the Crown depicts the Raj crumbling. A portrayal of imperial power on the wane may not immediately appear to constitute a veneration of British identity. However the spectator is distracted from the thematic thrust of the narrative by the visual celebration in the production. There are scenes of the Lake Palace at Udaipur providing a breath-taking background for the wedding party sequence and the garden at Rose Cottage presents a stunning "cocktail of shrubs and rare plants". The audience is presented with the "richness of the vegetation", the beautiful countryside together with a collection of "sumptuous palaces" (Robinson 1984: 50). Harlan Kennedy described Jewel in the Crown as: "double-standard movie making" comparing it to being "asked to bend over a luxurious perfumed ottoman while being given six of the best". He added: "Intellectually, we agree to eat humble pie about our imperial past. Emotionally, the impact of the India movies is to make us fall head over heels in love with the dear old days...when at least we had glamour" (Kennedy in *Film Comment*, July-August 1985, 52).

In narrative terms, the production offers a more complex analysis of British society in India than A Passage to India and consequently sends confusing messages to a contemporary audience. The disintegration of the Raj, which forms the dramatic core of the production, offers little apparent comfort for those seeking an affirmation of imperial authority. Threatened from within by rising Indian nationalism and from without by rampant Japanese imperialism a powerful sense of foreboding prevails. British imperialist nationalism seems undermined and weakened so that its resistance to foreign invasion is dangerously low. The purity of the Raj has become diluted and its sense of moral purpose suffused with doubt. Andrew Higson (1993) claims that the films attributed the fall of the Raj to a corruption of identity and found in A Passage to India and Jewel in the Crown an attempt to "recapture an image of national identity as pure, untainted, complete and in place" (Ibid.: 123). For him the fall of the Raj follows the "tainting of the pure identity". This "tainting" is given meaning in the interracial connections made between some of the characters.

A Passage to India is set at the height of imperialism. The interracial relations are limited in structure and extent to the friendship between Fielding and Aziz and the benign but ineffectual interest expressed by Mrs Moore in the welfare of the Indians. Interracial sexual relationships are limited to one, dubious and isolated act of sexual intercourse between Aziz and Adela which may not have been consensual. In Jewel in the Crown the interracial relationships are darker but more explicit. It is clear that Daphne Manners and Hari Kumar have sex and she dies giving birth to their mixed race child. Merrick luridly and brutally rapes Kumar. The racial boundaries are more obviously crossed and this occurs at a time when the Raj is crumbling. Thus, the greater extent and development of these interracial relationships reflects the swifter disintegration of imperial power and the "tainting" of the pure national identity is seen to have a more pronounced and damaging effect.

CHAPTER V - RECLAIMING NATIONAL IDENTITY

In <u>A Passage to India</u> Fielding, Adela and Mrs Moore share similar liberal values with comparable social, economic, and class roots. They are distinguished from Ronald Merrick in <u>Jewel in the Crown</u> and his lower middle class grammar school background. This social distancing is marked but he is a pivotal figure with real authority whose acts shape the narrative. His rank is presumably a reward for merit and endeavour making him an ambitious, proto-Thatcherite figure. Given that malevolence impels some of his actions and considering his evident character flaws, he is also a focus for a broadly liberal critique of Thatcherite values.

Both <u>Jewel in the Crown</u> and <u>A Passage to India</u> raise issues of national identity in terms of racial rather than ideological purity. It follows that a failure to achieve this purity will result in decay and destruction. Such a reconstructed national identity must also incorporate broadly liberal values into the dynamic or the exercise of unbridled authority will also have a corrosive effect. The two productions seem to attempt to offer a liberal foundation for a contemporary sense of national identity constructed from an imperial past made ethically and morally acceptable.

These productions are usually described as examples of Heritage Film along with <u>Chariots of Fire</u> (1981). (Higson 1993). When examining what it meant to be British, Sheila Johnston compared the period heritage of <u>Chariots of Fire</u> (1981) with the contemporary political drama <u>The Ploughman's Lunch</u> (1983). The latter contrasts sharply with <u>Chariots of Fire</u>'s 1920s vision of uncomplicated patriotism and creates a "modern and metropolitan world, of Victoria-line tube trains, squash courts, publisher's launches and smart wine bars" (Johnston 1984: 105). It's presentation of historic national identity was conspicuously refashioned for contemporary consumption. Penfield, the central character, is an ambitious journalist anxious to leave his lower middle class origins.

In one significant scene, Penfield buries his mother while looking anxiously at his watch. The reader may conclude that even at such a distressing occasion Penfield cannot afford to lose any time in his quest for social advancement. The scene conveys something of his selfishness and shallowness. In a production appearing in the aftermath of the Falklands War, Penfield is writing a history of the Suez crisis presented not as national humiliation but a matter of honour. We hear early in the film a BBC programme examining various Eastern European states and tacitly criticising them for distorting their national history. This revisionism is precisely what Penfield seeks to achieve with his forthcoming book.

Johnston (1984: 105) compares Penfield with Joe Lampton and the opportunism and brutal ambition at the core of <u>Room at the Top</u>. However a legitimate comparison may be limited. Joe Lampton made little attempt to deny his working class roots and displayed none of the artifice generally required to re-invent a life. In the words of his creator, John Braine, he simply wanted to "get the hell out of the working class". Lampton occupied a world where social divisions remained relatively clear and his difficulty lay in crossing these boundaries with little more than his sexuality and ambition to propel him over the threshold. In <u>Room at the Top</u> the working class were highly visible and portrayed as a vital, valid alternative life force. With James Penfield we are not even sure precisely what his social background is and he appears fully formed from somewhere in the grey, lower middle class. The working class is largely and notably missing from this production further underlining their increasing irrelevance in the Thatcher period.

There are, in the narrative and visually, suggestions that earlier perceptions of national identity are themselves inherently fraudulent. We see a supposedly typical 1930s family contentedly enjoying a bedtime drink only to discover that the whole scene was artificial. We discover that the eponymous "ploughman's lunch" was a 1960s advertising invention. The film criticises the conspicuous consumption and materialist vulgarity evident in the 1980s and takes this to the point of caricature. There are expense account lunches, over indulgence at Langans' brasserie and a champagne fuelled trip to the coast.

With the exception of Susi's mother, a radical historian, sympathetic characters are difficult to locate. Her political sympathies and age would locate her as an activist during the 1960s. She may have advocated some of the ideals and personified the prevailing sense of

CHAPTER V - RECLAIMING NATIONAL IDENTITY

national identity. The demonstrations of the peace campaigners and the poetry readings all resonate with values from another pre-Thatcherite time. The film emasculates these characters by keeping them firmly at the margins of power. Perhaps even more damning than the fraudulent reclaiming of the Suez affair these characters with their distinctive sense of identity are implicitly undermined by their portrayal as impotent and irrelevant individuals.

The Ploughman's Lunch (1983) was concerned with the Thatcherite politics of historical representation amidst the jingoism of the Falklands War.

Some of the cynicism about contemporary politics in The Ploughman's Lunch appears in Defence of the Realm (1985) which also takes an investigative journalist as its central protagonist. This examination of the use and abuse of power in 1980s Britain explored the secretive world of nuclear defence and is thematically linked to the contemporary television drama Edge of Darkness (1985). Defence of the Realm (1985) was concerned with the increasing wealth and sinister influence of the secret services, government and corporate enterprise over the nuclear power industry. The principal character Nick Mullen is a journalist who encounters a Pentagon inspired British governmental conspiracy to conceal a near nuclear accident at an American air base in East Anglia. This involves the Thatcherite proprietor of Mullen's own newspaper and the secret services who appear brutal, cynical and malevolent. A loner without friends or family the almost equally cynical Mullen begins to develop a political and social conscience matched with a determination to decode the airbase mystery. The final scene is ambiguous and Mullen may have died from an MI5 contrived explosion in his flat after firstly ensuring that the story breaks internationally.

However, there is no certainty that, despite possibly having made the ultimate sacrifice, he has thwarted the conspiracy. The essence of the film is in its depiction of a secret state. In Defence of the Realm the critical scene shows Mullen attempting to confront a highly placed civil servant whose calculated leaks to his own newspaper have driven him to the brink of exposing the intelligence cover up. He is immediately apprehended by three, apparently educated but burly men – none in uniform–in a quasi arrest, taken to MI5 headquarters and made to wait in a dimly lit office. He then faces the three senior civil servants behind the conspiracy, all nameless officials. This scene conveys Mullen's powerlessness and sense of isolation, and they know he has no political affiliations or likely allies. After questions about his patriotism and thinly veiled threats to his safety, he is turned into the dark deserted streets of Whitehall in the dead of night. Such a conspiratorial narrative resonates with the period. During Mrs Thatcher's term of office, the issue of national security became a frequent cause of political friction in the civil service between left and right. Sarah Tisdall, a clerk at the Foreign Office had been imprisoned for informing *The Guardian* newspaper of the arrival of the cruise missiles at Greenham Common airbase. Clive Pontin, an MOD official, had been tried (and acquitted) at the Old Bailey for giving Labour MP Tam Dalziel information concerning the sinking of the Argentinian cruiser, the General Belgrano, during the Falklands War.

However, Judith Williamson found the film's refusal or failure to address the identity of the conspirators as somewhat disappointing and incredulous. She asked in an article for the *New Socialist* (February 1986, 41) whether: "The State is really some kind of hidey-hole located, Narnia-like, behind a book case and leading out onto back streets? Is it really a shadow land full of statues and pointed questions?" Although this is a legitimate argument, it misses the relevance of the film for a 1980's audience. The significance of <u>Defence of the Realm</u> is not so much the depiction of a secret state but the depiction of a supra state. The film is concerned at a deeper level with the emergence of a "multi-nationalism". It is significant that the nuclear weapons are American, deployed by the United States Air Force at one of their own bases in the U.K. The real conspiracy and secrecy are in the unspoken acknowledgement that British national security, and with it military national autonomy and international security, has yielded to the demands of nuclear power itself. This power receives "essential needs" status and these needs transcend national boundaries. There is no clear division made in the film between the role of the Unites States Air Force, the British Government and British Intelligence in the

CHAPTER V - RECLAIMING NATIONAL IDENTITY

collusion. In the film the near nuclear accident at the US Air Force base results from a full scale military alert ordered by the United States military in response to the bombing of its Embassy in Ankara.

The film demonstrates that the results of a small cell of Turkish terrorists acting against the United States in an Embassy at the edge of Europe have direct and unavoidable consequences for the British Government. Significantly the Government cannot or will not prevent these consequences and are consequently impotent. John Hill (1999) refers to the final scene. Mullen and Nina, secretary to the disgraced Labour MP Dennis Markham, (who has himself been framed by the right-wing inspired leaks conspiracy), succeed in disseminating vital information about the cover up before the Security Services attempt to eliminate them. Hill finds that "...it is difficult to see just how newspaper revelations will lead to change" (1999: 152). These headlines appear in foreign newspapers but this if anything only serves to emphasise the cross national or multi national determining of nuclear power.

Defence of the Realm articulated the sense of powerlessness and distant paranoia felt by the liberal and left wing living in the midst of an increasingly politically proactive security service. I believe, however, it has a greater significance. Chariots of Fire may recreate imperialist nostalgia and the strand of patriotism evoked by images of British ships setting sail from British ports for foreign wars. The Ploughman's Lunch may depict a cynical historical revision and constitute an attempted representation of an historic national humiliation in terms suitable for a jingoistic post Falklands nationalism. Defence of the Realm suggests all this may be mere sabre rattling and impotent posturing. Real power and the literal defence of the realm has already moved into the shadow lands of the secret state or supra state which the film is unwilling or unable to identify further.

My Beautiful Launderette (1985) challenges the proposition that an imperialist regime can function in a liberal or morally acceptable fashion. This sharp, contemporary representation portrays a microcosm of modern suburban England inverting the old imperialist order so that the ethnic immigrant has economically colonised the indigenous white man. Lewisham is a reverse Raj with the Pakistani community holding positions of power, wealth and influence. The eponymous launderette is decrepit and neglected before Omar takes over. Symbolically it was formerly "Churchill's" invoking memories of Britain during "her finest hour". It is renamed "Powders" which is both a pun on the washing powders it uses legitimately but also wryly refers to the illegal sale of cocaine undertaken to raise the finance needed for refurbishment. This neatly establishes the duality of the 1980s and repeats the close connection between corporate enterprise and organised crime suggested by The Long Good Friday in 1979.

This close correlation of crime and business is a motif repeated throughout the film. The production opens with Salim and some Afro Caribbean henchmen forcing Johnny and Genghis out of their "home". Later, Nasser has Johnny perform a very similar service for him. In Nasser's opinion he is merely "squeezing the tits of the system" and he encourages the young Omar to follow his example. This tends to reduce Thatcherite values to naked opportunism. There is little evidence in the film of any liberal humanist counter culture and the only character with such a value system is Omar's father, Papa. Once a respected journalist, he now spends his time in bed, deeply depressed, drinking himself to death, and pointlessly complaining that the working class "are such a great disappointment" to him. The liberalism articulated in Papa appears to be an impotent, largely irrelevant and spent moral force. In giving representation to the reduced role of liberal values he calls to mind Suzy's mother in The Ploughman's Lunch. The white working class characters tend to illustrate the disappointment Papa feels by hanging around aimlessly on street corners and expressing themselves through violence.

The film foregrounds the interracial homosexual relationship between Johnny and Omar but also makes it clear that Johnny has made a choice. According to his white friend Genghis he has "cut himself off from his own people". John Hill finds the film "something of a riposte" to the Raj films of the 1980s (Hill 1999: 208). It clearly rebuts any suggestion that national identity can be rooted in exclusive white ideology. It suggests that oppression, violence and social disquiet are integral features of imperialism. There is a graphic illustration of violence when Genghis and Moose beat up Salim. The injustice inherent in imperialism and racism seems little changed even when the traditional imperial order is reversed and the ethnic immigrant becomes the oppressor. This critique of imperialism may implicitly espouse liberal values. It certainly avers that any reclaimed sense of national identity which purports to use as its base an imagined imperial past tempered by liberal humanism is fundamentally flawed, fanciful and self deluded.

5.5 Contributing to the Culture of Change

An assessment of the contribution to the culture of change made by the heritage film will be over several levels, socially, economically and perhaps above all politically. It is necessary to establish whether there were any significant changes in British culture during the 1980s affecting aspects of national identity. Interpretations vary. Some may incline to the view that the heritage film was nostalgic for an era of imperialism when Britain had been strong. They may feel that the 1980s productions celebrated a contemporary time of national renaissance when Britain was becoming truly "Great" once more. Others may take the view that the 1980s began the stark and unequal restructuring of society and that the heritage film is no more than comforting pastiche of history in moving pictures. Here I am once again returning to the themes, debates and modes of analysis first adopted in "Realist Nights and Heritage Mornings." (2001).

Immediately apparent in these films is the tendency to reduce the working class to marginal, servile and largely impotent figures. Even the very few heritage films to foreground a working class character place them in conspicuously ancillary roles. In Maurice Scudder appears to be present in the narrative in order to invest the principal character, and by extension the period, with apparent liberal humanist values. In Chariots of Fire Massabini appears only when Abrahams declares that he "wants that gold medal". Artisan characters tended generally to appear as nameless servants humbly attending to their masters. In this historical reconstruction of Britain, the working class is servile and reduced to the fulfilment of the ancillary and joyless roles they historically occupied in pre war society. There is effectively no reference to class struggle or efforts to improve in any of the influential heritage products. In <u>Brideshead Revisited</u> the pickets during the General Strike are stripped of their dignity in the presence of the upper class protagonists. These scenes would have made uncomfortable viewing for the economic victims of the New Right's harsh policies, which aggravated the industrial carnage of the early 1980s.

Andrew Higson (1993, 1996) and John Hill (1999) claim that the heritage films visually subvert the social criticisms made in their narratives. In <u>A Room with a View</u> the film successfully inverts the Emersons and instead of using them as a focus for a social satire of middle England and its bourgeois pretensions they appear to be lauded for their uncomplicated humanism. As members of the Edwardian merchant middle class, they stand comparison to the meritocracy espoused by Mrs Thatcher, although not in their humanism. Shorn of the social criticism intended by Forster they display liberal values, honesty and vitality. Their cultural credentials separate them from the masses but equally do not lead to intellectual corruption. The meritocracy is therefore distant from the old effete upper class represented by Cecil Vyse.

The early 1980s was a time of great social, political and economic unrest and <u>Brideshead Revisited</u> mourns the passing of a more certain, class ordered period. The house represents, metaphorically, the national community functioning as an imagined focal point for unity. There was clear evidence throughout the production of the emphasis given to a lavish visual celebration of the house and its associated artefacts. This elegy for simpler times perhaps functioned as a palliative during the turbulence of 1981. Its veneration of wealth and privilege would have particular resonance for the 1980s generation of aspirants. The production broadcast as the 'Yuppy' culture surfaced and the celebration of 'style' became more overt. This apparent triumph of style over substance helped produce Peter York, a man who became conspicuously famous as a 'style guru' selling the idea that style was simply a commodity. Style could therefore be acquired or created at will and utilised to help construct a fantasy lifestyle and perhaps by extension a fantasy version of national identity.

"Heritage" was recognised as an "industry" for the first time and assisted by government legislation reflected a desire to supplement the eroded manufacturing base with the service sector. Having led the world into industrialisation Britain was fast becoming the developed world's first post-industrial society, converting factories into museums and manufacturing into memory. This limited the options for the traditional workers who had built solid communities around the sturdy manufacturing locations of shipyards, mines and mills. The imagery and the metaphors are striking. Former manufacturers became tour guides showing visitors around their own industrial heritage and no longer able to produce anything more tangible than nostalgia and history. This version of 'heritage', largely unwelcome to the working class communities affected, resonated with the New Right and their pastoral, imperial fantasies.

The heritage film did however express a new moral perspective that featured in the Thatcherite ideology. Making no secret of her admiration for Victorian England and by extension imperialism, she wished to invoke their supposed virtues of thrift, enterprise and self-sufficiency. In practice the adoption of these 'virtues' in the early 1980s and the encouragement given to the 'free market' and by extensive de-regulation did not lead to the creation of wealth which would benefit the entire nation. Instead, it operated to promote greed, avarice and the supremacy of self-interest. These tendencies have been present throughout history but the heritage film seemed determined to celebrate them and articulate the pursuit of personal advancement in terms of a moral crusade. In <u>Chariots of Fire</u> the lightly varnished ambition of Abrahams and Liddell is disguised in purportedly moral terms. They claim to run for their faith but the narrative exposes this artifice and ultimately they seek personal glory. Had the film contented itself with a veneration of success it would have some relevance for a contemporary audience but would have added little to any imagined reconstruction of national identity. It was the preference for personal ambition over consensus beliefs and the celebration of the emerging meritocracy that delineates the film as fundamentally Thatcherite.

Attempts at a more liberal, humanitarian formulation are not generally convincing. Jewel in the Crown and A Passage to India both concern imperialists in India. Each production purports to locate within the Raj traditional liberal values. Characters displaying strong liberal values are foregrounded and depicted influencing the narrative development. However, this narrative imperative flounders in the face of the overwhelming visual celebration of imperialism. It is also possible to attribute other motives to the conduct of some of these characters such as Fielding in A Passage to India. The liberal influence on the period is thus at best restricted and the cry of "there's nothing I can do" becomes a mantra for the liberal white women in Jewel in the Crown. The heritage film attempts to soften recollections of imperial splendour and suggestions that this amelioration may integrate into contemporary conceptions of national identity fail.

These efforts to blunt the harsher edges of imperialism are significant in that any liberal humanist values belong to the middle class characters. In Jewel in the Crown the only working or sunken middle class white character is Ronald Merrick who is portrayed in brutal terms. There are no significant efforts to invest working class characters with a 'moral' configuration. This absence in the heritage films is in a sense aggravated by some non-bourgeois heritage productions which appear to be trying to create a working class heritage of immorality, illegality and deviancy. Dance with a Stranger and Scandal deal exclusively with real life working class characters who fell by the legal and moral wayside, and therefore should not be included in any nostalgic reconstructed version of national identity. The working class is either servile or dominantly criminal.

Both, the heritage films and 1980s culture in general had little scope for perceptions of England that differed materially from imperial notions. Concepts of liberal humanism were introduced into historic recollections of imperial grandeur in order to justify the reconstruction and to foster the contemporary belief that this represented a solid basis for recreating national identity. Chariots of Fire recalled an era when Britain was not the weaker and subservient sister to the U.S.A but an independent, equal partner in

CHAPTER V - RECLAIMING NATIONAL IDENTITY

the 'special relationship'. Released at the time of the Falklands War it encouraged a nationalist belief that Britain had become once more capable of sending ships and men to fight foreign wars in far off places. The irony of fighting an essentially 19th century colonial war at the end of the 20th century did not undermine the imagined restoration of national pride and military might. Even the gangster Harold Shand sneers at American cultural influence at the end of The Long Good Friday.

Mrs Thatcher and her government consciously moulded perceptions of national identity and their attempted political interference with particular television documentaries was evident. Death on the Rock, Who Bombed Birmingham and Tumbledown questioned the integrity of the national security services. Such challenges to Thatcherite notions of national identity provoked extreme political pressure in efforts to change the productions. Of course, there were alternative views. The Ploughman's Lunch suggested history was capable of political interpretation and revision. In this production Britain appeared to be as capable as any Communist dictatorship of re-writing its own history and changing its identity for current consumption. Defence of the Realm exposed the flawed and deluded thinking that in the 1980s Britain remained a vigorous independent nation capable of self-defence revealing it to be largely mythology. This production detailed the extent to which national independence relied upon the international use of nuclear power. This force transcends domestic or national authority.

What I have articulated here is the attempted reclamation of a particular bourgeois and rather imperialist nationalism, foregrounded by the cultural and political themes of the Thatcherite 1980s as they have been represented and mediated through the British Heritage film and television artefacts of that decade.

Conclusion

There is within British society an omnipresent social and political imperative to construct an imagined community of allegedly homogeneous individuals at various levels. The focus may vary and the centrifugal dynamic may shift but the fundamental need remains constant. Pre-war society was rooted in sharply defined class differences with a preordained structure as the foundation for this construction. I have discussed the social and cultural influences, which impacted on and re-aligned these values. External tensions also act as a defining agent for national identity. These tensions become most acute during times of war and the shaping of a unified national response becomes in turn most apparent.

The 1940s threat of invasion provided a real and powerful focus for national unity. The need to survive defined the terms and produced a clear expression of national identification. There are numerous examples of wartime cinema, which demonstrate national unity by representing the differing social classes working together for the common national good. These films celebrated the ability of all classes to unite and act collectively to serve a common purpose but carefully avoided any didactic critique or analysis of the inherent validity of the class system. <u>In Which We Serve</u> (1942) is characteristic wartime cinema in that the class differences are clearly delineated. The upper class is personified by the Captain played by the aristocratic Noel Coward, the middle class by the Petty Officer portrayed by Bernard Miles whilst Richard Attenborough as the rating clearly conveys the working class. They effortlessly overcome class differences to serve the wider national interest.

This narrowly defined structure survived the War and persisted well into the 1950s. The restrictions of class that pervaded the war era remained evident in peacetime and a nation that had helped to save itself from Nazi tyranny appeared curiously repressed and restrained. There was little obvious sense of liberation once the street parties were over. Post war rationing remained until 1953 and codes of conduct, modes of moral behaviour and social expectations found definition in predominantly class terms. In terms of cinematic representation the middle class had barely progressed from the grey, clenched emotional austerity of Brief Encounter (1945) when for Alec and Laura, honour, loyalty and duty prevailed over romantic longing and personal happiness. Typically, the working class characters portrayed in this successful film were loveable rogues or comic caricatures. Generally, the working classes were expected to identify and uncomplainingly occupy their place within this rigid and ordered structure and were frequently represented as comic characters or criminals. Cinematic portrayals rarely strayed from these caricatures and stereotypical depictions.

However, from the mid 1950s, as the national identity literature suggests, it is possible to observe equally clear countervailing pressures towards divided identities, plural groupings and cultural diversity. (Anderson 1985, Nairn 1977, 1997, Cannadine 1983, Smith 1984, 1991, Laing 1986, Hill 1986, Scannell 1988, Sinfield 1989, Marwick 1998). This counter culture conflicted with the pressure to construct an imagined community and the tension created by the clash forges new perceptions of national identity. During periods of social change, these tensions are often articulated in the cultural domain. This is perhaps especially so in popular culture which both reflects and influences our modes of self understanding and leads to our sense of shared identity and of 'nation'.

The second half of the 20th century witnessed two such significant periods of change which will bear serious examination in these terms: the late 50s into the 60s and the 1980s. In both periods there is palpable social change and we can see the tensions in available modes of identity construction being worked through within cultural products. It is my contention that Empire lies at the core of these tensions and changes in British national identity. Although India achieved independence shortly after the Second

World War, the remainder of the Empire remained in place some 10 years later. The various pluralist responses to both the decline of Empire in the 1950s and an imaginary reconstruction of Empire in the 1980s shape perceptions of national identity.

A war weary 1950s Britain suffered from economic exhaustion, political sterility and unsustainable imperial commitments. These factors conspired with increasing colonial demands for independence to undermine the British national will to govern and an Empire that had lasted for 400 years was largely dismantled in less than 20. This increasing reluctance to shoulder Rudyard Kipling's "white man's burden" found representation in contemporary attitudes towards class, affluence and social mobility. Although this decline may have had perhaps its most marked affect upon the class structure, it also influenced issues of morality and the effects of post imperialism created hybrid representations of Englishness and shifting constructions of contemporary national identity. The pre-war class certainties, which appeared to survive the war, would slowly dissolve as the Empire declined. The emergence of pluralist groupings coincided more closely with the headlong retreat from imperialism in the 1950s than with the defeat of the external enemies in 1945.

A victorious and superficially somewhat reassuring and safe existence of post war class dominated society was ill prepared for the apparently bitter social tensions suggested by the savagery and vitriol of "Look Back in Anger" in 1956. The lead character Jimmy Porter found few "good brave causes" left in a post imperial, morally decaying Britain. He railed against the apparent destruction of more noble and traditional working class ways of life including the Music Hall, a symbol of working class cultural vitality. Jimmy mourns the dearth of such causes and finds nothing to put in their place. He passionately and volubly laments the decline of the traditional working class and the bourgeois influence that follows widening affluence.

Jimmy Porter typified a working class response to a declining imperial order which found increasing expression throughout the late 1950s and early 1960s. In retrospect, the Second World War, like the First, appears to have begun as an imperial conflict. In

CONCLUSION

1939 the Allies consisted of the British Empire and a flagging French Empire trying to resist a rampant Nazi Germany whose aspirations, although primarily ideological in intent, were imperialist in execution. Loosely aligned with Germany was the aggressively expanding Japanese Empire and Mussolini's Italy with its fantasies of creating a new Roman Empire. The overwhelming wartime need for a unified national response to a marked and clearly defined external threat diminished and as the imperial influences declined a more pluralist society began to emerge. By the early 1960s, international British influence was fading and the nation began to look increasingly inwardly. The contemporary cultural artefacts gave expression to this tendency and the Social Realist cycle of films gave expression to this plurality.

There is little consistency in the responses to these changes and it is not possible to detect a collectively didactic critique of the existing social order. There is no suggestion of a new hegemonic order or of a specific polemic response. For instance Joe Lampton, in Room at the Top, cared little for the traditional aspects of working class life and in the words of his creator, John Braine, simply "wanted to get the hell out of the working class". The film was released with a then rare "X" for "Adults Only" Certificate which drew attention to the relatively explicit reference to sex. It portrayed Joe Lampton as an unapologetic upwardly mobile upstart, prepared to use his sexuality in order to gain material success and social advancement. He does not lament the passing of the finer working class traditions in the manner of a Jimmy Porter. Joe has little regard for the class he simply wishes to discard as quickly as possible.

The divergence of possible identities for a "new" working class is further illustrated and explored in Saturday Night and Sunday Morning. Arthur Seaton simply wants to have a good time because he believes that anything else is "propaganda". He does not seek rank and privilege being content to remain on the factory floor. He does however distance himself from the values of his parents whom he considers "dead from the neck up". Arthur does not apologise for his high income and dismisses one of the older but poorer paid workers by telling him "he must have had a fine time starving".

Contemporary advertising for the film tends to diminish its force by describing it as "the adventures of a working class Don Juan". The film concludes with Arthur, rock in hand insisting to Doreen that it will not "be the last stone I throw". Given that he and Doreen are about to embrace conventional domesticity in the particular housing estate he symbolically attacks this threat is unconvincing. Arthur represents an affluent 1960s version of a traditional working class male. He does not seek a way of life that radically differs from his father's but he does refuse to submit and be like his parents who had "their hash settled before the war".

The distinct characters of Arthur, Joe and Jimmy, three depictions of working class change in the late 1950s, tend to undermine any suggestion that they represent an ordered social or political rejection of society. They demonstrate the plurality, tensions and differences that can exist within one class. Thus, Vic Brown in A Kind of Loving does not react to the news of his girlfriend's pregnancy in the manner of Arthur Seaton or even Joe Lampton. He submits to an essentially clinical marriage, which he describes as "a kind of loving". He regrets the decision almost immediately.

This regret contrasts with the reactions of the other characters, in particular Christine who disappoints Vic by behaving in such a manner that she reminds him of his mother. The misery caused by this marriage invited the viewer to review an institution, even at this time of social change, which continued to underpin society and shape national identity. Vic clearly feels trapped but he fails to free himself from his predicament and appears to accept it. A Kind of Loving also addressed the increasingly apparent "consumerist" tendencies of the working class, which it sought to compare with more "traditional" working class values. There was at this time something of a paradox in that whilst national wealth declined along with international influence many working class individuals had never known such prosperity. Many sections of the working class genuinely had, in the words of the Prime Minister Harold MacMillan "never had it so good".

This contrast provides some explanation for the shift in focus away from external international and imperialist affairs to more domestic and immediately relevant local issues. During the early

1960s, this change of focus also found expression on British television, which also considered various ways of constructing a "new" working class identity. This is particularly noticeable in the contrast between early Coronation Street episodes and Z Cars. The founder of Coronation Street, Tony Warren, spoke of his desire to preserve a rapidly disappearing working class lifestyle threatened, presumably, by increasing affluence and social mobility. This urge led him to create Coronation Street in which characters were located by reference not only to their exact class but also to their precise street. Coronation Street began broadcasting as the bulldozers were demolishing many of the clustered and cloistered communities the programme sought to preserve.

Shortly after Coronation Street the BBC began showing Z Cars, a gritty urban drama dealing not with an imagined working class sense of community spirit but social alienation and communal collapse. This series questioned whether notions of traditional working class solidarity would survive social displacement into the new housing estates and tower blocks that were increasingly dominating town planning in the 1960s. The decade began therefore with two diametrically distant television productions. Coronation Street clearly functions as an elegy or lament for the passing of an essentially community centred society. Here the working class compensated for material deprivation with cohesive and binding communal ties and an exaggerated recognition and veneration of local affiliation. The working class credentials of the programme were established, defined and delineated by no more than a dozen houses on one very particular cobbled street.

Z Cars simultaneously charted the social alienation and fragmentation that follows the destruction of the close knit community so celebrated by Coronation Street. Set in the fictional but significantly named "Newtown" Z Cars portrays a world of concrete tower blocks, neighbours who are strangers and a sense of transplanted community. The production is notable for an absence of local identity and is intrinsically rootless. A diminished sense of regional identity is advanced and class divisions are muted. Some of the Officers, notably "Fancy" Smith, appear to exist in order to articulate concerns the viewer might share about this apparently increasing social alienation. Their dramatic role as simply policemen seems to be largely secondary.

The disappearing working class lifestyle lamented by Tony Warren represented one of the principal dimensions of change, which included increasing prominence of forms of social, cultural and ethnic differentiation. Questions of race, sexuality and the newly nascent post-war youth culture came to the fore. The decline of Empire and its concomitant need to present a unified moral response to external threats permitted the exploration of plural groupings and diverse cultures largely unknown to mainstream contemporary society. A Taste of Honey examined aspects of race and sexuality and also challenged the established pre-eminence of the nuclear family by suggesting an alternative. This groundbreaking issue posed one of the most fundamental questions about perceptions of national identity. It pointed to the existence of an underclass, a group of people effectively sliding through the fissures in society and starkly challenged middle class notions of comfort, security and order. This representation of family life stood some distance from the avuncular and hermetic existence of The Grove Family or The Huggetts and ran counter to the desire for a united common identity. Films such as A Taste of Honey allow a degree of positive response to the newly expressed differences in society.

The questioning of class boundaries received further representation in The Loneliness of the Long Distance Runner. Using the Borstal Ruxton Towers as a national metaphor, the central character Colin Smith conspicuously rejects both by refusing the privileges that conformity would bring. In a scene towards the end of the film, the Public School boys are introduced to the Borstal boys shortly before the climatic race. After some initial hesitation, they identify with each other and both sections of society are depicted as equally imprisoned by an essentially anachronistic imperialist class order. Just as these notions of a securely class ordered society were challenged the Social Realist cycle also addressed the decline of 'certainties' of the imperial past with its sense of Britain as an imperial power.

CONCLUSION

This significant dimension of change was addressed in <u>The Entertainer</u> which examined national decline on the world stage. The film presented Britain, metaphorically, as a tired old Music Hall act now descending into mild pornography and cheap, alien, American driven mass culture. The younger characters considered emigration seeing no apparent future in a decaying impoverished post imperial Britain. This thematic premise is emphasised by the treatment given to Archie's son, a serving soldier in the British Army. When called to fight in Suez in support of an ill-advised, essentially imperialist mission he parodies Lord Kitchener saying "my Queen and country need me" mocking any feeling of nostalgia for implied imperial grandeur. The fiasco results in his death and highlights the contradictions apparent in imposing an outdated imperialist agenda on contemporary youth. By contrast nostalgic longing for Edwardian certainty and imperial might lead Billy Rice and the older characters to look for comfort in some of his old songs. Billy sings one in public and receives a rousing reception from the older members of his audience. Billy feels genuinely saddened and perplexed that his country is now "always in the wrong". Like Jimmy Porter, Billy Rice is a character without a cause.

Politically the 1960s witnessed the manifestly Edwardian Harold (MacMillan) give way to the new classless Harold (Wilson). The latter adopted the trappings of the working class, smoking his pipe and walking his dogs, but spoke of the "white heat of technology" and mastered the relatively new medium of television. His ascendancy coincided with the abrupt end of Social Realism. By 1963, the cycle had largely run its course. The end became almost certain when one of the principal financial backers of the films, Harry Saltzman, transferred his expertise and investment to the cinematic representation of James Bond.

Described by film critic Jeffrey Richards as "last hero of the British Empire" Bond, and in a different way Harry Palmer, locate Britain's international position rather differently. Distant from attitudes typifying the pre-war period Bond is more attuned to changes in class in 60s Britain and to the Cold War situation. As a Commander in the Royal Navy, Bond is below the rank of Captain or Admiral but somewhat above the sunken middle class rank of

Petty Officer. Consequently, he defies to some extent normal class recognition. Furthermore, his motif of casual insubordination further separates him from the conformist Officer class we might expect him to identify with. The Soviet Union is usually the historic sponsor of his enemies but the association is diffuse. Bond relies primarily upon his own ingenuity and initiative but significantly requires the backing, at critical moments, of the CIA and by association the might and technological expertise of the United States. Treating Bond as a national metaphor places the United Kingdom on the side of the USA. Although the nation still has the strengths of rugged individuality it is no longer able to function in the manner of a dominant power and therefore becomes increasingly reliant upon brilliant and essentially classless cavaliers.

Also popular at this time was the Harry Palmer trilogy, which presented a defiant and reluctant spy who appears to be overtly working class. Yet, it is also clear that he has cultural and intellectual finesse. He resents his superior Officers and rues the circumstances that have compelled his duty to the Crown. The contemporary viewer may have interpreted Palmer as a metaphor for a working class challenge and questioning of bourgeois assumptions traditionally made concerning working class loyalty to the Crown.

The Social Realist films depicted the emergence of the differing strands of the working class and the more influential of these films addressed the refusal of the protagonist to accept a destiny predicated upon pre war social and class assumptions. The overall impression is of a collection of disparate individuals emerging separately from the previously homogenous mass of the working class. This emergence occurred some time after the critical strains caused by the Second World War and mirrored the national withdrawal from Empire, which gathered pace in the 1950s. In these aspects of the 50s and 60s the balance between centrifugal and centripetal tendencies is broadly in the centrifugal direction. I have discussed this movement towards divided identities, plural groupings and diverse cultures in the socio-historical account in Chapter 2. Thus, culture articulated and reflected peoples' sense of a social, political and economic collective identity.

CONCLUSION

In the 50s and 60s we can see perceptions of national identity challenged and questioned and the embryonic fracturing of the traditional working class becoming evident. There is a notable lack of any alternative hegemonic order. This fracturing did not seem to produce an immediate and cohesive moral, social or political response. The imperative to restore to the nation a sense of an imagined community of allegedly homogenous individuals would make no real appearance until the 1980s. The 1979 General Election returned a Conservative Government led by the first ever woman Prime Minister, Mrs Thatcher. Her electoral success followed a prolonged period of political and industrial unrest and economic decline. Mrs Thatcher brought with her a clearly defined ideology, which rejected consensus, and sought to repair the social, political and economic damage she attributed to consensus. The following decade produced a further series of social fractures as the new Conservative Government applied with suitably Thatcherite conviction this new ideology. Dominating the film and national identity literature documenting this period of change is the development of Heritage cinema, which appeared to give expression to some of the New Right policy.

Mrs Thatcher made little secret of her admiration of the national imperial heritage and conspicuously sought to adopt the "Victorian values" system that underpinned the Empire. Her frequent references to historic imperial glory seemed reflected in the Heritage media. This film cycle gave expression to an imaginary reconstruction of national identity. Presented for contemporary consumption this imaginary identity incorporated predominantly imperialist themes and ideology. The films were cohesive with strong thematic and narrative links. Stylistically similar, they also offer a degree of uniformity in the mise en scene. Some of the more influential heritage films share as source material the novels of E. M. Forster. Merchant and Ivory produced some of the more influential films and drawing from the same pool of actors gave an impression of an upper class repertory company.

Forster wrote prolifically satirising the pretensions and bourgeois aspirations of the then upwardly mobile merchant class. It is therefore somewhat ironic that some of his more influential work should be adapted for use as the foundation for films which quintessentially celebrated the rise of bourgeois values. Now numerically superior, the middle classes had by the early 1980s assumed social and economic dominance and effectively supplanted the working class as a dynamic cultural focus. Just as the Social Realist films were preoccupied with the working class, the largest contemporary cultural grouping of the 1950s, the Heritage film resonated more closely with the mercantile or meritocratic middle classes, which had become numerically dominant.

The Heritage film revisited the recent past and attempted to recycle images of national unity and racial purity for contemporary application. Social dissent, class division and ethnic diversity would have little role to play in this processed version of nationality. The Social Realist films treated Empire with, at best, ambivalence, personified by the conflicting attitudes toward imperialism shown by the Rice family in <u>The Entertainer</u>. The Heritage depiction varied between the elegiac and nostalgic mourning evidenced in certain productions and the more straightforwardly revisionist approach favoured by others. The mourning for loss finds clear expression in <u>Brideshead Revisited</u>.

This production occupied 6 months of prime television broadcasting time and eulogised the pre-war class system by celebrating the effortless elegance and stylish lives of the landed aristocracy. The working class characters were either located in the margins or reduced to acquiescent servility, happy, apparently, to humble themselves to their masters' needs. The only direct criticism of this ostentatious wealth and privilege enjoyed by the Flyte family came at the end of the series and was voiced by the manifestly bourgeois Hooper.

The portrayal of any countervailing pressure towards divided identity or discontent is minimised. The General Strike of 1926 merits only a single episode and seems primarily to emphasise the dash and elan displayed by the aristocratic protagonists. The strikers receive little attention. Viewers were permitted to locate the Brideshead estate as a metaphor for the nation and a focal point around which an imagined national unity may form. Constructed in dominantly heritage terms the production shared the sense of loss and remorse felt by Evelyn Waugh, the writer of the original novel. Significantly, this production attracted large audiences at a time when unemployment approached three million, traditional industries were closing down and civic dissent had given way to rioting. The class based and evidently well ordered community depicted by the production drew audiences of around 12 million. This suggests the existence of a receptive market for the consumption of the reassurance and apparent social certainty offered by this nostalgic, reconstructed and imagined sense of community.

During this time the Government actively encouraged the development of an essentially nostalgic heritage industry and passed legislation in 1980 and 1983 to enable this. Ironbridge in Shropshire, generally considered the world's pioneering manufacturing region, became a working museum. Contemporary visitors to industrial museums and country houses did not of course bear witness to the poverty, misery and disease that often surrounded the original construction of these reclaimed icons of national identity. The arduous and often life-threatening toil needed to create the industrial revolution is anaesthetised by slide shows, on site videos and aesthetically designed information boards. The authentic working classes become mere background for a nostalgic celebration of a collective industrial enterprise.

The industrial revolution coincided with the rise of Empire. The roots of Empire lay in trade and there exists a historic intertwining of imperial expansion with the burgeoning and flowering of the bourgeois, merchant classes. Celebrating and commemorating the genesis of the industrial revolution inevitably implicitly invites a commensurate celebration of imperialism. The histories then become complicit. This duality finds expression in the Heritage films and in their recreation and redefinition of imperialism as the basis for a specific sense of reclaimed national identity. However, the Heritage film also attempted to distance the contemporary spectator from the harsher realities of life for the subordinate class and therefore ease any inherent tensions.

The Social Realist films revealed a diversity of working class responses to the social changes and tensions emerging at a time of imperial decline. The very diversity and plurality of these responses serves to illustrate the marked lack of any new paradigm or alternative hegemony. The Heritage film purports to invest an imaginary imperialism with liberal humanist values and suggest this as the new paradigm or basis for a reconstructed national identity. The strict social order that underpinned imperial Britain requires qualification to enable re-presentation as a basis for an imaginary reconstructed national identity. This qualification usually took the form of imbuing one of the central characters with overtly liberal humanist qualities. Occasionally one of the central characters would reject the imperial order entirely.

In Maurice, for example, the eponymous, privileged central character sacrifices his mercantile standing for the love of a working class grouse beater. This may represent the ultimate liberal humanist act, forsaking the shallow advantages of social and economic prestige for the more worthy, higher values of romantic love. Some may see it as a selfish betrayal of traditional middle class notions of public service. Jeffrey Richards considers it an act of subversion, casting aside responsibility in order to pursue personal happiness (Richards 1997). However given that the relationship is gay what is important here is that this underlines the film's liberal humanism.

The Edwardian novelist E.M Forster sought to satirise the more pretentious aspirations of the then emerging mercantile middle class and used the Emersons as a vehicle for this social criticism in his novel A Room with a View. Yet by the time the film was completed the Emersons emerge in almost heroic light imbued with common sense, an unpretentious interest in the arts and an inclination towards liberal humanist values. In the transition from book to film the antipathy shown by Forster towards the class personified by the Emersons has significantly been changed to approval. The characters have therefore ceased to be objects of counter cultural criticism but instead members of the allegedly homogeneous community. Contemporary spectators of the film may have identified common ideological ground in the Edwardian merchant class inhabited by the Emersons and the 1980s meritocracy promoted so avidly by Mrs Thatcher and the New Right. Edwardian vices of artifice, vulgarity and greed become 1980s virtues of enterprise, individuality and endeavour.

CONCLUSION

A clutch of films and television productions about the Raj appeared further cementing the association between 1980s Heritage literature and the Empire. A Passage to India typified the paradoxical Heritage approach to imperialism. Stunning visuals and lush production values celebrate and recreate the trappings and ritual splendour of the Raj. These tend to undermine and contradict any restricted narrative criticism of either the ethics or execution of imperialism. The film does foreground particular characters who appear to espouse liberal and humanist values and these characters are presented to us as the conscience of the Raj mitigating the more brutal aspects and implications of imperialism.

This is a typical heritage device. The visual and ritual glories of the Empire are celebrated but the harder edges that might otherwise appear in the narrative are softened by the interplay of the liberal characters. This selection of the more appealing aspects of imperialism viewed through a liberal humanist filter enables an imagined reconstruction based fundamentally upon national fantasy. Even this limited concession to liberalism is at risk when the sincerity of the liberal values expressed by some of the principal characters is questioned. Thus in A Passage to India Fielding is initially presented to the viewer as a genuine liberal prepared to sacrifice his standing in the Raj in the pursuit of justice for Aziz. Yet towards the end of the film the viewer is left to ponder whether or not he may be acting in this way for somewhat less noble frustrated, homo-erotic romantic reasons.

Mrs Thatcher spoke often of the national imperial heritage and sought where possible to evoke memories of imagined or authentic imperial splendour. When British troops recovered the islands of South Georgia from Argentina she urged the nation "rejoice, rejoice, rejoice". She compared herself to Winston Churchill and felt that Britain had regained national pride. She sought to compare a six week colonial encounter with terrified teenage troops conscripted and forced into battle by a third world dictatorship with an epic six year struggle for survival. The comparison recalled a time of apparently complete national unity but such a comparison was essentially jingoistic and the stuff of imperial fantasy. Despite this the illusion resonated with 1980s audiences and finds some reflection in

Chariots of Fire which articulated nationalistic concerns at this time.

This film was replete with images of stirring national solidarity uniting under the flag a Scot, a Jew of Lithuanian extraction and an English aristocrat. Set in the 1920s the film evoked memories of a time when Britain could match the United States and could dismiss the French with the contempt traditionally accorded to "unprincipled frogs". By extension this portrayal of the French helped to distance the reconstructed sense of national identity from the supranational aspirations of the E.U. The renegotiations over Britain's E.U. contributions conducted volubly by Mrs Thatcher would also lend credence to this apparent reclamation of an individual and traditionally robust British national identity.

This film appears to endow the meritocracy with a strong moral force encouraging the belief that the pursuit of individual excellence is a worthy prize justifying the reduction of the interests of the majority. Thatcherism swiftly became a distinct ideology and unusually for a political creed placed morality at its centre. The Prime Minister tended to reduce complex ethical issues to simple moral certainty. The Falklands War was for Mrs Thatcher a straightforward struggle between the "good" democracy of Great Britain and the "evil" dictatorship of Argentina undertaken to ensure that liberty prevailed. Moral conviction would be rewarded with the success that in turn justifies the certainty.

In applauding moral conviction, initiative and individual achievement in such forthright terms Chariots of Fire subtly undermines consensus values and liberal ethics. Compromise is "the Devil's work" and Corinthian values are consigned to the "Prep school playground" since they would, if adopted, interfere with the "pursuit of excellence" and obstruct Abrahams in his mission to "carry the future". The dialogue resonates more closely with the 1980s than the 1920s period in which the film is nominally set. Disguised as religious faith Liddell and Abrahams run essentially for personal glory and self-satisfaction. The manifestly aristocratic Lord Lindsay performs the only act of *noblesse oblige* in the film and then steps aside for the upwardly rising meritocracy represented by Liddell and Abrahams. The implicit undermining of traditional notions of middle class public service reflects contemporary Thatcherite ideology. Even the personal sacrifices made by Eric Liddell appear ultimately to serve his athletic ambitions and not his faith and reflect Thatcherite ideology.

The Empire is re-presented and re-packaged by the Heritage film for contemporary consumption. These imperial fantasies are re-presented as a solution for contemporary ills and as the basis for an imaginary community of alleged homogeneity. The suggestion of community is emphasised by the avoidance of overt class tensions, which are minimised. The Heritage film gives little expression to the emergence of pluralist groupings and divergent moral responses depicted in the Social Realist film. Moral complexities become simple ideological certainty.

There is also apparent in 1980s literature evidence of countervailing cultural influences rejecting imperialist re-construction as a basis of national identity. (O'Shea 1984, Horne 1984, Hewison 1987, Samuel 1989, Riddell 1989, Corner and Harvey 1991, Higson 1993, 1995, 1996, Marwick 1998) Some 1980s productions suggest that the past being re-constructed is in any event inherently fraudulent. In The Ploughman's Lunch the central character Penfield re-presents the Suez crisis as an inspiring example of British statesmanship instead of a post imperial fiasco. The film suggests that images regarded as typifying an era, such as a typical 1930s family enjoying a bedtime drink, were nothing more than the artful creations of advertising agencies. The eponymous "lunch" is in fact a marketing device constructed by a 1960s art director.

The Raj is inverted in My Beautiful Launderette as the Asian immigrant community gains the upper hand by "squeezing the tits of the system". They treat the indigenous white working class inhabitants as colonial subjects reversing the historical working of imperialism. A clear link between organised crime and commercial enterprise is made, questioning the moral foundation of imperial hegemony. The Cook, The Thief, His Wife and Her Lover highlights the perceived cultural vandalism implicit in the ideological assertion of the Conservative Government. Other contemporary productions suggest that social change taking place in the 1980s is so fundamental that there is no possibility of an imagined community. Britannia Hospital expresses such a bleak view of society that complete anarchy and total disorder seem unavoidable.

The tensions produced by this period of change are evident in media representations of the Falklands War. It seems likely that Mrs Thatcher would have enthusiastically embraced a film celebrating in straightforward narrative terms this national military success. When the producers of Tumbledown were making the drama the Government and the Ministry of Defence made overt attempts to influence and even distort the narrative and its inherently anti war theme. Social tension will normally produce open debate and the director Richard Eyre stated that he feared a liberal period, with healthy debate, and social and political questioning encouraged, was ending. There is therefore a suggestion that the tensions arising would be eased by the imposition of the prevailing political and cultural ideology.

There is some evidence for this in that other contemporary television productions and documentaries that did not fit the Thatcherite model of national identity were also subject to some degree of governmental interference, (although on the other hand it must be stressed here that the BBC refused to make Richard Curteis's The Falklands Play). This also supports the premise that any version of national identity propounded at this time was in the form of a deliberately reconstructed model. To this extent the imagined community of the 1980s did not emerge but was an ideological imperative meeting the need for alleged homogeneity. The existence of ideology in this period of social change differentiated the period from the 1950s when the changes emerged through greater social fragmentation amidst rising affluence rather than polemically.

I have articulated the changing perceptions of British national identity during two periods of significant social change: 1955-65 and 1980-90. The key to both periods is Empire: the reaction to the loss of Empire during the first period of social change and the attempts to recreate Empire as a basis for a re-constructed national identity during the second period.

I have analysed and illustrated the hybrid construction of national identity through the representation of a narrow, fractious

CONCLUSION

nationalism. Manifested in the cultural and social changes occurring during the dismantling of Empire in the late 50s and early 60s this questioned traditional pre-war interpretations of an imperialist class bound national identity.

This period also witnessed the coming into prominence of differing forms of social, cultural and ethnic differentiation. Greater expression was given to divided identities, plural groupings and diverse cultures. The changes emerged organically and not ideologically with little overt political influence. There is no evidence of any collective polemic and suggested new paradigm or alternative hegemonic order.

I have then considered the other period of significant social change. This articulated a reclamation of a specifically exclusive bourgeois and essentially imperialist nationalism promoted by the Thatcherite 1980s. This followed a prolonged period of industrial unease, social uncertainty and economic decline and was highly ideological. In this book I have returned to the arguments, themes and concerns I first raised in my 2001 Theses "Realist Nights and Heritage Mornings: Comparing Representations of British National Identity 1955-65 and 1980-1990.

The new Conservative Government embraced conviction politics and Thatcherism swiftly became a distinct political ideology. This found considerable expression in the Heritage film and in the cultural impetus towards gentrification of the emergent bourgeois middle and merchant classes. This required the effacing of the "other" national cultural history of class struggle, workers rights and inclusive sectional interests, so fore-grounded in the 1960s, in order to impose a strident national character and moral certainty. Predicated upon a Right Wing simulacra of British imperial history, this notion of nationalism privileged and represented the superficial values of enterprise, individual conviction and personal commercial gain over the beliefs of community and negotiated consensus.

It was once said that Britain had lost an Empire but not found a role. By the 1980s, she may still not have found a role, but had at least found a National vision.

Appendix

Selected Filmography

Alfie (1966). Director: Lewis Gilbert. A Sheldrake Production. Actors (characters): Michael Caine (Alfie), Shelley Winters (Ruby), Millicent Martin (Siddie).
Another Country (1984). Director: Marek Kaniewska. A Goldcrest Production. Actors (characters): Rupert Everett (Guy Bennett), Colin Firth (Tommy Judd), Cary Elwes (Harcourt).
At the Edge of the Union (1985). A BBC TV production. Documentary.
Billy Liar (1963). Director: John Schlesinger, Assistant Director: Frank Ernst. A production by Vic Films in association with Woodfall. Actors: Tom Courteney (Billy Fisher), Julie Christie (Liz), Wilfred Pickles (Geoffrey Fisher).
The Bostonians (1984). Director: James Ivory. A Merchant/Ivory Production. Actors Christopher Reeve, Vanessa Redgrave, Madeline Potter.
Brideshead Revisited (1981). Director: Charles Sturridge. A Granada TV production. Actors (characters): Jeremy Irons (Charles Ryder), Diana Quick (Julia Flyte), Anthony Andrews (Sebastian Flyte).
Britannia Hospital (1982). Director: Lindsay Anderson. A Channel 4 Films production. Actors (characters): Malcom McDowell (Mick Travis), Graham Crowden (Dr Miller), Marcus Powell (Sir Anthony Main).
Buster (1985). Director: David Green. A Vestron production. Actors (characters): Phil Collins (Buster Edwards), Julie Walters (June Edwards), Larry Lamb (Bruce Reynolds).

APPENDIX

Chariots of Fire (1981). Director: Hugh Hudson. A production by Goldcrest in association with Allied Films. Actors (characters): Ben Cross (Harold Abrahams), Ian Charleston (Eric Liddell), Nigel Havers (Lord Andrew Lindsay), Ian Holm (Sam Massabimi).

The Colditz Story (1956). Director: Guy Hamilton. A production by British Lion- Ivan Foxwell. Actors (characters): John Mills (Pat Reid), Eric Portman, Lionel Jeffries, Christopher Rose.

Coming Thro' the Rye (1923). Director: Cecil M. Hepworth. A Hepworth Picture Plays production. Actors (characters): Alma Taylor (Helen Adair), Shayle Gardner (Paul Vasher), Eileen Derves (Sylvia Flemming).

The Cook, The Thief, His Wife and Her Lover (1989). Director: Peter Greenaway. Produced by British Film Institute Channel 4. Actors (characters): Michael Gambon (Albert), Helen Mirren (Georgina), Alan Howard (Michael).

Coronation Street (1960). A Granada TV production. Devised by Tony Warren. Actors (characters): Pat Phoenix (Elsie Tanner), Ena Sharples (Violet Carson), William Roache (Ken Barlow), Doris Speed (Annie Walker).

The Dambusters (1955). Director: Michael Anderson. Produced by ABPC-Robert Clark. Actors (characters): Michael Redgrave (Hugh Barnes Wallace), Richard Todd (Guy Gibson), Basil Sydney (Sir Arthur Harris).

Dance With a Stranger (1985). Director: Mike Newell. A Channel 4 Films production. Actors (characters): Miranda Richardson (Ruth Ellis), Rupert Everett (Blakely), Ian Holm (Cussens).

Darling (1965). Director: John Schlesinger. A Vic-Appia production. Actors (characters): Dirk Bogarde (Robert Gold), Lawrence Harvey (Miles Brand), Julie Christie (Dianne Scott).

Death on the Rock (1988). A Thames TV production. Documentary.

Defence of the Realm (1985). Director: David Drury. An Enigma production. Actors (characters): Gabriel Byrne (Nick Mullen), Greta Scacchi (Nina Beckman), Denholm Elliott (Vernon Bayliss).

Dixon of Dock Green (1955). Director: Ted Willis. A BBC TV production. Actors (characters): Jack Warner (P. C. Dixon),

Arthur Rigby (Sergeant Flint), Moira Mannion (Sergeant Grace).

Dr No (1962). Director: Terence Young. Eon Productions. Actors (characters): Sean Connery (James Bond), Joseph Wiseman (Dr. No), Ursula Andress (Honeychild Rider).

The Edge of Darkness (1985). A series devised by Troy Kennedy Martin for BBC TV. Actors (characters): Bob Peck (Craven), Joe Don Baker (Jedburgh), Joanne Whalley (Emma).

The Entertainer (1960). Director: Tony Richardson. A Woodfall – Holly production. Actors (characters): Laurence Olivier (Archie Rice), Joan Plowright (Jean), Roger Livesey (Billy).

The Europeans (1978). Director: James Ivory. A Merchant Ivory production. Actors: Lee Remick, (Eugenie Baroness Munster), Robin Ellis, (Robert Acton), Tim Woodward (Felix).

Everyday Except Christmas (1957). Director: Lindsay Anderson. A Graphic production. Documentary.

Flame in the Streets (1961). Director: Roy Baker. A Rank/Somerset production. Actors (characters): John Mills (Jackie Palmer), Sylvia Syms (Kathie Palmer), Brenda de Banzie (Nell Palmer).

From Russia With Love (1963). Director: Terence Young. An Eon production. Actors (characters): Sean Connery (James Bond), Daniella Bianchi (Tatiana Romanova), Robert Shaw (Donald 'Red' Grant).

Ghandi (1982). Director: Richard Attenborough. A Goldcrest production. Actors (characters): Ben Kingsley (Ghandi), Candice Bergen (Margaret Berg-White), John Gielgud (Lord Irwin).

Goldfinger (1965). Director: Guy Hamilton. An Eon production. Actors (characters): Sean Connery (James Bond), Gert Frobe (Goldfinger), Honor Blackman (Pussy Galore).

The Greengage Summer (1961). Director : Lewis Gilbert. A Colombia/PKL production. Actors: Kenneth More, (Elliot) Danielle Darrieux, (Madame Zizi), Susanah York, (Joss), Jane Asher (Hester).

The Grove Family (1954). Devised by Michael Purtwee. A BBC TV production. Actors: Edward Evans, (Mr Groves), Ruth Dunning, (Mrs Groves) Christopher Beeny, (Lenny).

APPENDIX

The Hidden Agenda (1990). Director: Ken Loach. A Granada TV production. Actors (characters): Jack Shepherd (John Stalker), T. P. McKenna (Sir John Herman), Brian Cox (Kerrigan).

High Hopes (1988). Director: Mike Leigh. Produced by Channel 4 Films in association with the National Film Finance Cooperation. Actors (characters): Philip Davis (Cyril), Ruth Sheen (Shirley), David Bamber (Rupert Booth Brain), Lesley Manville (Letitia).

Jack and Knaves (1961). Devised by Colin Morris. A BBC TV production. Documentary.

Jewel in the Crown (1983). Director: Christopher Morahan. A Granada TV production. Actors (characters): Art Malik (Hari Kumar), Tim Piggott Smith (Ronald Merrick), Susan Wooldridge (Daphne Manners).

A Kind of Loving (1962). Director: John Schlesinger. A Vic/Waterhouse production. Actors (characters): Alan Bates (Vic), June Ritchie (Ingrid), Thora Hird (Mrs Rothwell).

The Knack (1965). Director: Richard Lester. A Woodfall production. Actors (characters): Rita Tushingham (Nancy), Michael Crawford (Colin), Ray Brooks (Tolan).

The Long Good Friday (1979). Director: John Mackenzie. A Calendar production. Actors (characters): Bob Hoskins (Harold Shand), Helen Mirren (Victoria), Derek Thompson (Geoff).

The Leather Boys (1963). Director: Sidney J. Furie. Produced by Raymond Stross Productions. Actors (characters): Rita Tushingham (Dot), Colin Campbell (Reggie), Dudley Sutton (Pete), Gladys Henson (Gran).

Look Back in Anger (1959). Director: Tony Richardson. A Woodfall production. Actors (characters): Richard Burton (Jimmy Porter), Claire Bloom (Helena Charles), Mary Ure (Alison Porter), Dame Edith Evans (Mrs Tanner).

Maurice (1987). Director: James Ivory. A Merchant/Ivory production. Actors (characters): Hugh Grant (Clive Durham), James Wilby (Maurice), Rupert Graves (Scudder).

Meet the Pioneers (1948). Director: Lindsay Anderson. A Sequence Films production. Documentary.

My Beautiful Launderette (1985). Director: Stephen Frears. A Working Title Ltd/SAF production for Channel 4. Actors (characters): Daniel Day-Lewis (Johnny), Gordon Warnecke (Omar), Saeed Jaffrey (Uncle Nasser), Rita Wolf (Tania).

Oscar Wilde (1960). Directors: Gregory Ratoff and Scott McGregor. A Vantage production. Actors (characters): Ralph Richardson (Sir Edward Carson), Robert Morley (Oscar Wilde), Phyllis Calvert (Constance Wilde), John Melville (Lord Alfred Douglas).

A Passage to India (1984). Director: David Lean. Produced by John Brabierres, Richard Goodwin in association with John Heyman and Edward Sands and Harver Box Office Inc. Actors (characters): Peggy Ashcroft (Mrs Moore), Judy Davis (Adela), James Fox (Richard Fielding), Victor Banerjee (Aziz).

The Ploughmans Lunch (1983). Director: Richard Eyre. A Channel 4 Films production. Actors (characters): Jonathan Pryce (James Penfield), Charlie Dore (Susan Barrington), Tim Curry (Jeremy).

Reach for the Sky (1954). Director: Lewis Gilbert. A Rank/Pinnacle production. Actors (characters): Kenneth More (Douglas Badder), Muriel Pavlo (Mrs Badder), Linden Brook, Lee Patterson.

Rock Around the Clock (1955). Director: Fred F Sears. A Columbia/Sam Katzman production. Actors: Bill Haley and the Comets, The Platters, Little Richard, Tony Martínez and His Band.

Prick Up Your Ears (1987). Director: Stephen Frears. A Zenith Productions/Channel 4 Films production. Actors (characters): Gary Oldman (Joe Orton), Alfred Molina (Kenneth Halliwell).

The Private Life of Henry VIII (1933). Director: Zultan Korda. An Alexander Korda/Zultan Kordan production. Actors (characters): Charles Laughton (Henry VIII), Merle Oberon (Jane Seymour).

Room at the Top (1959). Director: Jack Clayton. A Remus production. Actors (characters): Laurence Harvey (Joe Lampton), Simone Signoret (Alice Aisgill), Heather Sears (Susan Brown), Donald Wolfit (Mr Brown).

APPENDIX

A Room With a View (1985). Director: James Ivory. A Merchant/Ivory production. Actors (characters): Helena Bonham-Carter (Lucy Hornchurch), Julian Sands (George Emerson), Denholm Elliott (Mr Emerson).

Sapphire (1959). Director: Basil Dearden. An Artna production. Actors (characters): Nigel Patrick (Hazard), Michael Craig (Leroyd), Yvonne Mitchell (Mildred), Paul Massey (David).

Saturday Night and Sunday Morning (1960). Director: Kavel Reisz. A Woodfall production. Actors (characters): Albert Finney (Arthur), Shirley Anne Field (Doreen), Rachel Roberts (Brenda), Hylda Baker (Aunt Ada).

Scandal (1989). Director: Mike Newell. Produced by Palace in association with British Screen. Actors (characters): Ian McKellen (John Profumo), Joanne Whalley (Christine Keeler), John Hurt (Stephen Ward).

Scotland Yard (1960). Devised by Robert Barr. A BBC TV production. Documentary.

This Sporting Life (1963). Director: Lindsay Anderson. An Independent Artists production. Actors (characters): Richard Harris (Frank Machin), Rachel Roberts (Mrs Hammond), Alan Badel (Weaver), William Hartnell (Johnson).

A Taste of Honey (1961). Director: Tony Richarson. A Woodfall production. Actors (characters): Rita Tushingham (Jo), Dora Bryan (Helen), Robert Stephens (Peter).

The Trials of Oscar Wilde (1960). Director: Ken Hughes. A Warwick Viceroy production. Actors (characters): Peter Finch (Oscar Wilde), John Fraser (Lord Alfred Douglas), Yvonne Mitchell (Constance).

Thunderball (1965). Director: Terence Young. An Eon production. Actors (characters): Sean Connery (James Bond), Martine Beswick (Paula Caplan), Adelpho Celi (Emilio Largo).

Tumbledown (1988). Director: Richard Eyre. A BBC TV production. Actors (characters): Colin Firth (Robert Laurence), Paul Rhys (Hugh Mackessac), David Calder (John Laurence).

Upstairs Downstairs (1973). Devised by Jean Marsh. A London Weekend TV production. Actors (characters): Jean Marsh (Rose), Gordon Jackson (Hudson), Simon Williams (Captain Bellamy), Lesley Anne Down (Georgina).

Victim (1961). Director: Basil Dearden. A Parkway production. Actors (characters): Dirk Bogarde (Melville Farr), Sylvia Syms (Laura Farr), Dennis Price (Calloway), Nigel Stock (Phip).

Wish You Were Here (1987). Director: David Leyland. A Channel 4 Films production. Actors (characters): Emily Lloyd (Lynda), Tom Bell, (Eric), Clare Clifford (Mrs Parfitt).

Who Bombed Birmingham (1990). Director: David Boulton. A Granada TV production. Actors (characters): John Hurt (Chris Mullen), Martin Shaw (Ian McBride), Niall Toibin (Paddy Hill).

Who Me? (1960). Director: Robert Barr. A BBC TV production. Documentary.

You Only Live Twice (1967). Director: Lewis Gilbert. Produced by Eon Productions. Actors (characters): Sean Connery (James Bond), Donald Pleasance (Stavro Blofeld), Akiko Wakabayashi (Aki).

Z-Cars (1962). Director: John McGrath, scriptwriter: Troy Kennedy Martin. A BBC TV production. Brian Blessed (Fancy Smith), Stratford Johns (Inspector Barlow), Frank Windsor (John Watt).

Bibliography

ADAIR, G., 'Another Country', *Monthly Film Bulletin,* vol. 51, no. 2, (1984), 148-149.

ADENEY, M. and LLOYD, J., *The Miner's Strike 1985-85: Loss Without Limit.* (Routledge and Kegan Paul, 1986).

ADONIS, A. and HAMES, T. (eds.), *A Conservative Revolution? The Thatcher-Reagan Decade in Perspective* (Manchester University Press, 1994).

ALDGATE, A., *Censorship and the Permissive Society: British Cinema and Theatre 1955-65* (Oxford: Clarendon Press, 1995), 45-150.

ANDERSON, B., *Imagined Communities: Reflections on the Origin and Spread of Nationalism* (London: Verso, 1985), 11-17, 41-50, 80-104, 129-141.

ANDERSON, L., 'Stand Up! Stand Up!', *Sight and Sound* (Autumn 1956), 63-69.

ANDERSON, L., 'Review of A Taste of Honey', *Encore,* vol. 15 (July 1958), 42-43.

ANDREW, D., *Concepts in Film Theory* (Oxford: Oxford University Press, 1984).

ARTS COUNCIL, THE, *The glory of the Garden* (HMSO 1984).

ARTS COUNCIL, THE, *A Great British Success Story* (HMSO 1985), 11.

ASCHERSON, N., 'Why Heritage is Right Wing', *The Observer* (8 November 1987), 9.

AUTY, M. and RODDICK, N. (eds.) *British Cinema Now* (London: British Film Institute, 1985).

AVON, LORD, *The Memoirs of Sir Anthony Eden, Full Circle* (Cassell, 1960).

BAHRO, A., 'Ecology Crisis and Socialist Idea', *Socialism and Survival* (Heretic Books, 1982), 35.

BARKER, SIR E., *National Character* (London: London Press, 1927).

BARKER, SIR E., *Character of England* (Oxford: Oxford Press, 1947).

BARNETT, A., *Iron Britannia: Why Parliament Waged the Falklands War* (Allison and Busby, 1982), 148-165.

BARR, C., 'Review of Saturday Night and Sunday Morning', *Granta*, vol. LXIV, no. 1204 (1960).

BARR, C., *'Amnesia and Schizophrenia in All Our Yesterdays: 90 Years of British Cinema'* (London: British Film Institute, 1986).

BENNETT, T., *The Making of The Spy Who Loved Me* (Open University Press, 1977).

BENNETT, T. *Bond and Beyond* (Milton Keynes: Open University Press, 1992).

BENNETT, T. (ed.) *Popular Culture: Past and Present* (Milton Keynes: Open University Press, 1982).

BENNETT, T., MERCER, C. and WOOLLACOTT, T. (eds.), *Popular Culture and Social Relations* (Open University Press, 1986), 1-80.

BHABHA, H. K., *Nation and Narration* (Routledge, 1990), 1-10, 25-40, 50-60.

BISHOP, P. and WITHEROW, J., *The Winter War: the Falklands* (Quartet, 1982).

BLAND, L., MCCABE, T. and MORT, F., 'Sexuality and Reproduction: Three 'Official' Instances' in Barret, M. *et al* (ed.), Ideology and Cultural Prodution. (London: Croom Helm, 1979), 84.

BOGDANOR, V. and SKIDELSKY, R. (eds.), *The Age of Affluence* (Macmillan, 1970), 35-75.

BOOTH, A., 'A Gap Final Left to God', *The Guardian* (16 April 1990).

BORDWELL, D., *Narration in the Fiction Film* (Chatto and Windus, 1985).

BRADLEY, I., *The Call to Seriousness* (London, 1976), 40-65.

BRAGG, M. (presenter and compiler), *The South Bank Show: Coronation Street* (Special. ITV, December 1995).

BRAINE, J. *The Spectator* (December, 1961), 948.

BRANDT, G. W. (ed.), *British Television Drama in the 1980s* (Cambridge University Press, 1993).
BREUILLY, J., *Nationalism and the State* (Manchester University Press, 1985), 1-75.
BRIGGS, A., *Competition. The History of Broadcasting in the United Kingdom* vol. V (Oxford University Press, 1995).
BRUNSDON, C., 'Crossroads: Notes on Soap Opera', *Screen*, vol. 22, no. 4 (1981), 32-37.
BRUNSDON, C., 'Problems with Quality', *Screen*, vol. 31, no. 1 (1990), 67-90.
BRUNT, R., 'A Divine Gift to Inspire? Popular Cultural Representation, Nationhood and the British Monarchy' in Strinati, D. and Wagg, S. (eds.), *Come on down? Popular Media Culture in Post-war Britain* (London: Routledge, 1992).
BUTT, R., 'Political Union in Europe', *New European*, vol. 3 (Summer-Autumn 1990), 45-51.
CAIRNS, C., 'Rooms Without a View', *Sight and Sound*, vol. 1, (London: BFI, June 1991), 10-13.
CAMPBELL MOSINER, E. and SIMPSON, I. R. (ed.), *The Correspondance of Adam Smith* 2nd edition (Oxford University Press, 1987).
CANNADINE, D., 'The Context, Performance and Meaning of Ritual. The British Monarchy and the Invention of Tradition (1820-1977)' in Hobsbawm, E. and Ranger, T. (eds.), *The Invention of Tradition* (Cambridge University Press, 1983).
CANNADINE, D., *The Pleasures of the Past.* (London: Collins, 1989).
CANNADINE, D., 'Gilbert and Sullivan: the Making and Unmaking of a British Tradition' in Porter, R. (ed.), *Myths of the English* (Polity Press, 1992).
CARDIFF, D. and SCANNELL, P., 'Broadcasting and National Unity' in Curran, J.; Smith, A. and Wingate, P. (eds.), *Impacts and Influences* (Methuen, 1987).
CARTER, E., 'Chariots of Fire: Traditional Values / False History', *Jump Cut,* no. 28, (Berkeley USA, 1982), 14-16.
CASHMORE, E., *United Kingdom? Class, Race and Gender Since the War* (Unwin Hyman, 1989).

CAUGHIE, J., 'Broadcasting and Cinema: Converging Histories' in Barr, C. (ed.). *All Our Yesterdays: 90 years of British Cinema* (London: British Film Institute, 1986).

CHANDAVARKAR, K., 'Strangers in the Land: India and the British Since the Late Nineteenth Century' in Bayley, C. A. (ed.), *The Raj: India and the British 1600-1947* (London National Portrait Gallery, 1990), 368-379.

CHESHIRE COUNTY COUNCIL, *Tatton Park: the Mansion* (1987), 38.

CHURCHILL, W. (1950), cited in *Europe Unite! Speeches* 1947-1959 (1960), 417-418.

CLARKE, K., *Conservative Party Conference Speech* (Blackpool, 11 October 1985).

COLLEY, L., *Britons* (New Haven, 1992), 40-75.

COLLINS, J., *Uncommon Cultures: Popular Culture and Postmodernism* (London: Routledge, 1989).

CONRAN, S., *Castle Howard: The Official Guide* (Castle Howard Estate Ltd, 1997).

CONTE-HELM, M., *Japan and the Northeast of England* (Athlone Press, 1989).

COOK, P., *The Cinema Book* (British Film Institute, 1987).

COOPER, D. E., 'Looking Back on Anger' in Bogdanor, V. and Skidelsky, R. (eds.) *The Age of Affluence* (Macmillan, 1970).

CORNELIUS, A. AND MILNER, M., 'EFTA Nations Queue Us To Find Their Place In Brave New World Of The Super Market', *The Guardian* (6 March 1990).

CORNER, J. AND HARVEY, S. (eds.), *Enterprise and Heritage: Crosscurrents of National Culture* (Routledge, 1991).

CORNER, J. and HARVEY, S. 'Introduction: Great Britain Limited' in *Enterprise and Heritage: Crosscurrents of National Culture* (Routledge, 1991), 1-20.

CORNER, J. AND HARVEY, S., 'Mediating Tradition and Modernity' in *Enterprise and Heritage: Crosscurrents of National Culture* (Routledge, 1991).

CRAIG, S. and WODDIS, C. 'How the Arts Council Keeps it in the Family', *City Limits* (18-24 February 1983).

CRITCHLEY, J., 'How the BBC Provokes the Tories', *The Guardian* (13 February. 1989), 21.

CSEPELI, G., 'An Inorganic Nation' in Schlesinger, P. *Media, State and Nation: Political Violence and Collective Identities* (Sage, 1991), 137-193

DAHRENDORF, R., 'Reflections on the Revolution in Europe' in *A Letter Intended to Have Been Sent to a Gentlemen in Warsaw* (Chatto and Windu, 1990).

DAVIDSON, B., *Modern Africa: a Social and Political History* 3rd edition (Longman 1994).

DAVIES, N., *Europe: a History* (Oxford University Press, 1996).

DAVIS, F., *Yearning for Yesterday: a Sociology of Nostalgia* (Methuen, 1979).

DEARLOVE and SAUNDERS, *Economics in Postwar Britain 1945-1963* (Macmillan, 1991).

DEHN, P. *Daily Herald* (September 15, 1996) cited in Higson, A. *Dissolving Views: Key Writings on British Cinema* (Cassell).

DELANEY, S., *A Taste of Honey* (Mathuen, 1959).

DENNING, LORD, *Lord Denning Report* (London: HMSO, 1963).

DERBYSHIRE, J. and DERBYSHIRE, I., *Politics in Britain: From Callaghan to Thatcher* (W&R Chambers Ltd., 1990), 15-170.

DHONDY, F. 'All the Raj', *New Socialist*, no. 16 (March-April 1984), 47.

DIMBLEBY, D. and REYNOLDS, D., *An Ocean Apart* (BBC Books and Hodder and Stoughton, 1988).

DRESSER, M., 'Britannia' in Samuel, R. (ed.), *Patriotism*, vol. 3 (1989), 26-49.

DRIVER, F., 'Fields of Vision. Visualizing Landscape', *Journal of Urban History*, vol. 21, no. 6 (1995), 64.

DUKE, V. and EDGELL, S., 'Public Expenditure Cuts in Britain and Consumption Sectoral Cleavages', *International Journal of Urban and Regional Research* (1984).

DUNLEAVY, P. and HUSBANDS, C., *British Democracy at the Crossroads* (George Allen and Unwin, 1985).

DURGHAT, R., *A Mirror for England* (London: Faber and Faber, 1970).

DYER, R., *Coronation Street: A Television Monograph* (British Film Institute, 1981), 3-52.

DYER, R., *The Matter of Images: Essays on Representations* (London: Routledge, 1993).

DYER, R., *White* (London: Routledge 1997).

ECO, U., *The Bond Affair* (London: Macdonald, 1966).

ELSAESSER, T., 'Images for Sale: the New British Cinema' in Friedman, L., *British Cinema and Thatcherism* (London: University College London, 1993).

ERIKSON, K. T., *Wayward Puritans* (London: Wiley, 1966).

FIELD, J. 'Police Monitoring: the Sheffield Experience' in Fine, R. and Millar, R. *Policing the Miner's Strike* (Lawrence and Wishart, 1985).

FINCH, M. and KWIETNIOWSKI, R., 'Melodrama and Maurice: Homo Is Where the Het Is', *Screen*, vol. 29, no. 3, (1988), 72-80.

FINE, R. and MILLAR, R., *Policing the Miner's Strike* (Lawrence and Wishart, 1985).

FISKE, J., *Television Culture* (London: Methuen, 1987).

FLEMING, I., *From Russia With Love*, (London: Pan, 1961).

FORBES, J., 'Maurice', *Monthly Film Bulletin,* vol. 54, no. 646 (November 1987), 324-325.

FOSTER, K., 'To Serve and Protect: Textualising the Falklands Conflict', *Cultural Studies*, no. 11 (1997), 235-52.

FRANKEL, J., *British Foreign Policy 1945-1973* (Oxford University Press, 1975).

FRANKENBERG, R., *Communities in Britain* (Penguin, 1966).

FRIEDMAN, L., *British Cinema and Thatcherism* (London: University College London, 1993).

GALBRAITH, J. K., *The Affluent Society* (Riverside Press, 1958).

GELLNER, E., *Nations and Nationalism* (Basil Blackwell, 1983), 1-30, 80-105.

GERAGHTY, C. 'Women and Sixties Cinema: The Development of the 'Darling' Girl' in Murphy, R. (ed.), *The British Cinema Book* (British Film Institute, 1997).

GIDDENS, A., *A Contemporary Critique of Historical Materialism* (Macmillan, 1981).

GILLIAT, P., *The Observer*, 15 April 1962.

GILROY, P., *There Ain't No Black in the Union Jack: The Cultural Politics of Race and Nation* (Hutchinson, 1987), 43-72.

GIROURARD, M., *Return to Camelot* (New Heaven and London, 1981), 80-105.

GOFTON, L., 'Back to the Future', *Times Higher Education Supplement* (20 January 1989).

GRAY, R., 'The Falklands Factor' in Hall, S. and Jacques, M. (eds.), *The Politics of Thatcherism* (Lawrence&Wishart 1983b), 271-281.

GREENFIELD, L., *Nationalism: Five Roads into Modernity* (Harvard University Press, Cambridge MA and London, 1992).

HALL, M., 'The Consumer Sector 1950-60' in Worswick, G and Ady, P., *The British Economy in the 1950s* (London: Oxford University Press 1962b).

HALL, S. and WHANNEL, P., *The Popular Arts: A Critical Guide to the Mass Media* (Boston: Beacon, 1964).

HALL, S., 'Jimmy Porter and the Two-and-Nines', *Definition* (February 1960), 100.

HALL, S. and JACQUES, M. (eds.), *The Politics of Thatcherism* (Lawrence&Wishart, 1983), 257-290.

HALL, S., *The Hard Road to Renewal* (London: Verso, 1988), 1-60.

HAMES, T., 'The Special Relationship' in Hames, T. and Adonis, A. (eds.), *A Conservative Revolution? The Thatcher-Reagan Decade in Perspective* (Manchester University Press, 1994b), 114-143.

HAMES, T. and ADONIS, A. (eds.), *A Conservative Revolution? The Thatcher-Reagan Decade in Perspective* (Manchester University Press, 1994), 238-252.

HARRIS, R., *Gotcha!: The Media, the Government and the Falklands Crisis* (Faber and Faber, 1983), 13-26; 92-120.

HEALD, D., *Privatisation: Analysing its Appeal and Limitations* (MacMillan, 1984)

HEBDIGE, D., *Hiding in the Light: On Images and Things* (London: Comedia-Routledge, 1988), 55-95.

HELGERSON, R., *Forms of Nationhood: The Elizabethan Writing of England* (Chicago and London: University of Chicago Press, 1992).

HELLER, A., *A Theory of History* (Routledge, 1982), 67-284.

HENDERSON, N., *Channels and Tunnels, Reflections on Britain and Abroad* (Weidenfeld and Nicolson, 1987).

HETHERINGTON, P. and ROBINSON, F., 'Tyneside Life' in Robinson, F. (ed.), *Post-Industrial Tyneside. Newcastle-upon-Tyne City Libraries and Arts* (1989b), 189-210.

HEWISON, R., *The Heritage Industry: Britain in a Climate of Decline* (Methuen, 1987), 9- 12; 35-43; 83; 91-102; 133; 142-4.

HEWISON, R., 'Commerce and Culture' in Corner, J. and Harvey, S. (eds.), *Enterprise and Heritage: Crosscurrents of Natural Culture* (Routledge, 1991b), 162-178.

HIBBIN, N., 'Review of Room at the Top', *The Daily Worker* (26 January 1959).

HIGSON, A., *Representing the National Past: Nostalgia and Pastiche in the Heritage Film* (London: Univeristy College London Press, 1993).

HIGSON, A. (ed.), *Dissolving Views: Key Writings on British Cinema* (London: Cassell, 1996).

HIGSON, A. 'The Heritage Film and British Cinema' in *Dissolving Views: Key Writings on British Cinema* (London: Cassell, 1996).

HIGSON, A., 'Space, Place, Spectacle: Landscape and Townscape in the Kitchen Sink Film' in *Dissolving Views: Key Writings on British Cinema* (Cassell, 1996).

HIGSON, A., 'British Cinema' in Hill, J. and Church-Gibson, P., *The Oxford Guide to Film Studies* (Oxford and New York: Oxford University Press, 1998b).

HILL, D., 'Review of Coronation Street', *The Spectator* (29 December 1961), 948.

HILL, J., 'Working Class Realism and Sexual Reaction: Some Theses on the British 'New Wave' ' in Curran, J. and Porter, V. (eds.), *British Cinema History* (London: Wedenfeld and Nicolson, 1983b).

HILL, J., *Class, Sexuality and the British Cinema 1956-63* D. Phil Thesis (University of York, 1985).

HILL, J., *Sex, Class and Realism: British Cinema 1956-1963* (London: British Film Institute, 1986), 15-230.

HILL, J., 'British Cinema as National Cinema: Production Audience and Representation' in Murphy, R. (ed.), *The British Cinema Book* (London: British Film Institute, 1997b).

Hill, J. and Church-Gibson, P. (eds.), *The Oxford Guide to Film Studies* (Oxford University Press, 1998).

HILL, J., *British Cinema in the 1980s* (Oxford: Clarendon Press, 1999).

HIMMELWEIT, H., *How Voters Decide* (Open University Press, 1985).

HINCHCLIFFE, A., *British Theatre 1950-70* (Basil Blackwell, 1974).

HINDMARSH, J., "Realist Nights and Heritage Mornings: Comparing Representations of British National Identity 1955-1965 and 1980-1990". (York University Press, 2001).

HJORT, G. and MACKENZIE, C. (eds.), *Cinema and Nation* (Oxford University Press, 2000).

HOBSBAWM, E., 'Observations on the Debate' in Jacques, M. and Mulhern, F. (eds.), *The Forward March of Labour Halted?* (New Left Books, 1981), 19-182.

HOBSBAWM, E. and RANGER, T., *The Invention of Tradition* (Cambridge University Press, 1983).

HOBSBAWN, E., 'Falklands Fallout' in Halls and Jacques (eds.), *The Politics of Thatcherism* (Lawrence&Wishart, 1983b), 257-271.

HOBSBAWM, E., *Nations and Nationalism Since 1780: Programme, Myth and Reality* (Cambridge: Cambridge University Press, 1990).

HOBSBAWM, E., *Nations and Nationalism since 1780: Programme, Myth and Reality* 2nd expanded Ed. (Cambridge: Cambridge University Press, 1993).

HOGGART, R., *The Uses of Literacy* (Harmondsworth: Penguin, 1957), 15-45, 50-125.

HOGGART, R., *The Uses of Literacy* (Harmondsworth: Penguin, 1958).

HOLLINGHURST, A., 'Suppressive Nostalgia', *Times Literary Supplement* (November 1987), 1225.
HOPKINS, H., *The New Look* (Secker and Warburg, 1963).
HORNE, D., *The Great Museum: the Representation of History* (Pluton Press, 1984).
HOUSE OF COMMONS, *Public and Private Funding of the Arts* (HMSO, 1982), x-xvi.
HOUSE OF COMMONS, *The Export of Works of Art 1985-1986* (HMSO, 1986).
HOUSTON, P., 'Review of Look Back in Anger', *The Spectator*, (5 June 1959).
HOWARD, SIR M., 'Escape from History', *The Guardian* (13 March 1990).
HOWE, G., *The Conservative Revival of Britain* (Conservative Political Centre, 1988).
HUTCHINSON, J. and SMITH, A. D. (eds.), (Oxford and New York: Oxford University Press, 1994).
IMESON, J., 'Review of Chariots of Fire' in *Monthly Film Bulletin* (May 1981), 90.
JACKSON, B., *Working-Class Community* (Harmonsworth: Penguin, 1972), 39.
JACKSON, P. (ed.), *Implementing Government Policy Initiatives: the Thatcher Administration 1979-83* (Royal Institute of Public Administration, 1985).
JAMESON, F. 'Post-Modernism on the Cultural Logic of Late Capitalism', *New Left Review*, no. 146 (July-August 1984), 53-92.
JENKINGS, R., in Riddell, P. *The Thatcher Decade: How Britain Has Changed During the 1980's* (Blackwell, 1989b), 194-195.
JENKINS, P., *The Guardian* (6 October 1982) cited in O'Shea, A., *Formations of Nation and Peolple* (Routledge and Kegan Paul, 1984), 37.
JENKINS, P., *Mrs Thatcher's Revolution: the Ending of a Socialist Era* (Jonathan Cape Publishers, 1987).
JESSOP, R. and BENNETT, K., 'Authoritarian Populism, Two Nations and Thatcherism', *New Left Review*, no. 147 (September-October 1984), 32-61.

JONES, D., *The English Nation* (Chatto &Windus, 1998).
JONES, W. and KAVANAGH, D., *British Politics Today* (Manchester University Press, 1991), 10-36.
JORDAN, M., 'Character Types and the Individual' in Dyer, R., *Coronation Street: a Television Monograph* (British Film Institute, 1981).
KALTEFLEITER, W. and PFALTZGRAFF, R. (eds.), *The Peace Movements in Europe and the United States* (Croom Helm, 1985).
KAPLAN, E. A. (ed.), *Women in Film Noir* (London: British Film Institute, 1978).
KAVANAGH, D., *Thatcherism and British Politics: the End of Consensus?* (Oxford University Press, 1987).
KEINER, R., *The Politics of the Police* 2nd Edition (Harvester, 1992).
KELLY, C. and BREINLINGER, S., 'Identity and Injustice: Exploring Women's Participation in Collective Action', *Journal of Community and Applied Social Psychology*, no. 5 (1995), 41-57.
KENNEDY, H., 'The Brits Have Gone Nuts', *Film Comment* (July-August 1985), 52.
KENNEDY, P., *The Rise and Fall of the Great Powers* (Unwin Hyman, 1988).
KETTLE, M., 'John Paul's Grand Design for Europe', *The Guardian* (27 April 1990).
KNIGHT, A., 'Review of Room at theTop', *The Saturday Review* (11 April 1959).
KOENING, C. F., 'Europe's Spiritual Guidelines', *New European*, no. 2, vol. 1 (Spring 1989), 20-23.
LAING, S., *Representations of Working Class Life 1957-64* (Macmillan, 1986), 3-51, 20-95, 109-93.
LAING, S., 'Banging in Some Reality: The Original Z Cars' in Corner, J. (ed.), *Popular Television in Britain: Studies in Cultural History* (British Film Institute, 1991b), 125-145.
LAING, S., 'The Politics of Culture: Institutional Change' in Moore-Gilbert, B. and Seed, J., *Cultural Revolution? The Challenge of the Arts in the 1960s* (Routledge, 1992b).

LASKI, H., *The Rise of European Liberalism* (London, 1936).
LEADBEATER, C., 'The Tory Years', *The Observer* (4 May 1997).
LESTER, R. (compiler and presenter), *Hollywood U. K.* (BBC TV, 9 September 1993).
LEWIS, P., 'Z Cars', *Contrast*, no. 1 (1961-62), 305-318.
LIGHT, A., 'Englishess', *Sight and Sound* (July 1991), 63.
LOACH, L., 'Can Feminism Survive a Third Term', *Feminist Review* no. 27, (1987), 24-36.
LOVELL, A., 'Review of The Entertainer', *Tribune* (19 August 1960) cited in Hill, J., *Sex, Class and Realism: British Cinema 1956-1963* (London: British Film Institute, 1986).
LOVELL, A., 'Free Cinema' in Lovell, A. (ed.), *Studies in Documentary* (London, 1972b),52.
LOVELL, T., 'Coronation Street' in Dyer, R., *Coronation Street: A Television Monograph* (London: British Film Institute, 1981b), 32-90.
LOVELL, T., 'Landscapes and Stories in 1960s British Realism', *Screen,* vol. 31, no. 4 (winter 1990), 357-376.
LUKES, S., 'The Future of British Socialism?' in B. Pimlott (ed.), *Fabian Essays in Socialist Thought* (Heinemann, 1984), 269-83.
LUMLEY, R., *The Museum Time-Machine: Putting Cultures on Display* (Routledge, 1988).
MACCABE, C., 'Realism and the Cinema: Notes on Some Brechtian Thesis', *Screen*, no. 2, vol. 15 (1974), 7-27.
MACINNES, C., 'A Taste of Reality', *Encounter*, no. 4, vol. 12 (March 1959), 70-71.
MACINNES, J., *Thatcherism at Work: Industrial Relations and Economic Change* (Open University Press, 1987).
MACLAREN, J., 'Review of Room at the Top', *The New Yorker* (11 April 1959).
MACMILLAN, H., 'Speech in Cape Town, South Africa' (3 February 1960) cited in Horne, D., (1989), 195.
MALCOM, D., 'Review of Room With a View', *The Guardian* (10 April 1986), 13.
MARQUAND, D., *The Unprincipled Society: New Demands and Old Politics* (Fontana, 1988).

MARSHALL, G., NEWBY, H., ROSE, D. and VOGLER; C., *Social Class in Modern Britain* (Routledge, 1988), 114.

MARWICK, A., *British Society Since 1945* (Penguin, 1990), 308-393.

MARWICK, A., *Culture in Britain Since 1945* (Basil Blackwell, 1991), 138-191.

MARWICK, A., *The Sixties: Cultural Revolution in Britain, France, Italy and the United States 1958-1974* (Oxford University Press, 1998).

MARWICK, A. (ed.), *The Arts, Literature and Society* (London: Routledge, 1990).

MATTAUSCH, J., 'CND: The First Phase 1958 to 1967' in Klandermans, B. (ed.), *Peace Movements in Europe and the United States* (JAI Press, 1991).

MATTHEWS, T., *Censored* (London: Chatto Press, 1994).

MAYNE, R., 'Bad Boys', *Sight and Sound*, vol. 53, no. 2 (Spring 1984), 148-149.

MCGRATH, J., 'Better a Bad Night in Bootle', *Theatre Quarterly*, vol. 5, no. 19 (1975), 42-43.

MCNEIL, M., 'The Old and New Worlds of Information Technology in Britain' in Corner, J. and Harvey, S. (eds.), *Enterprise and Heritage. Crosscurrents of Natural Culture* (Routledge, 1991b), 116-137.

MELLOR, A., 'Enterprise and Heritage in the Dock' in Corner, J. and Harvey, S. (eds.), *Enterprise and Heritage. Crosscurrents of Natural Culture* (Routledge 1991b), 93-116.

MELLY, G., *Revolt into Style: the Pop Arts in Britain* (Penguin, 1972), 1-35.

MICHIE, A., 'Scotland: Strategies of Centralisation' in Barr, C. (ed.), *All Our Yesterdays: 90 Years of British Cinema* (London: British Film Institute, 1986b).

MIDDLEMAS, K., *Politics in Industrial Society* (Deutsch, 1979).

MILLAR, G., 'The Real India?', *Sight and Sound*, vol. 54, no. 2 (Spring 1985), 139-140.

MONK, C., 'Sexuality and the Heritage', *Sight and Sound* (October 1995), 33-34.

MONTICELLI, S., 'Italian Post-War Cinema and Neo-Realism' in Hill, J. and Church-Gibson, P. (eds.), *The Oxford Guide to Film Studies* (Oxford University Press, 1998b).

MOORE-GILBERT, B. and SEED, J., *Cultural Revolution? The Challenge of the Arts in the 1960s* (Routledge, 1992).

MOORHEAD, C., *Sydney Bernstein: A Biography* (Manchester University Press, 1984), 30-55.

MORAN, A., 'Film Policy: Hollywood and Beyond' in Hill, J. and Church-Gibson, P. (eds.), *The Oxford Guide to Film Studies* (Oxford University Press, 1998b).

MORGAN, K. S., *The Falklands Campaign - a Digest of Debates in the House of Commons* (HMSO, 2 April to 15 June 1982).

MORRISON, B., *The Movement: English Poetry and Fiction in the 1950s* (Oxford University Press, 1980).

MURPHY, R., *Sixties British Cinema* (London: British Film Institute, 1992), 20-75, 105-35.

MURPHY, R. (ed.), *The British Cinema Book* (London: British Film Institute, 1997).

NAIRN, T., *The Break-up of Britain (Crisis and Neo-nationalism)* (NLB, 1977), 11-92, 291-306, 325-329.

NAIRN, T., *The Enchanted Glass: Britain and its Monarchy* (London: Radius, 1988), 35-60.

NAIRN, T., *Faces of Nationalism: Janus Revisited* (London and New York: Verso, 1997).

NEWMAN, G., *The Rise of English Nationalism 1740-1830* (London, 1987), 10-35.

O'SHEA, A., 'Trusting the People: How does Thatcherism Work' in Bennett, T. and Williamson, J. (eds.), *Formations of Nation and People* (Routledge and Kegan Paul, 1984), 19-68.

OLSON, M., *The Rise and Decline of Nations: Economic Growth, Stagflation, and Social Rigidities* (Yale University Press, 1982).

ORBANZ, E., *Journey to a Legend and Back: the British Realistic Film* (Berlin: Volker Spiess, 1977).

ORWELL, G., 'England Your England' in Orwell, S. and Angus, I. (eds.), *The Collected Essays, Journalism and Letters of George Orwell*, vol. 2 (Harmondsworth: Penguin, 1970), 97.

OSBORNE, J., *The Entertainer* (London: Faber, 1957).

OSBORNE, J., 'And Other Views', *Encounter*, vol. XV, no. 3 (September1960), 64.
PALMER, J., 'Tory MEP's Fear Moves to Oust Them', *The Guardian* (13 January 1990).
PARK, J., *Learning to Dream: the New British Cinema* (London: Faber and Faber, 1984).
PARKIN, F., *Middle Class Radicalism: the Social Bases of the British Campaign for Nuclear Disarmament* (Manchester University Press, 1968).
PERKIN, H., *The Origins of Modern English Society 1780-1880* (London, 1969), 265-290.
PERKINS, V. F., 'British Cinema', *Movie* (1962), 2-7.
PETLEY, J., 'Reaching for the Stars' in Roddick, N. and Auty, M. (eds.), *British Cinema Now* (British Film Institute, 1985).
PETRIE, D., *Creativity and Constraint in the British Film Industry* (Macmillan, 1991).
PETRIE, D., *The British Cinematographer* (British Film Institute, 1996).
POOLE, M., 'Englishness for Export' cited in Kerr, P., 'Classic Series – To Be Continued', *Screen*, vol. 23, no. 1 (May June 1982).
POOLE, R., *Nation and Identity* (London: Routledge, 1999).
PORTER, V., in Tiratsoo, N. (ed.), *From Blitz to Blair -A New History of Britain Since 1939* (Weidensfeld and Nicolson, 1997).
POTTER, D., *The Glittering Coffin* (Gollancz, 1960).
POULANTZAS, N., *Political Power and Social Classes* (New Left Books, 1973).
PRINCE, R., 'Review of Saturday Night and Sunday Morning', *New Left Review*, no. 6 (November-December 1960), 14-17.
PRYKE, R., *Public Enterprise in Practice* (Chatto&Windus, 1981).
PYM, J., 'Review of a Passage to India', vol. 2, no. 615 (1985), 100-101.
QUART L., 'The Religion of the Market: Thatcherite Politics and the British Film of the 1980's' in Friedman, L. (ed.), *British Cinema and Thatcherism* (1993b), 15-34.

QUIGLY, I., 'Review of Room at the Top', *The Spectator* (30 January 1959), 144.
QUIGLY, I., 'Review of A Kind of Loving', *The Spectator* (12 April 12 1962), 512.
REAGAN, R., *An American Life* (New York: Hutchinson, 1990).
REES-MOGG, W., *The Political Economy of Art* (Arts Council, 1985), 34.
RHODE, E., 'Review of A Kind of Loving', *Sight and Sound,* no. 4 (Summer 1962), 143-144.
RICHARDS, A., *Miners on Strike* (Berg 1996).
RICHARDS, J., *Happiest Days: the Public Schools in English Fiction* (Manchester University Press, 1988), 1-80.
RICHARDS, J., 'New Waves and Old Myths: British Cinema in the 1960s' in More-Gilbert, B. and Seed, J. (ed.), *Cultural Revolution? The Challenge of the Arts in the 1960s* (Routledge, 1992).
RICHARDS, J., *Films and British National Identity: From Dickens to Dad's Army.* (Manchester University Press, 1997), 1-30.
RICHARDSON, T., *Encounter,* vol. XV, no.3 (September 1960), 64.
RIDDELL, P., *The Thatcher Decade. Blackwell: How Britain has Changed During the 1980's* (Blackwell, 1989), 1-204.
RIDGMAN, J., 'Inside the Liberal Heartland: Television and the Popular Imagination in the 1960s' in Moore-Gilbert et al. *Cultural Revolution? The Challenge of the Arts in the 1960s* (Routledge, 1992).
ROBINS, K., 'Tradition and Translation: National Culture in its Global Context' in Corner, J. and Harvey, S. (eds.), *Enterprise and Heritage. Crosscurrents of Natural Culture* (Routledge, 1991b), 21-45.
ROBINSON, A., 'The Jewel in the Crown', *Sight and Sound,* vol. 53, no. 1 (Spring, 1989), 47.
RODDICK, N., 'Brideshead Revisited', *Sight and Sound,* vol. 51, no. 1 (Winter 1981-1982), 58-60.
ROYAL COMISSION, THE, *The Royal Commission's Report on Marriage and Divorce* (HMSO 1955).
RUSHDIE, S., *Imaginary Homelands: Essays and Criticism 1981-1991* (London: Granta Books, 1991).

SAMUEL, R. (ed.), *Patriotism: the Making and Un-making of British National Identity*, vol. 3 (London: Routledge 1989).

SCANNELL, P., 'The Temporal Arrangements of Broadcasting in the Modern World' in Drummond, P. and Paterson, R. (eds.), *Television and its Audiences: International Research Perspectives* (London: British Film Institute, 1988b).

SCHLESINGER, P., *Media, State and Nation (Political Violence and Collective Identities)* (Sage 1991), 137-193.

SCHLESINGER, J., in *Hollywood UK* (BBC TV, 6 September 1993).

SCOTT, P., *The Jewel in the Crown* (London: Heinemann, 1966).

SCOTT, P., *My Appointment With the Muse: Essays 1961-75* (London: Heinemann, 1986).

SETON-WATSON, H., *Nations and States* (Methuen, 1977), 15-89, 417-443.

SHAW, R., *The Arts and the People* (Jonathan Cape, 1987).

SHILS, E., *Tradition* (Faber and Faber, 1981), 59.

SHILS, E. and YOUNG, M., 'The Meaning of the Coronation', *Sociological Review*, vol. 1. no. 2 (1956).

SIGAL, C., 'Review of Coronation Street', *The New Statesman* (12 January 1962), 63.

SILLITOE, A., 'What Comes on Monday?', *New Left Review*, no. 4 (July-August 1960), 59.

SINFIELD, A., *Literature, Politics and Culture in Post-war Britain* (London: Basil Blackwell, 1989).

SKED, A. and COOK, C., *Post-war Britain a Political History* 2nd Edition (Penguin, 1984).

SKEGGS, B., *Formations of Class and Gender: Becoming Respectable* (Sage, 1997), 139-160.

SMILES, S., *Self-help with Illustrations of Conduct and Perseverance* 1st edition in 1859 abridged by G. Bull (Harmondsworth: Penguin, 1986).

SMITH, A. D., *National Identity* (University of Nevada Press, 1984), 1-50, 75-115.

SMITH, A. D., *The Ethnic Orgins of Nationalism* (Oxford and Cambridge MA: Blackwell, 1986).

SMITH, A. D., *National Identity* (London: Penguin, 1991).

SOLOMONS, J., *Race and Racism in Contemporary Britain* (Macmillan, 1989).

STEAD, P., *Film and the Working-Class* (Routledge, 1989), 150-205.

STORRY, M. and CHILDS, P. (eds.), *British Cultural Identities* (Routledge, 1997).

STREET, S., *British National Cinema* (Routledge, 1995).

STRICK, P., 'Review of 'A Room With a View', *Monthly film Bulletin*, vol. 53, no. 627 (April 1986), 118-119.

SUDJIC, D., *Norman Foster, Richard Rogers, James Stirling: New Directions in British Architecture* (1986), 179-181.

SWANN, D., *Retreat of the State: Deregulation and Privatisation in the UK and US* (Harvester, 1988).

SWIFT, E., 'Tory Poodle Jibe for Sponsor Group', *Stage* (20 February 1986).

TARR, C., 'Sapphire, Darling and the Boundaries of Permitted Pleasure', *Screen*, no. 26, vol. 1 (1985), 54.

TAYLOR, M., 'John Bull and the Iconography of Public Opinion in England 1712-1729', *Past and Present*, no. 34 (1992), 93-128.

TAYLOR, R. and PRITCHARD, C., *The Protest Makers: the British Campaign for Nuclear Disarmament* (Manchester University Press, 1968).

TAYLOR, R. and PRITCHARD, C., *The Protest Makers: The British Nuclear Movement of 1958-65 Twenty Years On* (Pergamon Press, 1980).

TAYLOR, J., *Anger* (London: Methuen and Co., 1962).

TAYLOR. J., *Anger and After: A Guide to the New British Drama* (London: Methuen and Co., 1969).

THATCHER, M., *What's Wrong With Politics?* (Conservative Political Centre, 1968).

THATCHER, M., *Speech Given at Conservative Party Conference* (October 1975).

THATCHER, M., *Speech given at Scottish Conservative Party Conference at Berwick* (July 1978).

THATCHER, M., *Speech given at Conservative Trade Unionists' Annual Conference* (November 1979).

THATCHER, M., *Women in a Changing World* (Press Office Downing Street, 1982).

THATCHER, M., 'Speech in New York', *Financial Times* (31 August 1991).

THOMPSON, E. P., 'Revolution Again! Or Shut Your Eyes and Run', *New Left Review*, no. 6 (November-December 1960), 18-31.

THOMPSON, E. P., *The Poverty of Theory (and Other Essays)* (Merlin Press, 1978).

TOMALIN, C., 'Love Story', *Sight and Sound*, vol. 56, no. 7 (1987), 290.

TOOKE, N. and DAKER, M., 'Seeing is Believing: the Effect of Film on Visitor Numbers to Screened Locations', *Tourism Management*, vol. 17, part 2 (1989), 89.

TUDOR, A., *Image and Influence* (London: Allen and Unwin, 1974).

TUDOR, A., *Theories of Film* (London: Secker and Warburg/British Film Institute, 1974).

TURNER, G., *The North Country* (London: Eyre and Spottiswoode, 1967).

TWEEDY, C., 'Sponsorship in Partnership, Greater London Arts', *Quarterly* (Spring 1987), 22.

UNNAMED AUTHOR, *The Listener* (6 January 1955), 36.

UNNAMED AUTHOR, *The Spectator* (8April 1955), 440.

UNNAMMED AUTHOR, *Britain* (July 1982) cited in Samuel, R. (ed.), *Patriotism: the Making and Un-making of British National Identity*, vol. 3 (London: Routledge, 1989).

VELJANOVSKI, C., *Selling the State, Privatisation in Britain* (Weidenfeld and Nicolson, 1987).

VINCENT, D., *Literacy and Popular Culture: England 1750-1914* (Cambridge University Press, 1989).

WADE, R., *Where the Difference Began* (BBC Television Script Printed, 1975), 6.

WAGG, S., *The Football World: a Contemporary Social History* (Harvester, 1984).

WALKER, A., *Hollywood England: The British Film Institute in the Sixties* (Michael Joseph Ltd, 1974), 80-200.

WALKER, A., *National Heroes: British Cinema in the seventies and Eighties* (London: Harrap, 1985).

WALKER, A. and WALKER, C. (eds.), *The Growing Divide: A Social Audit 1979-87* (Child Poverty Action Group, 1987), 29-89.

WALSH, J., 'There'll Always be an England: The Falklands Conflict on Film' in Aulich, J. (ed.), *Framing the Falklands War: Nationhood, Culture and Identity* (Open University Press, 1992b), 33-49.

WALKER, J. (ed.), *Halliwell's Film and Video Guide* (Harper/Collins, 1999).

WANDOR, M., *Look Back in Gender: Sexuality and the Family in the Post-war British Drama* (Methuen, 1987).

WARE, V., *Beyond the Pale: White Women, Racism and History* (London: Verso 1992).

WAUGH, E., *Brideshead Revisited* (Penguin, 1980).

WEATHERBY, W. J., 'Granada's Camino Real', *Contrast*, no. 1 (1961-2), 278-290.

WESKER, A., *The Wesker Trilogy* (Harmondsworth: Penguin, 1979), 59.

WHITEBATT, W., 'Review of Room at the Top', *New Statesman* (3 January 1959) no. 1, 144.

WHITEHOUSE, M., *Who Does She Think She Is?* (London: New English Library, 1971).

WIDDONSON, P., *E. M. Forsters' Howards End: Fiction as History* (Sussex University Press, 1977).

WILLIAMS, R., *Britain in the Sixties: Communications* (Penguin, 1962).

WILLIAMS, R., 'British Film History: New Perspectives' in Conran, J. and Porter, V. (eds.), *British Cinema History* (1983b).

WILLIAMS, R., 'Problems of the Coming Period', *New Left Review*, no. 140 (July-August 1983), 7-18.

WILSON, E., *Women and the Welfare State* (London: Tavistock, 1977).

WILSON, E., 'Thatcherism and Women: After Seven Years' in R. Miliband *et al* (eds.), *Socialist Register* (Merlin Press, 1987b), 199-235.

WOLLEN, T., 'Over Our Shoulders: Nostalgic Screen Fictions for the 1980s' in Corner and Harvey (eds.), *Enterprise and Heritage – Crosscurrents of National Culture* (London: Routledge 1991b).

WOOD, M., *In Search of England - Journeys into the English Past* (Harmondsworth: Penguin, 2000).

WOOLLACOTT, J. 'The James Bond Films: Conditions of Production' in Curran J. and Porter V. (eds.), *British Cinema History* (London: Weidenfeld and Nicolson, 1983b), 208-26.

WORSTHORNE, P., cited in ASCHERSON, N., 'Why Heritage is Right Wing', *The Observer* (8 November 1987), 9.

WRIGHT, P., in Bennett, T., *Formations of Nation and People* (Routledge, 1984).

WRIGHT, P., *On Living in an Old Country: the National Past in Contemporary Britain* (London: Verso, 1985).

WRIGHT, P., 'Misguided tours', *New Socialist* (July-August 1986), 34.

WYNDHAM, G., *Facing the Nation: Television and Politics 1936-1976* (Bodley Head, 1977), 224.

YOUNG, A., *Femininity in Dissent* (Routledge, 1990)

YOUNG, H., *One of Us: A Biography of Margaret Thatcher* (Macmillan, 1989).

YOUNG, H. and SLOMAN, A., *The Thatcher Phenomenon* (BBC Books, 1986).

YUPE, A., *David Puttnam: The Story So Far* (Sphere Books Ltd., 1988).

ZWEIG, F., *The Worker in an Affluent Society* (London: Heinemann, 1961).

About the Author

Dr Justin Hindmarsh is a leading exponent in the academic study of Film-Theory and Practice, Media, Radio-Theory and Industry and Sociology. Following graduation from Staffordshire University with an Upper Second in BA (Hons) Film, TV and Radio Studies, Justin completed an MA at the distinguished Centre For Mass Communications Research at Leicester University before embarking upon lecturing and research projects including Hollywood Cinema, Czech and French New Wave, Italian Neo-Realism, British Cinema, The Study of Audiences and Mass Media and Violence. It was then that Justin developed an academic interest in the notion of a 'British National Cinema' and to this end published *British Cinema-Style and Context: An Examination of "British New Wave films*.

Other academic publications soon followed by way of *Genre and Narrative Analysis* and *Documentary As Media Text*. These last two works each formed the basis of a unit in the pioneering global MA e-Learning in Mass Communications in which he devised and wrote lectures, assignments and activities.

Justin then progressed to The University of York, where he taught pure Sociological Theory. It was here where Justin researched and wrote *Realist Nights and Heritage Mornings* - a seminal PhD Theses concerning debates centred around theories of British national identity - upon which this latest publication is based.

www.ingramcontent.com/pod-product-compliance
Lightning Source LLC
Chambersburg PA
CBHW022058090426
42743CB00008B/644